SO-BKZ-694

DYNAMICS OF LEARNING

DYNAMICS OF LEARNING

by

Nathaniel Cantor

Foreword *by* George E. Miller, M.D.
Director, Center for Educational Development
University of Illinois College of Medicine

AGATHON PRESS, INC., New York

Distributed by

SCHOCKEN BOOKS, New York

Library of Congress Catalog Card Number: 71-166546

ISBN 0-87586-026-5

Printed in the United States

1719846

Foreword

The reader who looks first at its publication history will find that *Dynamics of Learning* is twenty-five years old; but the one who starts with its substance might conclude that the book had been written yesterday. For in spite of impressive advances in the quantity, scope and technology of education during the last quarter century, the most serious institutional impediments to individual learning are still those about which Nathaniel Cantor wrote with such insight and feeling: the obstacles which teachers create.

My daughter and her friends who attend one of the most highly regarded public high schools in America regularly describe that institution as a prison, and are able to document the accusation with persuasive evidence. The students at Berkeley and Columbia may have produced the most overt eruption, but an undercurrent of discontent with dehumanized, impersonal and irrelevant programs smoulders throughout the world of higher education. From the late elementary school through graduate and professional school the feeling is widespread among the young that schooling represents a sentence imposed by society rather than an opportunity granted each individual. This observation does not deny the impressive islands of faculty sensitivity or institutional responsiveness to individual student needs; it merely highlights the inescapable evidence that the dominant educational practices in the latter half of the twentieth century are still coercive and authoritarian, in which rewards go most regularly to students who can produce the required answers rather than to those who can ask the perceptive questions. And so *Dynamics of Learning* though twenty-five years old is still new; the problems it addresses are with us yet; and the solutions it proposes are still fresh, for they have not been dulled by widespread use.

At the heart of Cantor's argument is the recurrent theme that learning is both individual and personal, continuous and uninterrupted, shaped by many forces internal and external. The greatest challenge which teachers face is to understand these elements with sufficient clarity that their efforts encourage and facilitate student learning in a manner that serves the long term interests of both the individual and society, rather than inadvertently establishing a learning pattern which meets the immediate requirements of a school but defeats the ultimate goals of education. It is these heady issues that are so exquisitely explored in this book.

It is difficult, of course, for anyone who knew Nathaniel Cantor well to tease apart the power of the man and the force of his ideas. But there can be no question that he had a profound effect upon the learners who fell under his spell. The experience of a small group of medical educators with whom he worked so closely during the final years of a tragically shortened life is probably not atypical. Few of them were ever quite the same again for he helped each to gain a new appreciation of the professional responsibility embodied in the title "teacher". It often made their task more difficult for this insight generated within them a basic shift from concern for teaching to concern for learning. It was in fact a giant step toward the goal Comenius sought in ". . . a method of instruction by which teachers may teach less but learners may learn more".

The universality of the learning dynamics about which Cantor wrote can no longer be questioned. Although his academic career was lived chiefly in a university where he dealt mostly with undergraduate students, the validity of what he professed and practiced there has by now been confirmed at every level of education where the purpose is more than acquisition of facts or technical skills. Nathaniel Cantor believed with all his heart that ". . . education is for the making of Man", which meant to him not only a knowledgeable and skilled man, but also "an integrated, cooperative and creative individual". Anyone who reads this book thoughtfully cannot fail to be moved by the persuasiveness of his argument, nor to be unmoved by its implications. Whether readers are able to translate principle into practice will be the test of his talent. But there are many of us who have already tested him — and he has not been found wanting.

GEORGE E. MILLER, M.D.

Center for Educational Development
University of Illinois College of Medicine
March, 1972

Table of Contents

To My Students Who Have Taught Me

How To Learn To Teach

"Let the main object of this, our didactic, be as follows: To seek and to find a method of instruction, by which teachers may teach less, but learners may learn more."

The Great Didactic of Comenius
(1628-1632)

Introduction

We are in the midst of a radical reexamination of American education. It is true that we have periodically examined our formal educational institutions. What has been happening during the past fifteen years or so, however, is not merely another one of the episodic, superficial criticisms of our educational endeavors. Many of us are currently concerned with a *fundamental* inquiry into the content, methods, and goals of education in the United States.

There are many factors which have led to the contemporary critical appraisal of what is happening in our schools and colleges. One of the major ones is the precipitous changes in the world accompanying the present technological revolution.

The curricula of our primary and secondary schools and colleges have, over the decades, been modified to meet some of the needs of our changing society. Thus, for example, during the past thirty years the secondary schools and colleges of liberal arts and sciences have been markedly influenced in their offerings by the vocational and professional needs of the students. School certificates and college degrees have a cash value. "It pays to have an education." We are not discussing the merits of the vocational emphasis or the meaning of education. We are merely pointing out the change.

The kinds of modifications in the curricula made to meet the domestic problems in the United States are, however, far removed from the revisions required for an understanding of the far-reaching changes in the institutional life of the world. With the exception of a few colleges and graduate schools concerned with "area studies" little attention is given to the life, culture, and history of the peoples of Africa, Asia, or the Soviet Union. We are still primarily concerned with the Western European traditions ignoring the tremendous shifts in the roles which Western Europe and more particularly, the United States are assuming in world affairs. The foreign press correspondents, and official and unofficial reports of government representatives, give us truncated views of what is happening in the world. The uncritical reader is at the mercy of argument by authority. He simply does not possess the information or insight to attempt a critical appraisal of what he reads and sees in the widely circulated weekly pictorial magazines or even to judge between the "authorities" upon whom one can rely.

Very few people, including school teachers, comprehend the radical transformations taking place in the world, and the many sided implications of the technological revolution. A new intellectual climate is developing regarding the physical, biological, and social sciences. The foundations of the traditional beliefs in which most of today's adults have been nourished have all but disintegrated. Many of us "know" and talk about a great many things that aren't so. The problem is to unlearn a great mass of traditional beliefs about the world and man which has been invalidated by contemporary science.

Our schools and colleges have hardly begun to incorporate this altered picture of the physical and social world of the middle of the twentieth century. This has led many responsible leaders of American education to criticize the content offerings of the schools.

Another factor which has led to criticism of our educational "systems" is dissatisfaction with the products of our secondary schools, colleges, and professional schools.

Most laymen are probably unaware of the views of many educational administrators in the professional schools of law, engineering, medicine, business administration, and nursing. Official national and state committees of the various professional associations are disturbed over the fact that the professional schools are graduating tradesmen and specialists rather than educated professionals. The students "take" the professional courses, memorize the data, "pass" the examinations, graduate, and start practicing their specialties. The majority of professionals, however, have little awareness of the social and human contexts in which they practice.

This is what Dean Erwin N. Griswold of the Harvard Law School stated in a recent address:

Of course, all law deals with human relations. But my point is that it exists in its more or less scientific form, and as it is taught, it does not deal very much with people. Yet lawyers constantly deal with people. They deal with people far more than they do with appellate courts. They deal with clients; they deal with witnesses; they deal with persons against whom demands are made; they carry on negotiations; they are constantly endeavoring to come to agreements of one sort or another with people, to persuade people, sometimes when they are very reluctant to be persuaded. Lawyers are constantly dealing with people who are under stress or strain of one sort or another. How do people act in such situations? Do law students ever learn anything about this at all?[1]

Dean George Packer Berry of the Harvard Medical School declared: It [professional education in medicine] is being infiltrated today by the spirit of the trade school . . . when the educational experience fails to foster the student's growth and maturation, medical education tends to become vocational training.[2]

F. N.[1] "Law Schools and Human Relations," Address delivered at Washington University Law School, April 19, 1955.
F. N.[2] Report of the Second Teaching Institute, Association of American Medical Colleges, Chicago, Ill., 1955.

Too few professionals exercise their creativity, few continue in serious study, and too few recognize social and community responsibilities attached to the practice of their professions.

It is for the above reasons that some of the medical, law, and engineering schools are conducting or guiding long range experiments and explorations regarding new approaches to the learning and teaching of the professions. Their National Associations are calling for *educated* professionals.[3]

The "general education" movement in the high schools and colleges is one answer to the dissatisfaction with the narrow training given to the pre-professional students. The sheer accumulation of available knowledge, the minute division of labor required by our complex society, and the limitation of time demand a high degree of specialization. Specialization, however, can be carried to the point where one becomes skilled, without understanding the implications of one's practice of such skills. Dean Griswold's comments regarding the practice of law is a case in point. An experience, which many readers will easily understand, will make our point vividly clear.

Sometime ago the writer arrived at the appointed time, seven P.M. at a hospital clinic to undergo a routine physical checkup. Seven other men and women were present for the same service. The eight of us, unknown to each other, sat in a dimly lighted corridor, in our hospital gowns, trying not to feel strange and uncomfortable. The first of the team of six physicians who were to make the examinations arrived at ten minutes to eight, walked down the corridor between

F. N.[3] The author is privileged to be associated with such a program, at the University of Buffalo School of Medicine, which is supported by the Commonwealth Fund of New York City.

the two rows where we huddled on the hard benches, glancing straight ahead without uttering a word to any of us or even recognizing our presence. By eight thirty the remaining five specialists sauntered in and through the aisle past the eight cadavers. I recognized that I was alive, however, when a few minutes after eight thirty the "eye, ear, nose and throat man" called, "Hey, you, over there."

The Lords and Masters felt no need to explain their lateness to the patients as a matter of courtesy. Even more important they were insensitive to the poor rapport between patient and physician which was established. The doctors in question failed to realize that *men* and *women*, not bodies, were being examined.

Managers of well known business enterprises and industrial corporations are requiring that their executives become "generalists." Able administrators and managers, it is recognized, must understand the wider social contexts and backgrounds of their specialized operations. The "human relations" aspects of business and industry are being emphasized. Industrial organizations are not merely places where goods are manufactured. They are societies where men and women spend a major portion of their time.

Whether one considers the teacher, the professional, the administrator, staff man, executive or supervisor the problem of relating to others in a professional sense is the same. The helper must understand what happens when people are in any kind of teaching-learning situation.

Many of the critics of current educational practice assume that changes in curriculum will meet the needs revealed by the changes in our ways of living and will lead to more creative and civic-minded leaders. Others declare there is need for more classrooms, more teachers, higher salaries, and increased financial aid for talented youngsters

These approaches refer to the *machinery* of education. They are necessary conditions for sound educational practice. The keystone, however, is the teacher. We feel, rather strongly, that the most important problem in the contemporary examination of our education institutions has received the least attention, viz., how can the *quality* of teaching be improved?

The first edition of this study was published in 1946. It was a pioneer work representing one of the earliest efforts to examine the implications of modern psychiatry, mental hygiene, and the social casework process, for education. Since its appearance the author has had a rich and varied experience with many different groups. He has worked with undergraduates preparing for professional colleges, with groups of teachers and supervisors of teachers, members of medical faculties, personnel managers, training directors of industry, executives in industry, and groups of governmental officials. He has spent a year directing Workshops in six Western European countries as a Foreign Operations Administration Consultant to the O.E.E.C. (Office of European Economic Cooperation). He was visiting Professor of Sociology for one year at Columbia University studying the general education program under a grant from the Carnegie Foundation.

One of the outstanding results of these group experiences is the author's more profound conviction that the thesis expressed in the first edition is sound, namely, that *the teacher must understand what is realistically involved in the teaching-learning process.* Without this understanding, which includes the skill to put it to use, the teacher can talk, but the student is unlikely to learn in any vitally significant sense.

The student must be helped to want to learn, to learn how to learn, and to want to learn as long as life lasts.

Few realize how difficult this task is. The average pupil, by the time he reaches elementary school, has developed an involved system of security defenses which protect him against the threats of authoritative and significant people or situations. Each of us learns rather early in life to be cautious about expressing ourselves by gesture or language. We want to maintain the good-will of and feeling of comfort with the important adults around us. The need to protect one's self-esteem is basic to every one of us. We therefore learn to watch for signs in the other person which encourage or endanger our own performance. We want to avoid uncertainty, insecurity, and disapproval. Thus we develop many kinds of tricks to avoid the unpleasant feelings of anxiety which accompany disapproval or the threat of being disapproved. One of the chief defenses is to pretend to submit rather than to express our difference.

Most of us learn how *not* to learn. That is, we learn very early how to avoid tangling with the authority of adults who are significant in our lives. As youngsters we need the love and support of those upon whom we depend. Failure to meet their demands and expectations usually brings recrimination, disapproval or punishment in one form or another. We feel anxious and afraid when we express ourselves spontaneously. Now what happens?

We learn to curb self-expression a good deal of the time. We learn how to submit, run away, cut corners, rationalize, defend ourselves, and to distort. At any cost we want to avoid getting into trouble. In brief, we are driven "to adjust" to threats, anxieties, and fears.

We do not imply that infants and youngsters or adolescents should be permitted to do what they want when they want. We are describing what occurs. What occurs is this.

Generally, during the most important years of growth, that is, infancy and childhood, most learning acquires a negative character.

Behavior which lessens anxiety is adjustive not integrative.[4] The essence of integrative behavior is the capacity to exercise one's curiosity, to derive positive satisfaction from the *spontaneous* expression of one's skills and power. Motivation which leads to the spontaneous expression of one's self is different from the kind of learning which seeks to lessen anxiety and to avoid threat.

The essential problem, then, is to alter the traditional approach to learning from a negative to a positive one, to help students to learn how to learn, rather than to support their pattern of learning how to avoid exposing themselves for fear of being hurt and disapproved.

Learning will not become significant in the lives of students unless they want to learn. They can be helped to learn if they are encouraged to feel free to express their differences from authorities, whether teachers or texts. They can be helped to drop their defenses, to face their limitations, and to acknowledge their inadequacies. This holds true for teachers, too.

The central problem of education is self-discipline, self-motivation. The learner must freely accept responsibility for his decisions, his successes, and failures. This cannot be "taught," but it may be learned. Significant learning stems from the self-directed motivation of the learner who wants

F. N.[4] The research or clinical experiences of Miller and Dollard, P. S. Symonds, K. Goldstein, K. Horney, H. S. Sullivan, E. Fromm, R. May, to mention only a few of the recent writers, support this view. Activity which is the product of anxiety stresses partial action and compulsiveness (Goldstein). Impulses and desires do not become "drives" except as they are motivated by anxiety. They aim at safety not satisfaction (Horney).

something positive and creative for an unexpressed or un-filled need of his. No one can learn for another anymore than a mother can help her child grow physically by eating the child's meal.

This volume tries to contribute toward an understanding of how a teacher can help the student to want to learn and to become a responsible and self-disciplined individual.

Preface

WHAT THIS BOOK IS ABOUT

The release of atomic power can become one of the greatest blessings or one of the most devastating curses for mankind. Which it shall be depends upon the will of man. If men and women the world over continue to be divided in thought, feeling, and action as they have been in the past, there is little hope of avoiding a future holocaust, which, in self defense, freezes one's imagination.

If, on the other hand, enough of us rededicate ourselves to the task of building a world grounded upon a revivified faith in the essential dignity of and respect for the human being, there is still a fighting chance that man can create an orderly world of his choice. How?

Only fools or fanatics, the one without knowledge and the other without humility, rush in with completed blueprints. We are still far from understanding the complicated skeins of modern civilization. But we can discern the larger patterns which show us the general direction in which we should move, and the role which a more realistic education can play in leading us toward it.

Consider the following example. International trade should be expanded, not restricted. No sane economist or student of international relations doubts this, although there is certainly difference of opinion regarding many of its aspects.

Here is a simple statement: It cannot be perverted or misunderstood except by the mentally ill. ... The pestilence of racial bigotry and the blight of nationalism have turned Europe into bedlam and millions of hapless victims into ashes. Some of the outstanding scientists of the twentieth century planned, designed, and carried through the annihilation by fire, gas, and scalpel, of six million innocent and defenseless people. They performed this noble work not under the stress of bestial passion but with the dispassionate, icy calculation of the finest scientific spirit. This was the work of responsible leaders, counted among the flowering products of mind and spirit in Western civilization. What an utterly loathsome and ineffable degradation of human spirit. One feels ashamed and guilty in standing erect as man. What self-respecting adult—or child—doubts that the poisons of racial prejudice must be expunged from community life?

There are raw materials in the world. We have the machines, the power, and the skill to produce shelter, food, and clothing, an abundance of them. We haven't succeeded in providing the majority of people in this country or in any other country with the kind of shelter, food, clothing, or medical attention which is possible. The reasons for this are complicated. One of the principal reasons is that we have permitted the economic institutions of the eighteenth and nineteenth century to develop helter-skelter. The point has been reached in the middle of the twentieth century where we must plan, for good or for evil—or else be blown out of the need for planning. Does anyone aware of what is really happening in the world today doubt this?

We have mentioned the need for expanded international trade, ridding the world of insane racial prejudice, and the need for planning on a national and international scale as merely a few examples of the general direction in which the peoples of the world should move. To a degree, a pitifully small number of leaders realize these needs and are working in these directions. Unless and until masses of the citizens of each country share this realization and assume some responsibility in working for it, the atomic age of peace and plenty cannot be brought about. It is the creative and united will of men and women which can give mankind control over its destiny.

How can people be helped to understand the world in which they live and be motivated to undertake the planning of their destiny? There is no simple or single answer. Leaders in every area share the responsibility. I happen to place my unshakeable faith in the value of democratic professional instruction as one of the chief means of social change.

I am convinced that ten to twenty-five thousand *highly skilled, professional* teachers on all areas of education, placed in strategic, administrative and supervisory positions could redirect the thinking, feeling, and willing of millions of children, young women and men who are to become the adults of the next generation. The catch is in the phrase "highly skilled, professional teachers."

The Dynamics of Learning is an analysis of what is meant by a "highly skilled, professional teacher." It also tries to answer several basic questions. What happens, realistically, when living students and living teachers meet together in a classroom in the teaching-learning process? Do teachers really help students to develop or do they increase the fears and anxieties and timidities the students bring to the classroom? Does not most traditional teaching occur in a wilderness of waste logic and does not most "learning" consist of verbal ping-pong? What, precisely, is the source of the terrible confusion in education and the restless dissatisfaction felt by so many teachers, parents, and students?

It is uncomfortable to carry on the daily routine of teaching when it is accompanied by feelings that one isn't quite sure of what one is about, or the monotonous routine of learning when the student senses the wide gaps between life and language. I believe that the analysis of the techniques of teaching and the closely related problem of the psychology of learning presented in this study will help to illuminate what is wrong. The points of view represented in this study are a radical departure from traditional methods of instruction. Their acceptance, I am convinced, will lead to the only kind of genuine education there is, self-criticism, self-discipline, self-motivation, and a willingness to be responsible for one's own decisions.

It is a real pleasure to acknowledge my deep appreciation to those who have read and criticized the study, in whole or in part. I wish to thank Prof. Oscar Silverman, Dean Julian Park, and Chancellor S. P. Capen of the University of Buffalo, Dr. Daniel A. Prescott of the University of Chicago, formerly with the Commission on Teacher Education of the American Council on Education, and Dr. Karl Bigelow, Teachers College, Columbia University, and formerly, Director of the Commission on Teacher Education, Dean Kenneth Pray and Dr. Virginia Robinson of the Pennsylvania School of Social Work, Dr. Chester Pugsley, Principal of the State Practice School, State Teachers College, Buffalo, New York, and Mr. Herbert Aptekar, Director of the Queen's Jewish Community Service, Forest Hills, Long Island.

I owe a special debt of gratitude to Dr. James Plant of the Essex Juvenile Clinic, Newark, New Jersey, and to my wife not only for repeated readings and criticisms of the material but for the stimulating discussions of it.

I am keenly aware that it is only in an atmosphere of a genuinely liberal tradition such as exists at the University of Buffalo that experiments in teaching methods would not only be permitted but welcomed.

The dedication of this study to my students serves as some small penance for the guilt I feel over some of my teaching sins in the past and at present.

No one but myself is responsible for the final form and content of the study.

Nathaniel Cantor

Chapter 1

Education: The Handmaid to Reaction

The modern world has been plunged into chaos by the intellectuals, the products of Western European illiberal higher education. For the greater part, the dictators in Italy, Japan, and Germany had been supported by the intellectuals, not the illiterate peasants and workers. Mussolini, Hirohito, and Hitler were backed by the illiberally educated of their respective countries, the leaders in industry, art, science, literature, and philosophy.

The "educated" leadership supported, planned, and carried out the murder of millions of innocent civilians.

What may be said of the intellectuals, the so-called educated leaders of France, England, and the United States? To be sure, they have not tortured nor murdered. But they have shown an illiberality of spirit which has not been cleansed by our system of higher education. The "educated" leadership of England and the United States has, for the greater part, allied itself with the forces of reaction against democratic progress.

There have been and there are groups of genuinely liberal, educated young men and women and adults. They have always been and are now a very small minority. It is not easy to understand how liberal attitudes were formed. The influence of the home and the understanding of their own personal experiences certainly entered. In some cases the stimulus of exceptional teachers must have been present. In other cases, it seems that students make use of what education has to offer, despite the system and the instructors.

1

They can learn under the most adverse circumstances. In some way individual differences in native, creative ability enter.

For the vast majority of students, however, who pass through the various levels of education, *fundamental changes in basic attitudes* of childhood and adolescence do not occur. Education has not helped them much to outgrow opinions formed early. They remain stand-patters, protecting their prejudices. Education has not succeeded in creating the kind of *disinterested self-discipline* which provides a man with balance and perspective so that he can become self-critical, change, and adjust. Education has not led students to view themselves and their interests with detachment so that they might be led to wonder at themselves and to try to understand others, and the world they all inhabit.

Anyone who does not live a cloistered life is struck by the intolerant spirit of our generation of adults. Turn to any area of modern life, to the political, racial, religious, economic, business, or social relations in the communities of the United States. Observe the frightening amount of downright indecent human spirit. We do not refer to honest differences of opinion but to the mean and vicious spirit of educated adults. Is evidence for this required? It can easily be gathered from any area in modern life on a local, national, or international level. The examples cited here refer to race relations, one of the most disturbing and dangerous areas of social relations. One's attitude in these matters is an excellent test of the effectiveness of a liberal education.

Isn't it distressing that in our privately-owned colleges and professional schools, in our "institutions of higher learning," there is such potent lack of respect for learning and democracy that Italians, Jews, and Negroes have such a difficult time in gaining admission, despite their qualifications? Candidacy is not a matter of merit or character but of quota. The shameful silence of university faculties and administrators or their more shameful rationalizations is a sad commentary on the contributions of higher education in freeing and liberalizing the spirit of man.

Of what use is all the fancy jargon about new philosophies of education, the innumerable and interminable reports of revised courses of study, re-examinations of the objectives of education, and the re-dedication to democratic ideals? This is all eye-wash so long as quota systems are supported by shameful and discreet silence or, worse, shameless and dishonest apology.

Isn't it distressing that in the House of Representatives and on the floor of the Senate of the United States government, we witness national leaders distilling poison? The reactionary Congressmen and Senators from North and South, the products of our system of education, are not marshalling facts in support of a reasonable position. They are screaming, villifying, and brow-beating to maintain or stir up prejudices of group against group.

Isn't it distressing to learn that the college-trained executives of many of our large public utility corporations will not employ Jews in any capacity?

Isn't it disheartening to observe the position of the Daughters of the American Revolution, numbering among its members many graduates of our liberal arts and sciences colleges, regarding renting space to Negro artists in Constitutional Hall in Washington, D. C.?

A few weeks ago I was present at a discussion of a committee of women (most of them college graduates) in charge of the season's programs of a symphony program. The position was taken that "We don't want niggers in our hall."

So much for the products of our institutions of higher learning. What of the products of our primary and secondary schools? Have the public and high schools of this country liberalized the attitudes of 25,000,000 school chil-

dren? Has the present adult population become more democratic as a result of our system of education? Listen to college students, commenting on the family quarrels at the
dinner table when they report on what they have learned in
a course on racism. Read the scrawls in the washrooms of
the colleges, "Down with kikes and niggers."

Recently, during the War, at a neighborhood motion
picture, a film, *Hitler's Gang,* was shown. The theatre is
located in an upper-middle and professional class neighborhood. Hitler remarks that some device must be used to
enlist the support of the Germans for his program. Use the
Social Democrats, someone suggests. No, they are too powerful, replies Hitler. The Church, suggests another. No, it is
too well organized. I have it, let's blame the Jews, cries Goer-
ing. They caused the downfall of Germany. Splendid, says
Hitler. At this point, tremendous applause swept through
the theatre. The wives, mothers, and fathers, sisters and
brothers, of American soldiers exposing their lives in Germany spontaneously applauded. They are the products of the
American school system. Recent polls taken among the
American forces of occupation in Germany showed that over
one-fifth of the G. I.'s felt Germany was justified in its
treatment of the Jews. The signs are not very encouraging.
These soldiers are products of American secondary education.

So are the white adults who participated in the recent
race riots in Detroit, Mich.; Philadelphia, and other communities. So are the Oregon adults who burned the homes
of Japanese-American citizens. So are the youngsters in
Boston, Mass., New York City, Buffalo, N. Y.; and other
communities who led attacks against Jewish children, dis-
rupted services in synagogues, and desecrated Jewish and
Catholic cemeteries.

Why is it necessary to have the Anti-Defamation League
of the B'nai B'rith, the Association for the Advancement of
Colored People, the Urban League, the Fair Employment

Practice Act, the New York State Law against Discrimination in Industry, the Federal Anti-Poll Tax Law, and the numerous church groups, North and South, fighting prejudice? In part, because our school system has failed miserably in developing democratic attitudes.

How often has each of us been present at a social or professional gathering during a discussion when a religious or racial *group* has been slurred? How many of us have possessed sufficient integrity to challenge unequivocally such spreading of misunderstanding and hatred? Being tactful and well-mannered is considered more important than being integral and democratic. Hurting the feelings of an acquaintance is more important, we suppose, than tacitly acquiescing in the prejudice against minority groups. There is a time and place for taking a stand. Education should help one to determine the time and place. Does it?

I do not wish to be misunderstood. I am not trying to make our educational system the whipping boy of the ills of society. I certainly do not think it is the sole responsibility of educators to fashion angels out of monkeys any more than it is the sole responsibility of the church or the sole responsibility of parents. I am stating that something is radically wrong with a system of education which purports to train for leadership in a democratic society, which intends to prepare children to live as dignified, responsible, co-operative citizens in American communities, and which fails miserably in carrying out its goals.

The crisis of modern capitalistic society is due primarily to the mal-functioning of its economic institutions. An analysis of the reasons for this crisis is not relevant to this study. We should realize, however, that our political, social, legal, and educational institutions reflect the spirit of modern capitalistic economic enterprise. They support the existing economic system. If we are to reconstruct the social order instead of allowing it to plunge us into chaos, we must plan the techniques of control.

No one knows what the outcome will be. Different kinds of governmental and economic regulations must be discovered and invented if we are to avoid atomic disintegration. The struggle for power or for understanding, or for both, is occurring chiefly in the area of management-labor relations, on domestic issues, and in the United Nations organization on international issues. We shall need all the faith, good will, and understanding on the part of leaders and followers, which can be created. Institutions do not run themselves. They are managed, for good or evil, by human will. What contribution can our system of education make in shaping the attitudes which can create a different and better world?

The attitudes shaped by the press and radio, school, home, church, and industry are not always consistent. The pressures of getting ahead financially and becoming "successful" undo the feeble longings for becoming socially co-öperative. The task of education is not simple. Neither, do some of us believe, is it hopeless. In some way, education has a role to play in this process of making man, the animal, human. Education, all of us feel, should make a difference in the kind of people we become. Yet it does not seem to have made much of a difference.

Parents are anxious about the education of their children. They are not clear, however, about how the schools should educate. They are clear that neither they nor the schools do for their children what they want most of all. They want their children to have character. Our schools and the subjects taught do not seem to give it.

Our schools and colleges do help in preparing students to earn a living. It is proper that they receive such training. One must earn a living. For that, one must learn to read, write, add, draw designs, build bridges, cultivate the soil, remove an appendix, litigate a contract, repair a radio, preach a sermon, build a cabinet, sell shoes, or write a scenario. But there is a vast difference between earning a good living and living a good life. A good doctor, a good lawyer, or a good preacher is not to be confused with a good man or a good citizen. The distinction is of greatest importance.

What doth it profit a man to earn a living if he loseth his soul?

What is a good man? How are people made good or wise? What defines the useful citizen? Whose business is it to answer the question and to provide the education? This is the problem raised by Socrates over 2,000 years ago. What is virtue (wisdom, excellence, character)? Is it knowledge or an exposure of ignorance which humbles men and persuades them to continue the search for Truth, Beauty, and Goodness? Whatever it is, all of us would like to possess it. No life, however fortunate in other respects, is complete and rich without a certain harmony of character, a quality of experience which makes sense out of our striving and gives meaning to our suffering. It transforms animal bodies into human personalities and daily routine into occasional eloquence. Parents want it for themselves and expect it of their children. Character, virtue, wisdom, hope, courage, loyalty, spirit, goodness, beauty—call it what you will—ennobles life and distinguishes man from beast. Where do we search for it and how may we possess it?

Can we be taught, can we learn to live better? Is not our education, in part, responsible for what we become? Who educates us, our parents or our teachers? If the parents, then they, rather than the children, need to be educated. If the teachers, then they, too, must first acquire virtue before they can communicate it to others. Neither one possessing it, both justify their lack of it. The school asks for children better trained at home and the home demands children better trained at school. This results in parent-teachers associations and the children are forgotten.

Virtue, perhaps, cannot be taught. But the opportunity to search for it may be presented. When we have ceased to expect it from society or school, we will look for it in the only place where, if at all, it can be found, within ourselves.

Virtue cannot be taught but it may be learned. This is the implied thesis of this study. Several hundred pages will be required to try and convince the reader of its soundness. Perhaps we have tried the impossible in our system of education. We have tried to pound knowledge into students and extract it from them hoping that something would stick. We have been confused both about the nature of knowledge and its relation to virtue.

This study attempts to show what the trouble has been with our system of education and to indicate ways of improving it. An author in his right senses should be appalled at making such a statement in light of the vast literature on the philosophy of education. I, too, would be frightened but for the fact that during the past ten years I have lived through the insights which this study tries to communicate to the reader. I have become profoundly convinced of the soundness of the theses I am to present in this study. The techniques and principles which are to be discussed have been used with different kinds of groups: nurses in training, recently graduated from high school; social workers, groups of industrial supervisors who have never been to college; groups of adults; and regularly enrolled colleges of liberal arts and sciences students. The results have been highly provocative for the writer who has spent almost a quarter of a century in teaching thousands of students.

Briefly stated, I shall attempt to show what is essentially wrong with our education system; we have been using a false psychology of teaching and learning. What is of paramount importance is to try and demonstrate *systemati-*

cally what takes place when instructors and students get together to explore ideas. There have been many teachers engaged in their daily tasks, who have done excellent jobs and have won wide reputation. They have been exceptional. Without knowing in any systematic fashion what they were about, they were employing some of the ideas to be discussed in this study.

For several decades, psychiatrists have pointed out to educators that the insights of clinical psychology should be taken over into the field of education. Educators, in turn, have pleaded with the psychiatrists to tell them what meaning their disciplines held for education. Many articles have been written by both groups *about* the implications of psychiatry and mental hygiene for education. But there has been a pitifully meager amount of actual demonstration of how mental hygiene could actually be put to use in education.

It is of interest to note the difficult struggle that Freud had personally in introducing his ideas as well as the difficult path psychiatry generally had to travel in being accepted. The student of the history of psychiatric development knows the shabby treatment accorded Sigmund Freud by his colleagues in Vienna. It seems strange now to recall that Professor Freud never held a chair in any European university, let alone the University of Vienna, his home town, where he had been a life long resident, or that he had to come to the United States in 1911 to present publicly, for the first time, his ideas.

Psychiatry was ridiculed and abused for a number of years. It finally found a sympathetic hearing in the child-guidance clinics of the country, in the national mental-hygiene movement, and during the last twenty years has left its permanent mark in the field of social work. It has now, finally, reached Hollywood.

The rapid development of psychosomatic medicine in the last few years and the recent growth of mental-hygiene units and rehabilitation centers in the military establishments further evidence the increased understanding in human behavior made possible by modern psychiatry.

The influence of psychiatry on education to date has not been very significant. There are several areas in education where its mark has been left, in some "progressive" schools and in the field of nursery and kindergarten education. The skilled nursery-school teacher makes use of modern mental-hygiene concepts in her handling of the children. Strangely enough, the moment the child reaches the first grade of grammar school it enters one of the most rigid institutions in the United States—the American public school.

One wonders why there are so few state teachers' colleges in the country which make vital use of our new understanding of the dynamisms of human behavior. The pity of it is that we do have at hand a body of solid data and practical insights, which could revolutionize our whole American system of public education within one generation if only a sufficient number of teachers were given the opportunity to acquire the skill to use these insights.

I should like to emphasize that this study intends to be primarily a contribution to a new technique of teaching and learning. It purports to develop the implications of psychiatry, mental-hygiene, and social case work principles for education.

A theory of personality development is presented in Part One only to help the reader understand some of the basic ideas upon which Part Two of the study is based. The understanding of the process of teaching and learning, which is the core of the study, is not easy. For better or worse it is quite different from the usual analysis of teaching techniques and methods. It is difficult to find the language to express the complexities involved in the learning process.

The writer will employ such concepts as "Independence and Dependence," "Will and Guilt," "Resistance," "Ambivalence," "Projection," and "Identification." Many readers unacquainted with the technical literature describing these terms, will be impatient with or disturbed by this particular jargon (as was the author when first introduced to it). This is understandable. I have tried to make their meaning clear by avoiding technical expressions whenever possible. The labels, however, are unimportant. It is the realities behind the concepts which I shall try to describe. The question of choice of concepts used is unimportant if the reader recognizes in his own experiences the realities to which they refer. The reader is asked to judge for himself whether their selection illuminates the learning-teaching process described.

In order to anticipate possible misunderstandings I should like to add a few remarks.

I have been deeply involved in a teaching experience during the past ten years, which has shown me how knowledge can be used by students. There would be no special point in one teacher publishing a volume on his own experiences unless there is something of value for the field of teaching generally. I believe this to be the case. The teaching-learning process, discussed here, is valid in my opinion on all levels of primary and secondary education as well as in the college of liberal arts and sciences. The question of whether or not this approach is equally valid for all the courses of the liberal arts colleges (and even technical and professional schools) is an open one. The answer would depend on finding out in what areas it can be most effectively used. I am certain that the humanities and social sciences can be vitalized for students through the method dealt with here.

I believe there is a profession of teaching apart from what is being taught. The chapter on the function of the instructor indicates the nature of the principles of the profession of teaching. It is incomplete and sketchy, but it's a beginning. Would the reader agree that there is a profession of parenthood apart from the kind of children we have or how we spend our lives with them? Would not any parent be likely to be a better parent for the child, if some knowledge of the principles involved in child development were understood and utilized? A teacher of any particular subject will help the student learn, if that teacher realizes what happens when students do learn. For this, the instructor must know his function and must understand the responsibility of the student. This understanding constitutes the principles of the profession of teaching.

The problem of getting an author's insight across to the reader is always present—especially in a work of this kind which deals with *processes* of growth. Such insight as I may have has grown out of my professional and personal experiences. It has developed as a result of struggling to achieve the self-discipline which allowed me to permit the students to grow and develop in terms of themselves. Insight is achieved through overcoming one's natural tendency to have students believe what the instructor believes and feel as he feels. Every instructor must live through his own teaching experiences and develop his own professional self in order to learn how to apply the method described in this study.

One's skill in teaching cannot readily be translated for another, as every skillful teacher knows. It lies peculiarly in the realm of art or creation. Just as the artist or creator must subordinate himself to the quality and pliability of his material so, too, must the instructor, in the creative experience of teaching, subordinate himself to the students. It is the struggle *during* such experience which develops the understanding and capacities constituting skill in teaching.

I have tried to the best of my ability to communicate the understanding of the teaching-learning process. How successful this effort will be also depends upon what the reader brings of himself to this study. Whether the reader be a student, parent, businessman, or professional, he should find, if what is written is sound, something in his own experiences which corresponds to what I have found to be true.

Chapter 2

Knowledge For What?

The Goal of the College

Despite some differences of opinion about the goals of a liberal arts and sciences college education, it is generally accepted that its chief purpose is to train the mind by transmitting knowledge. President Maynard Hutchins of the University of Chicago vigorously maintains that colleges should not be concerned with problems of personality or character. Its business, he asserts, is intellectual pursuit. The object of the college is to train minds.[1]

Other college administrators feel that attention should also be given to the personality and character of the students as well as to their physical well-being. In the latter institutions, therefore, there is a well-defined place for college athletics, social activities, various art interests, and religious activity.

There is also a difference of opinion as to the most effective means of aiding students to acquire knowledge.[2] Whatever changes in administrative machinery have been made, with very few exceptions, the essential goal of the American college remains that of fact gathering.

F. N.[1] Hutchins, *The Higher Learning in America*, 1935. President Hutchins' point of view is supported by Van Doren, *Liberal Education*, 1944.

F. N.[2] It is encouraging that in nearly three-fourths of approximately two hundred colleges and universities on the approved list of the Association of American Universities some attempts are made through "honors work" to break the "academic lockstep." Frank Aydelotte, *Breaking the Academic Lockstep*, 1944. *General Education in a Free Society, Report of the Harvard Committee*, 1945. Harvard University Press. T. M. Greene and others, *Liberal Education Re-examined*, 1944. D. Henderson, *Vitalizing Liberal Education*, 1944. *Teachers for Our Times*, American Council On Education, 1944.

The college curriculum offers a variety of courses in the physical and biological sciences, mathematics, language, history, government, economics, sociology, psychology, philosophy, English, art, and Romance and classical language The courses one may take are rigidly prescribed in some colleges and completely elective in others. Still others require certain courses and permit a sufficient number of electives to make up the number required for the degree. The instructors present the facts or help the student to find them. The students take notes on the lectures or assigned or selected readings, take the required examinations, and turn in the required papers. If they reveal a satisfactory knowledge of the facts by way of description or interpretation, they eventually receive a diploma and a degree which allegedly signify they have received a liberal education.

There are two questions to be raised at this point. Just what kind of knowledge do our college graduates possess? What is the connection between having this knowledge and possessing a liberal education? I should like to examine each of these questions.

Ordinarily, a student registers during the first two years of college for general, introductory courses and during the last two years concentrates in one or more fields. Let us follow a student through a "typical" day. In his first class in the morning, there may be some reading of Homer, Chaucer, Spencer's *Faery Queen,* a play of Shakespeare, or an English poem. Instead, there may be a discussion of a written theme due that morning. He then goes to a class in English history where he is told about the contributions of Henry II of England to the development of English law, or to a class in *Contemporary Civilization* where he becomes acquainted with the background of the industrial revolution, or he passes to the smell of hydrogen sulphide in the chemical laboratory to try and discover what Boyle's Law is about, or to the physics laboratory to try and use a slide rule or to discover the coefficient of heat expansion or how to wire a series in parallel. He then proceeds to *Elementary German* where he struggles with the proper endings of the genitive and accusative cases.

Later in the day, in *Introductory Anthropology* he is told or reports on the ceremonies of the Blackfoot Indians or cross-cousin marriage of the Australian Arunta, and in the *History of Philosophy* he tries to understand Hume's answer to Berkely and Kant's critique of British empiricism. In psychology he is told about post-ganglionic fibres and conditioned-reflexes. In sociology he reads about the differential rate of delinquency in the city and country. He relaxes later in the afternoon by sitting through an art class, where he views slides on the paintings of the French Impressionists; or in a class on the Romanticists in music, where he hears a recording of a Schumann symphony. Multiplying this by four years and subtracting from the result the loss due to the passing of time and lack of genuine interest, still leaves quite a deal of knowledge and some technical vocabulary.

Now what kind of knowledge does our graduate possess? The data represent the more or less systematically accumulated facts or opinions about phenomena which had been gathered by scholars and imparted to students in classrooms and laboratories. What do the "facts" *mean* to the student? This brings us to the second question, What is the connection between this knowledge and a liberal education?

What is the significance of this knowledge in the life of the student? What do the facts in a given course mean to him? What real needs are they satisfying? What moving relation exists between the confusions and tensions in the living experience of the student and the knowledge he acquired? How are the perceptions of events around him heightened and enlivened? What difference in basic values and conduct is effected by the knowledge imparted in the classroom and laboratory? How is the mind trained or disciplined? Does the knowledge acquired in a liberal arts college fundamentally influence the subsequent lives of a majority of students? *Is the student really motivated in directions other than those which were followed when he entered college?*

The Entering Freshmen

Let us reconstruct an "average" college classroom. There are twenty-five young men and women approximately seventeen to nineteen years of age. They come from middle-class families. They have graduated from the public high school. There, they listened to authorities in the kinds of knowledge which prepare them to enter college.

Besides attending high school, they were members of clubs, they attended movies and parties, and had dates. They quarrelled at home and with their friends. They had good times. They read the "funnies." They listened to radio programs. They listened and participated in family discussions. Their parents were more or less regular "church-goers." Most of the students had attended Sunday School for various periods. They acquired the virtues and vices of a middle-class American community. They had received, and now live by, the opinions and prejudices of their families and friends.

The opinions and ideas which freshmen bring to college are less important than the emotions which accompany their beliefs and prejudices. This requires explanation so that we may better understand the problem facing the college teacher.

How do our children initially acquire their beliefs and views about family life, religion, what is good or bad and nice? How do they learn to react to authority and to difference? The answer seems obvious. Their parents "teach" them. The matter is not so simple. Parents teach children much less by talk than by manner.

Probably the greatest single mistake parents make in training their children is to project adult meanings into the experience of the child long before it has the need for or the capacity to understand what the adults are talking about. Infants and young children are quite dependent upon their parents. Parents represent the authority to which children must submit if their needs are to be satisfied. This process of early physical and social training is fraught with real danger to the child. The *way* in which the spontaneous freedom of the child is curbed will have tremendous significance during his lifetime. The *manner* in which parents exercise their authority will determine the child's habitual response during his subsequent relations with others.[3] The emotional responses of the child are most significant, least understood, and, very often, misdirected.

What impresses the child is not so much the statements made, the words used, as the feeling-tones and emotional tensions with which they are loaded. The language the parent uses means very little. What the child really responds to are feelings of warmth, security, love, affection, prohibition, deprivation, rejection, fear, resentment, hostility, and so on. The words, quite beyond his undertsanding, do not carry for the child the ideas they are supposed to represent. The calmness or harshness of voice, the smile or frown on the face, the hug or push, of those in authority determines the child's reaction.

Children must be inhibited. The kind of adjustments they make to authority, to society, to those who differ, to change, and the feelings which go along with the adjustment will, in largest measure, be influenced by the way in which parental authority is exercised. If the early training is administered firmly but kindly the child will not feel too frus-

F. N.[3] Edward Liss, "The Failing Student," American Journal of Orthopsychiatry, vol. 11, pp. 712-717, Oct. 1941.

trated. His resentment or hostility aroused over having to restrain himself will be modified by the affection which envelops him.

The growing child, of course, is unaware that the deep emotions he experiences become associated with particular words. Later, when the words or "ideas" are again presented, the early associated emotions are evoked. Not realizing what is happening, the child or adolescent or adult *finds reasons* to explain why his opinion or belief, or prejudice (emotion) is sound. The reasoning may be good, but it is not sound or valid. Reasons, good or bad, are found to justify the way one feels.[4] (This will be discussed in detail in Chapter Five).

In public and high school the children are again faced with new problems of adjustment. They, again, face authority. Instead of, or in addition to, their parents, they face teachers. Instead of, or in addition to, competing with brothers, sisters, and playmates, they face competition with fellow students. The whole business of elementary and secondary education occurs in a matrix of deep emotional experience. What they do with their new experiences is, in part, determined by the attitudes, formed in the home, which they bring to school. Both what they learn and how they learn will depend on their emotional sets, which, in turn, determine their present needs and interests.

One example will do although thousands could be given. A twelve-year-old youngster asks her dad to check her English assignment for the next day. She shows him her paper with the names of twenty poems followed by the names of the authors. She wants to know whether the correct author is listed with the poem.

"Who wrote Thanatopsis?" asks Dad.

"What's that?" inquires Junior Miss rather petulantly.

F. N.[4] Any reputable textbook on psychiatry or mental hygiene will contain innumerable illustrations of the degree of "rationalization" all of us engage in to protect ourselves from really seeing ourselves as we are.

"That is a poem," replied Dad drily. "Who is the author?"

"I don't know, and what difference does it make? Have I got the right author listed?"

"Well, it seems to me that if you are learning the names of poems and authors it does make a difference. Isn't that the purpose of this assignment?"

"Look, Dad," replies one of America's hopes, "don't take it so seriously. Pickle Puss wants the stuff and unless I hand this junk in tomorrow morning I'll have to stay after school and do it. The kids are all going skating and I don't want to miss the fun. Gee, you oughta see Betty's skates. I wish I could have a pair like hers. They're tubular."

Dad prided himself on knowing something about education. So he thought he would capture the interest of the child by reading Thanatopsis and try translating it into terms darling daughter would understand.

"Listen, dear.

> 'So be prepared that when thy summons comes to join that innumerable caravan which moves to those mysterious realms where each shall take his place in the silent halls of death, Thou go not like the quarry slave - - - ' "

"What do you think?" Dad smiled patiently.

"I think tubular skates are lots of fun."

Dad was far removed from the present need and interests of daughter.

High school students must acquire knowledge of a sort to pass the subjects before being certified for graduation. They possess facts. The facts, however, do not "possess" them. They are not stirred by what they have learned. The bookish facts lead a remote, sterile, conceptual existence hardly touching the vital daily experience of the students. What moves them are their feelings about their parents, their friends, their rivalries, their appearance, the opposite sex.

They live in accordance with rules of behavior and expected responses which have been sanctioned by the emotions impressed upon them during childhood training.

When the students enter college, their opinions about themselves and others and the world are sanctioned and supported less by logic than by habitual emotional responses.

The problem facing the college instructors is to find a way in which to help the student look at old facts in a new way and to give new facts sympathetic attention. Traditional sanctions have to be examined. The routinized sets of rules, previously governing their conduct, have to be exposed to criticism. The authority of and obedience to arbitrary ways of institutional life must be rationally justified, not compulsively supported. This is what getting a liberal education means.

The wise instructor will understand the range of feeling and emotion which accompanies the traditional points of view of the freshmen. When new ideas and points of view are presented or the old ones are critically examined, the students react in one of two directions. They treat ideas as a game of intellectual ping-pong, not daring to have their emotions disturbed, or else they treat the new horizons, being revealed, with seriousness, and accept the challenge of struggling through to modified or new vital attitudes. This is not an either-or matter. Different students react differently.

A sense of defeat and uneasiness takes hold of many of them. Without being able to make clear to themselves what is taking place, the students feel lost. They do not quite understand their place in the world, their relations to others, the processes of social change, and the forces which are so precipitously altering our life. They find it difficult to consolidate their accustomed emotional responses with the new feelings called forth by new and strange concepts. Their conception of self, their sense of importance, of self-esteem, of counting for something, which constitutes the core of a balanced personality, is obscured and distorted.

Along with this confusion of ideas, they have to struggle with their feelings regarding more intimate personal problems of sex, religion, clothes, dates, fraternities or sororities, personal appearance, family relations, competition, jealousies, grades, tuition fees, and future jobs. These are some of the living, dynamic realities brought into the college classrooms.

The curricula of the colleges of arts and sciences, it has long been recognized, have not met the needs of many students. It is unlikely that any single curriculum would fit the needs of all college students. The real issue, however, is not that the traditional subject-matter of the arts and sciences college should be surrendered and new programs substituted, or that all traditional methods of instruction are obsolete and any new method of instruction is preferable. Any curriculum plan, old or new, and any method of instruction, can be little better than the people responsible for implementing it. In the final analysis, the real issue concerns itself with obtaining sensitive, intelligent, and skillful teachers.

As one looks about at the present generation of adult leaders who had received college training, doubts arise as to whether the most effective use of the colleges of the country has been made; whether in the professional, political, business, social, family, or teaching area, we see too many college girls and boys hiding behind adult masks, pretending to be mature, rational, responsible citizens directing their own affairs and the affairs of their community in a socially-approved manner. In reality, too many of them are often confused, insecure, and dissatisfied. By and large, they seem to get along, but more intimate association with them would reveal a fundamental, inarticulated restlessness.

The meaning of their activity, the conception of self, their relationship to their fellow men, their interpretation of

the world and their place in it have remained basically un-
modified by knowledge acquired in the college classrooms.
They continue to live in the climate of feeling and opinion
which was received from their parents and carried through
college fundamentally unaffected by knowledge. The
economic bias, race prejudice, social distinctions, class status,
and moral attitudes reflected by the entering freshman remain *essentially* the attitudes of the senior, and the adult
personality.

The knowledge imparted in the college classroom equips
the student with a miscellaneous array of isolated data and
some new verbalizations, an additional language apparatus
which lulls him into a false sense of having really learned
something. In reality, his confusion is increased. The authority of the Word and its Devotees adds to the load of un-
digested symbols acquired before entering college.

The college curriculum itself is set up in terms of knowledge, not students. There are departments of economics,
sociology, history, biology, or divisions of the social sciences,
the humanities, and the physical sciences. *Subjects*, it seems,
are taught, not students, in spite of the earnest intentions of
most teachers. The curriculum consists almost entirely of
answers, not problems, answers to questions never raised by
students.

Knowledge, in itself, is sterile, whether it is in the form
of the Encyclopaedia Britannica on the library shelf, or in
the notebook of the student, or in his examination. It is
equally sterile and useless if it remains in the form of intellectual concepts retained by the student sufficiently long to
recall enough to pass the instructor's examination.

The lecture method of instruction and the discussion
or recitation method of teaching have been examined many
times. One of the outstanding conclusions of the different
kinds of experiments is that the lecture method is just as
good as the discussion method *so far as a survey and "mastery"*

of factual data are involved.[5]   Recently (February, 1946), the University of Wisconsin upper classmen, in response to a questionnaire distributed to 5,000 students, directed most of their criticism against teaching methods.   Lectures, the most common teaching method at the university, were considered least helpful.   The students favored small discussion sections.

The reader will miss the point we are trying to make if the issue is framed in terms of the lecture or discussion controversy, or the traditional *versus* progressive curricula, as it is usually discussed.   Our concern is with the nature of genuine, organic learning rather than with the best way of acquiring "facts."   The instructor may "lecture" for the entire hour or students may spend the entire period in discussion, but in neither case will the students necessarily learn in any genuine sense of the term.   *Talking is neither teaching nor learning.*

Indeed, the hundreds of experiments on methods of teaching in college have been concerned with how best *to transmit facts*.   This is not the problem.   The real problem, it seems to us, is how *to translate the data*.   The real question is: What method or methods are to be used to make knowledge *meaningful* for the student?

The instructor may speak for five or fifteen minutes, or the students may assume the responsibility for conducting the class.   In either case, the instructor must be aware of what is happening.   He must speak, or guide the discussion in the light of what the ideas or facts mean to the students. (This thesis is elaborated in detail in Chapters Six and Twelve.)

The task of general, not technical, education is not to train scientists or to develop scholars.   It is to give the life

F. N.[5] For a list of such experiments see Luella Cole, *The Background for College Teaching*, 1940, pps. 323-331. When classes are made up of a hundred to a thousand or more students it is difficult to proceed in any other way except to lecture. An alternative, of course, would be to break up this large number into smaller units, if the expense involved were not an important factor, as it usually is.

of the student new meaning, new significance, greater control over his conduct, to help him acquire liberal attitudes, to help him discover his capacities so that he might enjoy increased self-determination and self-realization.

In order to avoid possible misunderstanding, *we insist that knowledge is necessary*. Symbols, concepts, ideas are the instrumentalities by which an enlightened framework of beliefs is gradually selected and constructed. Knowledge is essential to make clear the conditions under which students will have to face the world. Knowledge is necessary to differentiate clear fact from exciting fancy, poisonous propaganda from rational planning.

It is impossible to achieve critical thinking without definite data. Content or subject-matter is not to be discarded but made significant in the light of student interest. Facts must be acquired in order to recognize the character of a problem or to realize its existence. Ideas are real weapons, and learning cannot take place without them.

It is the gap between knowledge and learning that is open to criticism. The belief that one acquires learning, as tested by standardized examinations, which will somehow prepare one for future competence, is belied by an instructor who remains close to and gains the confidence of college students.

Knowledge is not power. The *application* of knowledge is power. And power can be misdirected. The two important matters overlooked in the traditional imparting of knowledge are how to apply the concepts used, and how to determine the ends or goals which applied knowledge is to serve.

Knowledge must be instrumental and not an end in itself, otherwise it is symbolic of nothing in the lives of students.

Some readers may feel that this is precisely what is meant by "training the mind." One is free to define the phrase in this way. If this be the case, I think the conclusion is fair that the colleges fail to carry out their purpose.[6]

(Knowledge, of course, may be appreciated, enjoyed, or displayed. It then serves an esthetic end).

Indeed, the specialist in a field of learning is often incapable of understanding the *significance* of his own scholarship in his personal life, in the lives of students, and in the larger activity of society. He may be a skilled technician without being an educated person.[7]

Professor Kandel of Teachers College, Columbia University, writes: "A successful education can only be looked for as teachers become masters of what they teach, recognize the relation of what they teach to the society in which they teach, and have a sympathetic understanding of those whom they teach."[8]

Many years ago Ralph Waldo Emerson wrote in *The American Scholar*: "Action is with the scholar subordinate but it is essential. Without it he is not yet a man. Without it thought can never ripen into truth . . . The preamble of thought, the transition through which it passes from the un-

F. N.[6] The point of view of the chapter is supported, in general, by an increasing number of specialists professionally concerned with the development of the American college. See, for example, three articles by Daniel A. Prescott, "Non-intellectual Education," The Educational Record, 17:248-258, 1936; "Emotional Weather," *ibid.*, 20:96-106, 1939; "General Education and the Individual," *ibid.*, 20:409-421, 1936. Also, V. T. Thayer, "Current Trends in the Development of General Education," *ibid.*, 20:373-394, 1939. Also, L. K. Frank, "Fundamental Needs of the Child," Mental Hygiene 22:353-379, 1938; "The Reorientation of Education to the Promotion of Mental Hygiene," *ibid.*, 23:529, 1939; "The Task of General Education," The Social Frontier, 3:171-173, 1937; "General Education Today," *ibid.*, 3:209-211, 1937. D. A. Prescott, *Emotion and the Educative Process*, 1938. This latter volume is especially significant since it was sponsored by the American Council on Education. Dean Harold Benjamin presents his point of view in a small delightful volume, *The Saber-Tooth Curriculum*, 1939. See, also C. C. Fry and E. G. Rostow, "The Problem of College Mental Hygiene," Mental Hygiene 22:552-567, 1941 and H. A. Wann, "Mental Growth Through Education," *ibid.*, 25:18-21, 1941.

F. N.[7] "For, outside their special subjects, these men of science are as helpless as wasps on window panes . . . In a word, they are informed without being intelligent." C. E. M. Joad, *Guide to Modern Wickedness*, 1939, p. 294. Professor Joad's discussion of "Education," Chapter 14, is warmly recommended as a challenge to college instructors!

F. N.[8] I. K. Kandel, "The Fantasia of Current Education," The American Scholar, 10:297, 1941.

conscious to the conscious, is action. *Only so much do I know as I have lived.*" (Italics not in original).

The student cannot assimilate knowledge-symbols unless he is able to locate in his own experience the reality to which the symbol refers. Knowledge cannot be made meaningful unless the instructor recognizes the problem of helping the student translate that knowledge in terms of the latter's own emotional and intellectual experience.

The educated teacher must understand in a general way the underlying personality make-up and emotional reactions of the students when they enter his class. This is as much a part of the educational situation as the body of fact to be presented.

Dr. W. Carson Ryan visited schools throughout the United States to discover how wholesome the class atmosphere was. He concluded, "Simple friendliness in the schoolroom would seem to be one of those easily attainable and obviously desirable conditions for any human enterprise having to do with good mental health, but the visitor to schools *finds it in shockingly few of the places he visits.*"[9]

"The dilemma of education," Dr. L. K. Frank has stated, "arises from belief in man as a rational being in whom emotion can be controlled by reason and intelligence. Educational programs shrink from any frank acceptance of the underlying personality make-up and emotional reactions of students as entering into the educational situation because to do so would bring a widespread collapse of the whole educational philosophy and undermining of approved pedagogy."[10]

New Meanings for Old Values

Students enter the liberal arts college for a number of different reasons. The great majority would agree that if

F. N.[9] *Mental Health Through Education,* 1938, p. 31.

F. N.[10] L. K. Frank, "Dilemma of Leadership," Psychiatry, 2:247, Aug. 1939.

the college helped them to direct their personal life, the time, effort, and expense involved would be very much worthwhile. Students are curious and eager, contrary to the opinion of many instructors. Their apparent lack of interest in what the professor talks about is, in part, a commentary on the way the subject-matter is taught. The individual student craves confidence in his ability to amount to something. He does not particularly enjoy the feeling of defeatism and helplessness which overcomes him in face of vast institutional processes and complexities described in the courses to which he is subjected.

He has enthusiasm and seeks purposes through which it can be expressed. He wants understanding of himself and others. He seeks reassurance against his own frustrations. If in nothing else, every student, like each of us, is a specialist in living his own life. He senses the gap between what is talked about and what he has lived. His needs are not understood and, hence, are not met as far as his college classroom experience is involved. He is left pretty much untouched by the subject-matter of the course. He graduates and enters the competitive struggle for economic security in which, even if successful, he will not necessarily find inner security and rich happiness.

Here is the challenge to college teachers. How can knowledge be made part of the lives of the students? By interpreting it in the light of the needs of the students. By helping them to construct for themselves a new framework of ideas and feelings which relate to the actual world in which they live. This means they must be helped to develop broader meanings and enriched insights implied in the facts they obtain so that they understand themselves, their relations to others, and their role in society.

Knowledge must not be merely transmitted. It must be *translated* so that it becomes meaningful in the lives of students. Yet, there exists a system of values tested by time and experience which the community accepts as self-evident and wants its children to accept without question. Traditions must be preserved, even while society changes. The teacher is charged with transmitting tradition, but he also must understand what tradition means to the student.[11]

The position taken above implies that the college instructor should not be neutral in the description of the data in his field. He must help the student to discover and interpret the facts. It does not follow that he should become a propagandist for a pet cause. Any interpretation of data which leads to desired ends through action may be labeled propaganda. Every effort at convincing or persuading one of a particular significance implied by knowledge or opinion may be considered as a form of propaganda. However, such inclusive definition fails to make certain vital distinctions.

A propagandist in the vicious sense of the term is one who *manipulates* symbols or situations or persons in order to attain a predetermined objective. He may be sincere or insincere. The danger is that he deliberately conceals certain facts or interpretations which, if presented, would deter one from following him. If one has a point of view, and dearly holds to certain beliefs which he is willing to analyze with others, holding up his ends for criticism by others, he may be called a propagandist but certainly not a propagandist who is a manipulator.[12] Does not every instructor have certain points of view? Facts do not arrange themselves. They are selected whether or not one is aware of the criteria of selection. Knowledge is utilized, for good or evil, in a framework of feeling, beliefs, desires, hopes, and fears, conscious and sub-conscious.

F. N.[11] See Lewis Mumford, "The Social Responsibilites of Teachers and Their Implication for Teacher Education," Educational Record, 20:471-499, 1939.

F. N.[12] Max Lerner, "Propaganda in Our Time," The New Republic, Aug. 26, 1940.

Professors, students, the college administrators, and the public or private groups which support the college, all share and reflect the common values of the society in which they live. The common value elements define and determine more or less clearly why the college should exist, why certain subject-matters should be offered. To ask, "Why should there be colleges of arts and sciences?" "Why should men and women be educated?" brings a reply which must deal with the values, beliefs, and ideals held by the *community*. The issue is not whether the current values are desirable or not, but that the institution of higher education is an expression of *what the community considers desirable*. The college of arts, when viewed in this light, is seen to be an ethical institution, and teaching, an ethical profession.

The use to which institutions of learning had been put in the Axis states, reveals rather strikingly how closely they reflected the prevailing beliefs of those countries. The supremacy of the state in the lives of its individuals determined what was to be taught and for what purpose.

In America, the state operates to safeguard the personal and property rights of the individual. (This is our professed ideal, too frequently violated in practice). We believe that education is desirable so that the individual may discover and realize his capacities. We believe in freedom of contract, private property, equal opportunities for all, freedom of expression, and representative government. The American colleges reflect the ideas and ideals of a democratic way of life.

The controlling, administrative, and teaching personnel of our colleges share, along with others, the beliefs that constitute the American way of life. This does not mean that the beliefs are necessarily articulated nor that each individual does not interpret them somewhat differently when they are crystallized. It does mean that the facts of science, art, and literature are, in part, selected and presented in light of the attitudes and beliefs acquired through living in an American culture.

Students also share these common values of American life. The position taken in this study, however, is that education must give the life of the student new meaning, new significance, greater control of his conduct — so that he may be helped to discover his capacities and enjoy increased self-determination and self-realization.

If this process of self-development were carried through, if the *individuals' interests were the focal point* in evaluating knowledge, would not the existing common values of the community cease to play an effective regulating role in the lives of its members? We face the question of the relation between the individual and society.

Chapter 3

The Individual in His Society

The remark is commonly made that, "In the last analysis whatever anyone does is done to please oneself." The statement is not particularly illuminating. It says that people do what they want to do, which is obvious. Jesus did what He wanted to do. So did Judas. Jesus wanted to save Mankind and Judas wanted to save a few pieces of silver. What differentiates them? The behavior of Jesus has become an ideal of service to one's fellowman while the behavior of Judas has been symbolized as an act of betrayal of man's spirit to his greed. The *quality* of the self, not the fact that each acts to please himself, distinguishes an individual.

Every person feels, thinks, and acts as an individual. He becomes a different kind of individual depending upon his experiences with others. Every person associates with others and is influenced by them in thousands of ways. What he does, what he says, how he behaves, influences others and he, in turn, is similarly influenced by them. One's personality is a product of individual organic behavior expressing itself in, with, and through association with the world of objects and people. A simple analogy may make the matter clearer.

Each person's lung structure and capacity are somewhat different from every other person's. Each lung inhales a slightly different volume of air and expands in a slightly different way, which is normal for *each* individual under given conditions. But every lung must inhale air rather

than carbon monoxide or cyanide. Air is the normal gas for
every human lung however different its individual needs. A
lung without air is not a lung. It is just so much dead tissue.
Only so long as air is inhaled and exhaled does the organ
function as a lung. There is no lung *versus* air problem.

While every individual is different, without people to
associate with he wouldn't be a person. To associate with
people, one must conform to what they expect, to behave the
way one "ought to" behave.

How does one reconcile his personal idiomatic needs for
unique self-expression with his social needs to be like others?
There is a double standard which must be met. The problem
of this dual standard will be made clearer by briefly discussing each one.

Social Standards

There must be group standards. A society can exist only
if it is orderly. The majority or controlling group must
agree on ways of behaving. They must share in common
certain sentiments and beliefs. They expect others to conduct themselves in accordance with their sentiments and they
realize that they, too, must behave in the accustomed, expected ways. Without agreed-upon goals, purposes, and interests, social activity would be impossible. Furthermore,
the institutions of a society define, regulate, and control
the manner in which common goals and purposes are to be
achieved.[1]

Society expresses its goals and accepted ways of achieving
them through common symbols which carry, more or less, a
common meaning for a considerable majority of the population. Thus, for example, in the United States, we accept
the "Democratic Way of Life" as our goal. The lives of two
of our leaders, Thomas Jefferson and Abraham Lincoln,
symbolize this ideal. The pledge of allegiance to our flag in

---

F. N.[1] A. Kardiner, *The Individual in His Society*, 1939. T. Parsons, *The Structure
of Social Action*, 1937. T. Arnold, *The Folklore of Capitalism*, 1937.

thousands of schools every morning is another symbol of the same ideal. The ceremonies on Independence Day, the singing of *America*, the recitation of Lincoln's *Gettysburg Address*, these and hundreds of other activities are symbolic expressions of our common sentiments regarding political democracy.

The majority of citizens are influenced by the American attitude of "success." To be successful means to acquire financial security and the kind of social position, prestige, and possession which go along with wealth. This is one of the chief goals of American society. The ways of achieving the goal are also generally agreed upon. Freedom of contract, the right of private property, the equal protection of the law are some of the constitutional guarantees for economic activity which we support.

We also share common moral values regarding the disadvantaged, the sick, the aged, and the homeless. We feel it our duty to contribute to public funds for their support. In a broad sense we agree on what constitutes proper moral conduct. Such sentiments stem from our religious beliefs and ideals expressed through our religious training and religious institutions.

The political, economic, moral, and religious values just mentioned are imbedded in our social relations. They are reflected in our institutions. The common value sentiments which are accepted as an integral part of our daily life bind us together. There is an unquestioned sense of community solidarity which is taken for granted. Individuals expect certain behavior from others and act as others expect them to. The group standards thus serve to maintain order and stability.

The matter of group standards becomes complicated, however, as soon as different groups start questioning existing standards and seek to set up other norms of social conduct. When standards compete, social stability is threatened. As is well recognized, no society is ever completely static, else there'd be no change; nor completely chaotic, else there'd be no order. The more complex a society becomes, the more rapid and extensive its system of communication and transportation; and the more it welcomes or is subjected to outside forces, the greater the likelihood that traditional standards will have to compete with new values or even give way before them. The danger of too many standards is that it leads to no standards. In time, there would exist no influential group of people in the society agreeing on any beliefs or values which would motivate or control people's behavior or enlist their loyalty.

We have not reached such a divided state of opinion and uncertainty of standards in this country. There is, nevertheless, a tremendous amount of uncertainty as to what our fundamental goals are. We are uncertain of our international policies and of many of our national policies. There are too many conflicting groups competing for men's loyalties.[2]

The individual, not being sure of the standards of his own society, begins questioning not only them but also what he himself stands for. The situation is comparable to that of a youngster who is constantly exposed to the inconsistency of his parents. Not knowing where they stand, the youngster is unable ever to come to grips with what he himself wants or should want. He is uncertain from moment to moment of what to expect from his parents or what they expect from him. This leaves him, as it must, anxious and ill at ease.

If we are not certain about the direction toward which we wish to move, we will not be able to agree on a plan of action nor will we be able to build personal ideals for ourselves. In brief, we will not be able to reconcile our personal standards with those of the group around us if we are uncertain of both sets of standards.[3]

F. N.[2] K. Mannheim, *Man and Society in An Age of Reconstruction*, 1940. F. Alexander, *Our Age of Unreason*, 1942. E. Fromm, *Escape from Freedom*, 1941.

F. N.[3] H. D. Lasswell, *World Politics and Personal Insecurity*, 1935.

The central theme of this chapter, it will be recalled, is the relation of the individual to his society. The problem is to reconcile the peculiar needs of an individual who is different from everyone else, with his social needs to conform to the standards of his society. I know of no better way to illustrate the difficulties involved in understanding the role of the individual in modern society than to discuss briefly the main causes of individual and social mal-adjustment in our own time. **1719846**

In the following discussion, I want to show two things: (1) The need for new standards which a majority must support for effective social reconstruction, and (2) the need for socially-minded leaders who will assume positions of authority in public and private life. Without such leadership democratic government cannot be effective. We need individuals whose own creative needs and satisfactions will be identified with the values and standards of a revivified democracy.

I should like to state the conclusion first. The basic issue facing the people of the Western world is: Shall we try to avoid the crisis of modern society by democratic planning, or shall we permit the new age of machines to destroy us through dictatorship and war? There is a wide-open split on this issue. Few people understand what the modern crisis in Western society is. Still fewer understand how it might be met. *To prepare individuals who will get personal satisfaction out of active participation in this change and planning is,* it seems to me, *one of the important purposes of our educational institutions.*

The Crisis of Modern Society

The one fundamental difference between earlier European culture and modern European culture is found in the principle employed to explain the nature of man and his world. In the seventeenth and eighteenth centuries a few bold spirits questioned the authority of the Church and its views on the nature of man and of the universe. They felt that the only way of arriving at true knowledge was to rely upon their own observation, experimentation, and verification. Verifiable operations and not arbitrary faith were to determine what the "facts" were.

The scientists used this new method of research in many fields and the result was a series of inventions and discoveries which have radically transformed the modern world. The first great transformation effected by the new inventions is known as the Industrial Revolution which started in England after 1750, and subsequently spread throughout the world.

The technological advance which made the factory system and large scale production possible was dependent upon a series of factors other than the invention of the steam engine and textile machinery. Although feudalism was the prevailing pattern in the fifteenth and sixteenth centuries, the germs of a new basis for society were present. With the opening up of the New World, the possibility of large-scale markets came into existence. The large supplies of precious coin from America supplied the growing commercial world with a medium of exchange and a large surplus capital, which could be invested or used to create new enterprises.

The slowly-rising middle-class merchants gained in number and extended their activities. Markets were established at the outskirts of feudal estates. Towns grew up around the markets. The lending of money, at first forbidden by the Church, was later countenanced, and finally sanctioned.

More rational methods of cultivating the soil were discovered. Stock breeding was greatly improved. More efficient methods of transportation were accompanied by improved techniques in navigation. The production of food crops and wool could be entered upon at a distance since transportation of them was now possible. In short, more goods were produced and the possibility of exchanging them for a profit appeared.

A new way of life had been created. Instead of each family directly producing its *own* necessities for its *own* consumption, masses of men and women worked in huge factories at specialized tasks to produce specialized commodities to be sold throughout the world for a profit.

As we look back upon the last few hundred years of European history, we can see that the great revolutions, the Protestant Reformation, the English Revolution of 1688, and the French Revolution of 1789, were various forms of this basic struggle to shift power from the Church and landed nobility to the middle-class merchantmen. The struggle assumed the form of a religious revolt in Germany (although basically it was economic in character), a struggle for political power in England (so that the merchant could re-organize the political state for *his* purposes of trading), and a struggle for liberty, fraternity, and equality in France (the merchant had to be free to possess his own private property and have an equal say in the legislation necessary to employ it).

In the eighteenth and nineteenth centuries the state interfered as little as possible in the development of business enterprise. (As a matter of fact, the rising business classes used the legislative machinery of the state for their own interests). Freedom of contract, individual enterprise, protection of private property, as little government restriction as possible, every one minding his own business, and watching his own interests — these were the ideas of nineteenth century liberalism. It was supposed that without governmental interferences, prices would "naturally" adjust themselves. If everyone tended to his own interests, in the long run all of society would benefit.

Matters did not work out that way. The unregulated economic system of modern times breaks down periodically, resulting in unemployment, world-wide depressions, international struggle for markets, stifling of international trade, international monopolies, collapse of world-price structures, and war.

An unregulated economic system is a thing of the past. Planning we must have, good or bad.

The nineteenth and twentieth centuries witnessed the irrepressible growth of the industrial system throughout Western Europe and America. The industrial giant in recent years used capital as its motive power. Mass-production, the result of technological advance, became so efficient it could not work and at the same time yield private surpluses. Periodically, the income of the masses was not large enough to buy the goods produced. Hence, the inevitable depression.

Few of the 50,000,000 wage earners in this country recognize the workings of the economic system, and still fewer realize its implications. Nevertheless, the changes wrought by this system of finance-capitalism endanger the peace of the world. The government is forced to regulate more and more the economic life of the country in the attempt to lessen the frictions arising from unregulated private capitalist enterprise.

Thus far we have described the growth and impact of scientific method and technological knowledge upon the social and economic *institutions* of modern civilization. Equally far-reaching changes have been effected in the beliefs and *attitudes* of the people. There is less recognition of the latter changes since they operate more subtly and are less readily measurable.

An almost completely new basis for human society confronts us today. The Cathedral of Chartres, lovingly erected to the greater glory of God, with its incomparably-beautiful stained-glass and sculptural masterpieces and its twin spires pointing to heaven, is today a museum-piece for vacationists rather than a haven for the pious laden with the burden of sin. We, instead, possess the Empire State Building and its observation tower, from which we proudly gaze down upon the Metropolis of the World and admire the handiwork of man. Instead of the Catholic Synthesis, we find a world knit together by finance-capitalism.

The shifts in moral values are being accomplished in two directions. On the one hand, a small minority is able directly to assimilate the facts of the social sciences. Altered points of view toward man and his place in the universe result from a direct study of accumulated knowledge. The vast majority of people, however, are being indirectly influenced in their attitudes by the altered social, political, and industrial institutions.

Modern society is composed of many traditions. Science, technology, industry, and finance capitalism have been grafted upon the older Catholic Synthesis. Modern science of itself does not set up ideals. Machine products do not in themselves develop a new set of moral attitudes. Our dominant moral sentiments arose out of the inherited beliefs of traditional Christianity. The moral ideas and beliefs and attitudes which we share today are those which arose in the hills of Judea, the plains of Babylon, and which are expressed in the Old and New Testaments. Christianity taught respect for and the worth of the *individual*. It also impressed upon the masses the rule of authority.

Such moral ideas and basic emotional patterns have been inherited and remain those of our industrial civilization. Basically, we think in terms of individual soul salvation. But, under the impact of an industrial and business civilization, the road to salvation has been paved with dollars rather than with religious faith. The Christian ideals we have inherited are inconsistent with the new institutions which have arisen with the business practices necessary to maintain them.

Traditional morality was suited to the small groups of individuals whose activities were confined to small geographical areas. The disruptive acts of an individual directly affected the few who were in more or less immediate contact with him. Whether for good or evil, the individual is no longer self-sufficient, either spiritually or economically. The inter-dependence of the farmer, worker, banker, and baker, in town, state, country and the world is one of the basic characteristics of modern society.

The increased organization both in time and space, due to industrialism and capitalism, has resulted in extending the number and size of the groups which reciprocally influence each other. Large groups, indeed, states and nations, are the units affected.

Organized rather than individual effort must be emphasized. Larger organizations are gaining men's loyalties whether they are or are not aware of the change. The newer group attitudes, such as support of the United Nations, or support of government regulation of industry, often exist alongside of the contradictory individualistic attitudes. The inconsistencies are often overlooked, ignored, or denied. Thus, for example, a manufacturer may complain about government price ceilings ruining his business, but he will praise the regulation which puts a ceiling on the rent he has to pay for his apartment.

The conflict between our unregulated system of private economic enterprise and the need for planned control through democratic methods is becoming sharper. The unregulated economic and social forces of the world are not going to lead to a peaceful world by spontaneous adjustment. We must plan for the kind of society in which free men will choose to regulate their lives and voluntarily submit to a controlled social environment to gain greater freedom for all.

Individual Needs

Just as our institutions are relatively unstable and changing, so, too, is personality characterized by instability and conflict.[4] There are too many individuals who question the fundamental values of our modern society. They represent deviating types. Their fundamental questioning is not answered by the group symbols which they refuse to accept. Again, even the masses who accept the traditional beliefs as self-evident are not static personalities. They have all sorts of problems which arise in the daily routine of living, which throw them out of balance with themselves and with each other. They say the words half-heartedly and utter their faith with little conviction. What they believe in theory, they deny in practice.

In the machine age in which we are living, personality conflicts and tensions arise in our daily associations, personal and professional. They eat into the very vitals of our being. The activities of modern society, the complicated structures of government, business, and industry are too complex for any individual to understand. The average person is compelled to renounce his own understanding of what takes place even if he has the desire to grapple with the problem. His own interpretation of events is surrendered to the opinion of experts. He becomes suggestible. The danger is present that "experts" may become propagandists manipulating people for and toward ends which they do not perceive.

The repression of impulsive satisfactions and the frustration which accompanies having to do what one neither understands nor wants to do but must, leads to aggressive irrational impulses. They must, somehow, be absorbed in socially-acceptable outlets, lest they explode in socially-dangerous activities.

We have reached a point in the middle of the twentieth century where the norms of society as well as the standards

F. N.[4] L. K. Frank, "Social Order and Psychiatry," American Journal of Orthopyschiatry, 11:620-627, Oct. 1941.

of an individual are in such flux that we understand neither the world in which we live nor ourselves.

Ideally, the institutions of a culture should be stable enough to reflect an ordered world while at the same time flexible enough to permit the working out of individual tensions within its commonly-accepted values. Order and change should reciprocally influence each other, with institutions, as Emerson declared, riding in the saddle. In this manner, the standards of society and the norms of each individual would tend to coalesce.

Edward Sapir has so graphically described a genuine culture that no excuse need be offered for quoting him at some length:

"The 'genuine' culture is not of necessity either 'high' or 'low'; it is merely inherently harmonious, balanced, self-satisfactory. It is the expression of a richly varied and yet somehow unified and consistent attitude to life, an attitude in which one sees the significance of any one element of civilization in its relation to all others. It is, ideally speaking, a culture in which nothing is spiritually meaningless, in which no important part of the general activity brings with it a sense of frustration, of misdirected or unsympathetic effort. It is not a spiritual hybrid of contradictory patches, of water-tight compartments of consciousness that avoid participation in a harmonious synthesis. If the culture necessitates slavery, it frankly admits it; if it abhors slavery, it feels its way to an economic adjustment that obviates the necessity of its employment. It does not make a great show in its ethical ideals of an uncompromising opposition to slavery, only to introduce what amounts to a slave system into certain portions of its industrial mechanism. Or, if it builds magnificent houses of worship, it is because of the necessity it feels to symbolize in beautiful stone a religious impulse that is deep and vital; if it is ready to institutionalize religion, it is prepared also to dispense with the homes of institutionalized religion. It does not look sheepish when a direct appeal is made to its religious consciousness, then make amends by furtively bestowing a few dollars toward the maintenance of an African mission. Nor does it carefully instruct its children in what it knows to be of no use vitally either to them or in its own mature life. Nor does it tolerate a thousand other spiritual maladjustments such are apparent enough in our American life of today . . . It is not enough that the ends of activities be socially satisfied, that each member of the community feel in some dim way that he is doing his bit toward the attainment of a social benefit. This is all very well as far as it goes, but a genuine culture refuses to consider the individual as a mere cog, as an entity whose sole *raison d'etre* lies in his subservience to a collective purpose that he is not conscious of or that has only a remote relevance to his interests and strivings. The major activities of the individual must directly satisfy his own creative and emotional impulses, must always be something more than means to an end. The great cultural mistake of industrialism, as developed up to the present time, is that in harnessing machines to our uses it has not known how to avoid the harnessing of the majority of mankind to its machines. The telephone girl who lends her capacities, during the greater part of the living day, to the manipulation of a technical routine that has an eventually high efficiency value but that answers to no spiritual needs of her own, is an appalling sacrifice to civilization. As a solution of the problem of culture she is a failure,—the more dismal the greater her natural endowment. As with the telephone girl, so, it is to be feared, with the great majority of us, slave-stokers to fires that burn for demons we would destroy, were it not that they appear in the guise of our benefactors. A genuine culture cannot be defined as a sum of abstractly desirable ends, as a mechanism. It must be looked upon as a sturdy plant growth, each remotest leaf and twig of which is organically fed by the sap at the core. And this growth is not here meant as a metaphor for the group only; it is meant to apply as well to the individual. A culture that does not build itself out of the center interests and desires of its bearers, that works from general ends to the individual, is an 'external' culture. The word 'external' which is so often instinctively chosen to describe a culture, is well chosen. The genuine culture is 'internal,' it works from the individual to ends."[5]

Our present society tends to make the unhappy personality the average type. I do not, of course, mean that the average college student or the average adult is neurotic to the point where he requires professional assistance. I mean that very many of us are dissatisfied with ourselves and would like to be different.

Parents and teachers are no longer positive about the traditional beliefs of our society. No longer being sure of past values and not yet being convinced about new ones, they are unable to live by a faith firmly held or to present it convincingly to children and students. The child must, therefore, assume greater responsibility for his action, instead of finding it sanctioned by community values. This extra burden which modern society throws upon the child makes him more insecure and loads him with greater anxiety. Instead of cultivating himself, he collects things, the modern index of success. This compensation works for some for a while, but does not remove the restlessness and disquietude of spirit so marked in our generations, young and old, rich and poor.

F. N.[5] E. Sapir, "Culture, Genuine and Spurious," reprinted in Davis, Barnes and others, *Readings in Sociology*, 1927, p. 125.

The majority of people do not accept themselves. Most people rarely come to grips with an honest examination of what they are after. They strive for what the majority seeks and the majority does not really know.

More than any other time, our present epoch fails to provide the child and the adult with standards by which he can measure his worth. He is faced with the problem of developing his own attitudes and ideals without having been trained in the necessary self-discipline.

Paradoxically, the more self-disciplined a child becomes the more isolated he feels in comparison to the behavior of the majority of people. The healthy-minded person living in a "sick society" is looked upon as peculiar. He must become supinely acquiescent to be accepted by the majority, or remain different, and be considered neurotic. There is certainly no virture in being obnoxiously different merely for the sake of attracting attention. The self-disciplined individual will have better perspectives which enable him to judge the circumstance of time and place in which difference is to be expressed, and like-mindedness is to be observed.

The opportunity for the kind of discipline we are considering must be offered to millions of children. This is the great challenge to the public school system and to hundreds of colleges of the country.

The problem colleges must face is how to help people live together. The problem is not one of the individual or of the society, nor of the individual and society. It is one which must deal with preparing people to live together, in a world which is rapidly changing. The kind of relative order we want and the kind of social standards we desire must be kept in mind in educating individuals who will be freed to participate in community life in ways satisfactory to themselves. If attention is focused on the individual's satisfactions in expressing himself while social norms are under-estimated, people will not be united in common goals. Social cohesion will be endangered. This, in turn, will lead to greater tension since one will not be secure of one's social expectations. Logically, the end product would be a "community" of anarchic individuals. If, on the other hand, social order is the sole desideratum, men will become dissatisfied because self-expression and self-determina. on will be engaged in at one's peril.

Briefly, then, the essence of education, in the sense we are here dealing with it, lies in the individual taking over community points of view and in society reciprocally absorbing the individual's modification of the prevailing ideology.

The "justification" of modified community values which are being developed will have to rest on another set of accepted beliefs. If we are skeptical about the "way" of American life which has been handed down, we must, to avoid greater disintegration, construct a new "way" which we feel "ought to" guide us. "When shall we have the courage to admit that our judges, ministers, doctors, teachers, social workers, are, in a similar way, continually faced with the conflicts which confront the individual as he adjusts himself to changing condition? Now both the person who seeks for advice and the person who is expected to give it are at a loss to know to which norms and ethical standards they should cling. When shall we be willing to admit that, in the chaos in which the old conditions vanish and the new demands are not yet clearly established, systematic discussion of the pro and cons of different standards is badly needed? When shall we realize that the only way to prevent dictators forcing a new religion and a new code of ethics down our throats is for us to create a forum which is both scientific and democratic to give the lead to moral adjustment in a period of quick transformation?"[6]

F. N.[6] K. Mannheim, "War Education and Group Analysis," *Educating for Democracy,* Ch. XIX, edited by J. I. Cohen and R. M. W. Travers, 1939.

The momentous historical period in which we are living is, in a sense, favorable to the development of a living philosophy of education. Just because there is no certainty as to what it is we ourselves believe and accept nor what the next generation should believe, we are presented with the challenge and the opportunity to crystallize what "ought" to be our ultimate values. We have to recognize our newer conceptions of the nature of the universe, of man's place in it, of social relations, and personality development. The implications of these more recent conceptions cannot be verbally transferred by dealing only with the abstract concepts. They must be *translated* in terms of the readiness of students to assimilate what is talked about. The readiness of students will depend upon their needs. Unless *they want to learn,* teaching cannot readily take place. And if they do want to learn, nothing any instructor talks about will stop them. *All genuine learning,* in the final analysis, *is self-education.*

The student's personality is in continuous formation through his own choice of what he wants to attend to. Self and interests are two terms for the same phenomena. The self identifies with activities of one kind or another which tend to bring the conflicts of the person into dynamic equilibrium. Devitalized knowledge is too far removed from the vital, pulsating experience of the student. There is little reason to expect that knowledge which instructors possess or which books contain will lead to personal initiative and application by others. Knowledge-symbols, manipulated on a conceptual level, will, of course, have effect upon some conduct. One has to prepare for an examination, for example. Again, some people derive esthetic satisfaction in logic chopping or perceiving form. But knowledge gained through direct participation in translating ideas into personal significance modifies one's system of attitudes. The broad use to which "facts" are put depends upon its connection with personal disposition and interests.

Once the genuine interest of the student is stimulated there is no limit to how far he may go after the facts relevant to *his* curiosity. That search may lead him to study and contemplation which is not for the time being directed to "practical" ends (other than the immediate practical goal of understanding; the search for relations between ideas; their logical status).

The position maintained in this chapter does not underestimate the significance of critical thought based upon a solid array of facts. On the contrary, we have emphasized the *import*ance of knowledge as against sterile, impotent, lifeless abstraction. So long as the most rigid and formal concepts in some way relate to an interest of the student, they are not sterile, impotent, or lifeless. The "adventure" of ideas can become an exciting experience and possess a student. It is, we repeat once more, the translation of ideas which alone makes the transmission of knowledge into the experience of the student possible.

The democratic values of universal suffrage, freedom of speech, press, assembly, and petition, and representative parliamentary government are means of making the lives of individuals happier. That these traditional guarantees of democracy have, at times, been misused to exploit the vast majority of the people has been recently recognized. So long as democratic forms are maintained, the means of revaluation of democratic society, and correction of the abuses which distort and corrode the lives of people, remain. The test of the worthwhileness of education is the same.

Emotionally-unstable and personally-insecure people represent a grave threat to democracy. When individuals, in their helplessness, feel they have nothing to lose, they will seek emotional release in submitting to raucous "medicine-men."

Self-expression and social responsibility are made increasingly difficult by the de-personalized institutional pressures of modern economic life. The fear, anxiety, and hostility generated, for example, by the fear of economic instability and lack of opportunity lead to the ready acceptance of faith in the promise of propagandists. In their helplessness, people are ready to embrace cults and messiahs.

The reorganization of our culture, in the light of the needs of its members, is the gigantic and complicated task which faces us. Leaders in every area of institutional life must grapple with this problem. From the point of view of teaching it must be clear that the "mental-hygiene" point of view presented in this study is not a frivolous fad but almost identical with the conception of democracy itself. The promotion of human capacity for self-development and self-realization is the identical goal of mental hygiene and political and economic democracy.

Democracy is dedicated to the conservation of the individual; so is mental hygiene. Democracy, as a way of life, aspires to free the individual to realize himself in associated living; so does mental hygiene. Democracy implies differences of opinion, the right to differ; so does mental hygiene. Education, carried on in the framework of mental hygiene, aims to free individuals from personality distortions. By giving the student the opportunity to develop himself, he learns how to get along with others. A genuine educative process can aid in developing inner security, self-esteem, confidence in self, and courage to live with and in the conflict, characteristic of contemporary life.[7]

Dr. Winslow, who investigated the school health program of the New York State Regents Inquiry, the most extensive survey of education which has ever been undertaken,

F. N.[7] H. S. Ephron, "Mental Hygiene in Social Reconstruction," American Journal of Orthopsychiatry, 10:458-465, July, 1940. L. K. Frank, "The Reorganization of Education to the Promotion of Mental Health," Mental Hygiene, 23:529-543, Oct. 1939.

declared, "The principles of modern education are identical with the principles of mental hygiene. Both are directed toward cultivating self-confidence, self-respect, self-management, courage, the ability to take responsibility, the ability to overcome difficulties and to carry things through to completion; friendliness, sympathy, and co-operation with others, the development and expression of affection, tolerance of differences, the sharing of experience, the freer expression of initiative and creative abilities and interests; freedom from the stigma of guilt and shame, the ability to acknowledge an occasional defect frankly, the honest facing of unpleasant realities, and a capacity for assuming and submitting to authority in a spirit of good will."[8]

In the previous chapters we have discussed the educational and sociological premises underlying the learning-teaching process described in Part II of this volume. Before turning to the description of the process we wish to present the theory of personality development upon which it rests.

F. N.[8] *The School Health Program*, New York State Regents Inquiry, pp. 22-43, 1938.

Chapter 4

A Clinical Approach

In a recent distinguished text the author presents no less than fifty representative definitions of personality.[1] The present chapter does not intend to contribute to this confusion. Nor will the attempt be made to settle the difference of opinion as to the relative importance of "nature" and "nurture" in shaping personality. The questions of whether there are any laws describing personality development, and their character, are not in issue.

This chapter is limited to a description of personality traits and attitudes which is intended to help the reader understand the kind of learning-teaching to be described in subsequent chapters. When we speak of "personality development," we refer to those traits of personality involved in the learning process.

Such a partial picture of personality is, of course, artificial. As we try to describe the dynamics of the learning process, we will find it impossible to maintain, consistently, this shredding of the whole. In formulating a working definition for the purpose of this study, we do not pretend

F. N.[1] Gordon W. Allport, *Personality, A Psychological Interpretation*, Ch. II, 1937. The term has been complicated by being tied up with all sorts of philosophical, psychological, anthropological, and psychoanalytical questions as to the nature of the "ego" or "self." The extreme variation in the use of the term "personality" even on the part of experts may be gathered by reading *Proceedings of First Colloquium on Personality Investigation*, Lord Baltimore Press, Baltimore, 1938; *Proceedings of the Second Colloquium on Personality Investigation*, John Hopkins Press, Baltimore, 1930. Reprinted in American Journal of Psychiatry, 8:1089, 1928-29; 9:879, 1929-30.

that any individual personality is exhausted by the concepts we shall use. Even more, the whole phenomena of learning will not begin to be covered by the description which follows. It is recognized that others, with different points of view, can describe, and have described, the learning process, using a different set of concepts. All that we maintain is that the point of view to be expressed seems to us to be as real as experience itself.

Common-sense opinion and professional social scientists affirm that, in a general way, we can predict the behavior of people. No one seriously doubts that every normal adult's conduct is characterized by certain attitudes or traits. The behavior of our friends under all conditions is not accurately predictable, but they do act in relatively stable ways. There is pattern and order in each of our lives just as there are unpredictable reactions. Not only does each individual have patterned ways of behaving, but most people in a given culture also show some similar ways of reacting.

It is possible, therefore, to observe common traits, attitudes, and ways of behaving while, at the same time, recognizing that no two individuals are alike in many other respects. In a word, we agree with the common-sense view that every individual is a unique personality in some respects and that all of us are generally alike in other respects. Obviously, the more we know about any one individual's unique behavior, the less able will we be to generalize about most people. Contrariwise, the broader our generalization about common traits, the less likely are we to gain understanding of any particular individual. To understand any one individual's personality we must observe many of his organic, unified and "total" situations in their process of change and resolution. To understand a human being we must attend to the individual who is a living, conflicting, behaving, growing, changing, adjusting organism.[2] The transformations which actually occur in an individual's adjustment to and with his surroundings yield a clue to the kind of person he is. The peculiar way in which each individual selectively responds to a given situation, the total dynamic configuration, will illuminate what the individual is like.

The cautious observer, seeking knowledge of personality, refines this common-sense procedure in two ways. In the first place, his inferences or interpretations or insights are enriched by an existing body of more or less precise knowledge not shared by the layman. In the second place, the trained observer will always be on guard to return to the stream of individual behavior to check his inferences or insights, and will discard or alter or be confirmed in his interpretations of what he observes.[3] The greater his skill, the wider his observation, the more likely is it that his find-

F. N.[2] Dr. Henry A. Murray and his co-workers at the Harvard Psychological Clinic express this same point of view. "We thought that it would be an unprofitable expenditure of time merely to portray the skin of our material without attempting to get at the heart and bowels of it." *Explorations in Personality*, 1938, p 722.

The dynamic or holistic approach is being supported by an increasing number of outstanding authorities in biology, physiology, and neurology. For example, Ludwig von Bertolanffy, *Modern Theories of Development, An Introduction to Theoretical Biology*, 1933; J. H. Woodger, *Biological Principles — A Critical Study*, 1929; R. H. Wheeler, *The Science of Psychology*, 1929; G. E. Coghill, "The Genetic Interrelation of Instinctive Behavior and Reflexes," Psych. Rev., 37:264-266, 1930; Kurt Goldstein, *The Organism—A Holistic Approach to Biology Derived From Pathological Data in Man*, 1939; and *Human Nature in the Light of Psychopathology*, 1940: This point of view has also been applied to problems of human collaboration in the modern industrial scene. See Roethlisberger, *Management and Morale*, 1941, especially Ch. II. N. Cantor, *Employee Counseling*, 1945. Carl Rogers, *Counseling and Psychotherapy*, 1942.

I should like to call the reader's attention to the particularly keen analysis of Prof. John MacMurray, *Interpreting the Universe*, 1933,. Ch. VI, especially, has much in common with the point of view expressed in this chapter. Finally, the interested reader should study Andrus Angyal's stimulating study, *Foundations for a Science of Personality*, 1941.

F. N.[3] "No formulations about man and his place in society which do not prove strictly and literally accurate when tested by the experience of the individual can have more than a transitory or technical authority. Hence we need never fear to modify, prune, extend, redefine, arrange, and reorient our sciences of man as social being, for these sciences cannot point to an order of nature that has meaning apart from the directly experienced perceptions and values of the individual." E. Sapir, "Psychiatric and Cultural Pitfalls in the Business of Getting a Living," Mental Health, Publication No. 9 of The American Asociation for Advancement of Science, 1939, p. 237.

ings will be self-correcting and in correspondence with the conclusions of other observers.

This is precisely what has occurred in the recent approach to the study of personality. The attitudes or traits which we shall make use of in describing the basic patterns of individual behavior have been observed by many students. The language used may not be the same, but the patterns to which the concepts refer have been observed time and again.

The approach used in this study falls within the so-called "clinical" method. Several groups of students in different classes have been observed over a period of one or more years. On the basis of personal acquaintance with their behavior in the classroom, through personal conference, and through their written reports, inferences concerning their learning process have been made.

In light of the data being observed, we believe this approach is scientifically valid. It seems to us that *vague knowledge about an actual process is preferable to more precise statements about artificial, unlife-like situations*. Method must be bent to material.

The concepts or categories employed must be of a kind which will not destroy the unity of the situation described, but will remain close to it. At the same time, the concepts used cannot be based upon the subjective impressions of the observer. That is always dangerous. We must try to use a set of "insightful" categories which are based upon common-sense observation *and* the observations of those professionally trained in dealing with living human beings.

The point has not been reached in the study of living human beings, where all students either agree upon or use a set of concepts which have the same precise meaning for all observers. Nevertheless, there has developed a set of concepts which in a general way covers the dynamics of living situations. I refer to such categories as anxiety, tension, security, resistance, identification, projection, aggression, frustration, and so on.

These categories arising out of common-sense observations have been refined by recent students of human behavior and are now employed in a technical sense. Because all students do not entirely agree upon their meaning and implications, it does not follow that they should be discarded. Effort should be made to validate them by demonstrating their usefulness in increasing our knowledge of personality development. If empirical evidence fails to substantiate their usefulness, they can but lead to extravagant, and sometimes, wild claims which tend to discredit the search for useful categories.

What assumptions should an investigator of the learning process employ? There are many patterns which could be set up, in the light of which one could select the "facts." Thus, for example, the laws of frequency and recency have been established in the light of the repetition and time element of the stimuli. Again, curves of learning have been statistically demonstrated. Questionnaires, rating scales, and factor analysis devices have been employed.

Any number of patterns are possible depending upon one's interest. No one point of view can cover the complex process involved. In this chapter the basic patterns underlying the present study are described. No one is more keenly aware of their limitations and generality and provisional character than the author. Nevertheless, they appear to be useful in illuminating what is involved in dynamic learning on the college level.

The Dynamics of Learning

An individual is a system of dynamic, overlapping "forces" which actively strive for adjustment to each other and with the environment which affects them. One's native "temperament," expressed through traits acquired by a particular physical organism, is organized in a characteristic manner to engage in the kind of integrated activity called for by the particular problem faced at any given time. In simple language, an individual is acting in a particular way, toward a particular end, at any given time.

The organism seeks adjustment, finds balance, and is again faced with conflict to which a new adjustment must be made. There are both conflicting and stabilizing forces within the individual and his environment, which are never resolved into a permanent balance so long as life continues.

As we watch ourselves and other individuals, we are struck by this basic struggle to achieve more effective relationship between ourselves and our surroundings (including intra-personal adjustment). If this struggle could be described in general psychological terms, if we could answer the question: "What are some of the basic psychological drives?" we would have a better understanding of behavior.

Before attempting this, suppose an analogous question is asked: "What are some of the basic biological drives?" The person who responds, "Sex and hunger are two basic needs of the organism," would not be considered naive. Neither "sex" nor "hunger" are fixed drives. The sex drive is dressed up in all sorts of strange garb. Under its influence we engage in many kinds of activities, which, while independent, are nevertheless related to sex behavior. So, for example, a long discussion on musical criticism between a young man and a young lady, taking place on a park bench on a lovely spring evening, may have genuine merit on its own account. It may also serve as content to mark time before the more fundamental goal of the evening is reached.

Similarly, "hunger" can be satisfied in thousands of ways. Each manner of satisfying hunger consists of a series of habits, attitudes, or traits, which are independent of the context of hunger. But the hunger drive is the pivot which integrates these independent series of traits.

In like fashion we can speak of two general psychological drives. These patterns or drives are characteristic of individuals, especially when in association with each other, although they often characterize one's intra-personal conflicts as well. First, each one of us wants to be dependent on others. Second, each one of us wants to assert his independence.

We wish to emphasize that these needs of dependence and independence are not mechanisms or capricious spirits which exist somewhere in the organism. They are terms used to characterize, generally, the patterns of behavior of individuals organized toward particular ends.[4]

The kinds of dependence or independence sought for vary from individual to individual and in each individual from time to time. Seeking dependence or independence is a very complex psychological phenomenon. The traits and attitudes and habits involved in any quest may be organized into related system of behavior. But at any time they are integrated to help the individual attain the basic need of being wanted or of wanting to be left alone. In using these concepts of dependence and independence, then, we are trying to describe in general terms what occurs in the dynamic behavior of a person, especially when in relation to other persons. In subsequent chapters we shall deal with some of the particular forms in which these needs express themselves in the educational process. For the moment we turn to a general description of the two conflicting needs of every individual.

F. N.[4] Dr. Murray and his collaborators also emphasize the organization toward particular ends. They employ the concept of "need." "Need refers to an organic potentiality or readiness to respond in a certain way under given conditions. Need may refer to a temporary happening or to a more or less consistent trait of personality." *op. cit.* p. 61. "A need is a construct which stands for a force in the brain region, a force which organizes perception, apperception, intellection, conation and action in such a way as to transform in a certain direction an existing, unsatisfying situation." *op. cit.* pp. 123-124.

Dependence

Each one of us wants to depend upon other people. We want to be liked, loved, approved of, and understood. We want to feel that we belong somewhere. We long for the feeling of being wanted. This need drives us to join clubs, to visit each other, to agree with others, to make friends, to do the things which will win for us admiration and approval.

This need for dependence is easily observed in infants and young children. An infant cries to be held in the warm arms of the mother. A child falls or is hurt. Tearful and frightened, it runs to the parent for solace and sympathy.

The sense of security is primarily acquired during the first few years of one's life when deep contacts are made between the infant and the mother. The infant rapidly acquires a sense of "belongingness." This emotional tie is not a matter of logic. The enveloping affection is the result of the mother-child relationship and in no way depends upon the objective judgments of any kind. Whether the child is good or bad, ugly or handsome, healthy or sickly, all of this is irrelevant to parental love. A mother's arms is the child's harbor.

As the child develops from infancy to childhood and into adolescence, he is judged more and more by *what* he is and by *what* he can do. Comparisons with others are made, scoldings and naggings, praises and compliments fill the days. These judgments determine the child's feeling of adequacy or inferiority. Children who are secure, who sense they are loved, pay little attention to what their parents *say* about their inadequacies. Their pervasive awareness of security shields the child from the disquietude of not measuring up to brothers, sisters, or schoolmates. On the other hand, children who sense their rejection, and who feel insecure, seek to acquire feelings of adequacy which, however, never quite give them a basic sense of security. If they fail in showing that they possess some outstanding trait, the inevitable feeling of inferiority, in addition to the basic sense of insecurity, leads them to become "problem children."

It is difficult for children and adolescents to obtain basic security or love through accomplishments since affection is built on the "psycho-motor tensions" of the first few years. Reassurance against anxiety and insecurity is sought in another direction, that of doing something better than others, of attracting attention by asserting themselves. Security is dominantly an *emotional relationship*, while feelings of adequacy flow from what others *say* about one's abilities or achievements. The feeling of security rests upon *who* you are. The feeling of adequacy depends upon *what* you are. Security is rooted in affection. Adequacy floats with opinion. In either case the individual depends upon others. *He needs to be loved and approved of.*[5]

But man is set against himself. Every individual seeks security and dependence, but he also wants to assert himself, to be independent, to express himself in accordance with his own peculiar temperament. The harsh world of reality, in the form of dangerous parental and social prohibitions, and the relentless right-of-way of objects, cannot be easily overcome. Problems and dangers which cannot be conquered oppose the individual. The unknown is feared. Security, warmth, protection, and dependence are longed for, sought for, and achieved—only to be repudiated by the incessant demand to express oneself, to be independent, to dominate — and the pendulum starts its counter-swing. One rebels at being dependent and secure, settled and safe. The urge to dominate, to express one's peculiar difference, to be an independent individual, reasserts itself. More prohibitions and other dangers are encountered. The individual, fearful at the expression of his individuality, again seeks shelter in the

F. N.[5] James Plant, *Personality and the Cultural Pattern*, 1937, pp. 100, 275-276.

approval of others and seeks to behave in accordance with what others expect or demand.

A child, for example, wants to behave his way. Parents demand their way. The child's joy of spontaneous expression of his own needs must be weighed against his fear of losing the approval and love of those upon whom he depends. During infancy and childhood the parents win. The child submits — outwardly. Inwardly, resentment often accompanies his frustration. This breeds anxiety and hostility, which will manifest itself in devious ways sooner or later. The child, unaware of what is taking place, also experiences guilt. It is as if he said: "The Almighty Ones demand this. I want that. They must be right. I must be wrong. Something is the matter with me. If only they'd love me some more I'd feel better. I need them, so I guess I better do what they want so they'll like me — the Big Brutes."

Thus, the child's attempt to be independent is accompanied by fear, anxiety, and guilt. These reactions bring even greater need for dependence and security. The pendulum repeats the independent-dependent arc in a slightly different path directed by the ever new constellation of experience.

Every person faces this problem of self-expression versus repression. Most individuals are neither anarchic in their claims for self nor beaten into dulled submission by the claims of others. Most people achieve a working balance between their own needs and the demand of society, which is discovered and rediscovered in light of their own dynamic experience. The achievement is neither static nor gained without ceaseless struggle. The balance is constantly being shifted, redefined, and paid for at the cost of emotional disturbance to the self and to others.

Most of us are often out of balance with our environments and with ourselves. We refuse to recognize and accept this fact. We deny it. Without being aware of what takes place, we either conceal, distort, or create attitudes, and engage in the appropriate behavior which justifies our action. We have too much at stake. The pretty pictures we have built up about ourselves must not be spoiled. We incorporate into our own personalities the demands or wishes of others, whose approval we seek. If we do this often enough, the demands of others become identified with our "own" desires.

This process, however, is accompanied by resentment at the failure to express our difference and the necessity to conform with what others insist we shall become. We want to be like those around us, so that we may be liked by them, but we want to express our differences so that we might have the feeling of being somebody. If we dare to express our difference, we must be ready to face the disapproval of others. This makes us feel guilty. We become uneasy and afraid of such disapproval. We seek to re-establish ourselves in the good favor of those who disapprove of our conduct. On the other hand, if we succumb to the wishes of others in order to be like them and to win their approval, we feel resentful and hostile at having to suppress our difference.

Were we aware of this polar conflict, we would not be as twisted as many of us are in our thinking and feeling. We are often afraid to be ourselves. We deny that we do a lot of faking. We pretend that on the whole, we are consistent, rational, upright, kindly creatures. We conceal from ourselves that we are also, at times, inconsistent, irrational, unrighteous, cruel, hostile, and hateful.[6]

The trouble does not lie in being hostile, cruel, or irrational. That is an inevitable part of our make-up. We *are* that way, at times. *The trouble arises in our denying that we are that way.* It is the self-deception which does not permit us to recognize our conflicting selves. We engage in be-

F. N.[6] See Coignard, *The Spectacle of a Man*, 1937, pp. 194-199; F. Williams, *Russia, Youth and the Present-day World*, 1934, pp. 101-102, 203-206, for a convincing description of the need to hate. Also E. Fromm, *"Selfishness and Self-love,"* *Psychiatry*, 2:507, Nov. 1939.

havior which, unknown to us, compensates for our inadequacies and shields us from our faults. In time we become so accustomed to our rationalizations that we lose the ability to criticize and discipline ourselves.

Some such dynamisms which are not yet clearly understood operate in the life of every individual and in every personal relationship. The recognition of the dual nature of the self, i.e., the inherent ambivalence of every individual's behavior, is the basic psychological premise underlying the learning-teaching process described in Part II.

The Dual Nature of the Self

No one can doubt that an individual is constantly striving for a more effective balance between himself and his "inner" or "outer" environment. The phenomena of change in activity is real enough. Some kind of principle of effort is certainly involved in determining the direction of change. Instead of employing the concepts of dependence and independence, or approval and self-expression, we can try to describe the general way a person acts by employing the concepts of "will" and the correlative concept of "guilt."

The term "will" is so freighted with traditional meanings and misunderstandings that, before proceeding, it is well to define how we shall use it. By will we mean the *way* in which the energies, habits, traits, and attitudes of an individual are organized and integrated at any time toward achieving a particular end. One's relatively stable dispositions are organized and integrated in a given situation in order to do something, to reach some kind of objective. Thus a person, who is actively engaged in reacting to other persons, objects, situations, or to some inner problem, is exercising his will.

Names are often misleading. If there were another word which would better describe the phenomena of an individual organizing his energies toward some selected end, one could use it. It seems to me the common sense meaning attached to the term "will" best describes, in general terms, the be-havior of the organism integrated toward a particular end. *What* one wills at any moment is not the problem we are dis-cussing now. It is the characteristic way in which one reacts with the environment that we are attempting to describe.

With regard to any situation where an individual is ac-tively striving to reach a better balance between himself and what troubles him, there is present one of two basic orienta-tions (in various degrees of intensity) toward the problem, viz., "I will" or "I will not." The individual, organized in a certain way, is called upon to do something to meet the in-evitable factor of change with regard to persons or situations or within himself. He will assimilate or reject. He will go "toward" or "away from" the obstacle. He will unite with or separate from the problem.

Thus, there are two conflicting aspects of the willing process which one may call positive and negative. Funda-mentally, the organism *resists* changing itself. We tend to react to new experiences in terms of our biases, our accus-tomed ways of reacting. Once organization has been achieved there is a tendency not to disturb it.[7]

"A system tends to change so as to minimize an external disturbance," is a fundamental law of motion which holds true in every realm of phenomena.

The negative aspect of willing is fundamental. The individual, that is, avoids changing his way in accordance with the will of another. The individual will fight against altering his present wholeness, to defend it against encroach-ment by the will of others, and will, often, even refuse to recognize his own need to change himself. Since every indi-vidual shares the need to maintain whatever degree of in-tegration he has achieved, there is bound to be a conflict of

F. N.[7] Newton's First Law of Motion, the Law of Inertia, states that "every body persists in a state of rest or of uniform motion in a straight line unless compelled by external force to change that state."

wills whenever two or more individuals associate (as well as an inner struggle between one's positive and negative will).

Infants, children, adolescents, parents, teachers, adults, neurotics, artists, — every organism wants his will to be at the focus of his activity. The easiest way to meet change is to insist that the movement for adjustment proceed in the same direction as one's existing interests.

"*I will not* be other than I am" or "I will have things my way" is the general pattern which is observed in individuals when alone or in association with each other. An example, familiar to all, will illustrate this central reality of the developing experience of self-hood.

A group of acquaintances or friends are assembled to spend an evening. It may be a dinner party or a bridge party or any other social gathering. Sooner or later the conversation turns to some topic of the day. It may be some aspect of the European situation, the education of children, the defense program of the United States, the role of the United States in World War II, the relative merits of Jack Benny or Fred Allen, the activities of the Fifth Column, the virtues of the Philadelphia Symphony Orchestra, or of the latest best-seller. What happens?

Someone makes a passing remark. Someone else questions it or agrees. A third person disagrees. A discussion starts. In a few minutes it turns into an argument. The pitch of the still polite voices rises slightly. Proponents and opponents look to others for support. More irrelevant issues are introduced. The discussants move away from the original issue. Rhetorical questions are thrown at each other in a challenging way. Before answers are formulated the questioner has answered his questions and raised another. The pitch of voices rises proportionately to the absence of fact or lack of logic in the argument. The argument is in full swing. The time for adjectives and invectives has arrived. The name-calling stage has been reached. If the assembled guests possess intellectual manners the name-calling is less obvious but none-the-less present. One makes mental notes which are accompanied by ruffled feelings.

What has the conversation been about? Often the answer is relatively simple. Boiled down it comes to this: "Listen to me and I'll tell you. I'm pretty good and you'll have to admit it." "Oh, no. You all just listen to me. I'm better and I'll show you what's what." Rarely is the average discussion concerned with the merits of a genuine issue. Rarely is one vitally concerned with learning what another's and a different point of view really consists of. Many of such familiar conversations, no matter what their content, are about the personalities of the speakers. They are competing for the approval of the others who are present.

Imagine Mr. Martin Dies and Mr. Earl Browder sitting down for a serious three-hour or three-week conversation. How would it end? By each of them being more intensely confirmed in his respective opinion of the other. Each one lives, moves, and has his being in a system of ideas and feelings which the other will not enter. Neither one wants to change. Each wishes to convince or persuade the other.

Most of us, in many of our relationships with others, are acting pretty much in a similar fashion. The self resists changes from without and from within. We seek our likeness in those about us or wish to impose our likes and dislikes upon those who differ with us. We fight the alien will of another which threatens our sense of selfhood and wholeness. Fight as we may, normal association with others requires that we modify our sense of self. We must, or we choose to, reorganize our ways of responding. We bend or we break.

This continuous struggle of one's own will with the will of others is characteristic of all self-development. One's sense of wholeness, of self-hood, is challenged by ever-new configurations of experience. The self must be re-organized so that the challenge is met or assimilated or overcome, and a new sense of wholeness is achieved. The reorganization may be forced by outside threat or established by what one does to oneself.

We fear facing the new since it calls for changing the satisfying balance we have achieved, and we fear leaving the old for the same reason. To change means to surrender, in part, the comfort of the control which has been achieved. To change means to give up a sense of security for the insecurity of the strange.

The living experience of every individual constitutes a dynamic whole within which the self is being continually reorganized. When the particular organization of the self is more or less threatened, there is a proportionate rush of feeling or emotion. The sense of wholeness is lost. It can be recovered only by getting rid of the discomfort. The discomfort must be outwardly expressed or struggled with internally until a new sense of wholeness is momentarily achieved. Thus a child is hurt by falling or by being deprived of a desired toy. The tears or rage which follow are outward expression of discomfort and bring relief. Or the pain is borne within and is allayed by a sympathetic parent. In both cases, when the threat to the self has been done away with, the child is again at peace with himself.

When the individual seeks to get rid of a threat but refuses to or cannot change his own organism, he projects himself upon the environment or other individuals (or fights with himself).

When one projects the disturbance to self upon oneself, the individual is torn between competing selves. He "takes it out on himself." He feels depressed or despairs, or becomes fearful. It may take the form of phantasy, rationalization, guilt, or inferiority feeling. In extreme cases inner conflict leads to a neurosis or a psychosis. (The concept of projection is discussed in Chapter IX). He places himself at the center of the experience and seeks to have others or the environment conform to what he wants or wills.

This is the negative aspect of willing, the resistance to change. People, however, do change more or less radically. Individuals incorporate alien wills. Change proceeds in directions which are very uncomfortable for the individual. This is easily observed in the experience of youngsters who cannot remain as they are but are *compelled* to follow the direction (*wills*) of parents. This *forcible* imposition of an alien will is a threatening experience to the integrity of the self. What we are faced with in this situation is a conflict between the *negative* aspects of two wills, the child's and the parent's. The child wants his way but the parent wills his way.

Change need not occur in this manner. Movement may proceed by enlisting the *positive* aspect of one's will. A positive *willingness* to move in the direction of another is made possible if the one who is to change is given the right of self-determination. Thus, if the parent asks, "Would you like to help Mother?" the youngster feels that it is up to him to decide. He can express his own self. His own organization is not threatened. He is at one with the other. Part of *his* organization, at this moment, is the request of one upon whom he is dependent, and with whom he is united. His own willing being respected, he wills, positively, to help. Thus change is effected in his organization, and he becomes, for example, a more co-öperative individual. He retains a sense of wholeness and yet determines for himself that he will change.

Suppose the child determines not to help. The parent replies, "I'm disappointed but, if that's the way you feel, I suppose there's nothing to be done about it." Now the conflict between wills becomes an intra-personal one. Instead of the parent's and child's wills being in conflict, the child faces a struggle between the dual aspect of his own willing process. Whatever change occurs comes from within. The child's struggle arises because *he* willed not to help but feels that he should have helped. His own negative and positive willing aspects are in conflict. "I will not help" retains his sense of self-hood. But part of his organized self-hood is a mother with whom he is closely identified and who has not threatened him. This brings the feeling "I should have helped." The tension in this case is resolved, let us say, by the child responding, "I'll help, Mother." Here re-organization takes place not through pressure of others but through the positive act of willing controlling the negative. If the child had not helped, he would have willed negatively.

The child might help and still will negatively. Suppose the mother replied to his refusal to help, "I say you will help me at once, or else I'll spank you." The child, in fear, helps but does not *co-öperate*. He is not willing to help. Under threat he does, but at the same time he is reacting defensively, although not necessarily verbally, against differences which threaten his own identity and sense of self-control. His negative will controls.

When the individual seeks to get rid of what disturbed his sense of wholeness, of what interfered with his past comfortable control of himself, by choosing to do something positive in the direction of changing himself, he identifies himself with the new experience in the environment or with others. He willingly accepts an organization other than his own. He accepts difference and seeks to make it part of an altered self. A new wholeness results.

Identification can also take place if the one who insists upon his point of view is accepted by the other upon whom he projects. The "projector" finds himself accepted and experiences satisfaction, but he has not changed. Rather he has been fortified by the environment or the people he uses. He has not learned anything new. A wholeness results, but it is not so much a new organization as a re-organization of old patterns. The new whole which he accepts is merely his old self in altered forms.

Both of these movements of identification are usually accompanied by some kind of disturbance. Generally, the more intense the struggle to maintain oneself as one is, or to become other than one is in relation to others, the greater is the emotional disturbance one undergoes.

Every individual faces not only inner conflict because of the duality of his own willing but also conflict arising because of the conflict of wills in association with outer situations and people. The resolution of the conflict from without depends upon whether or not one's feeling of self-determination and also of identity are threatened. When the self is not threatened, we will positively, we "want to be with," and we wish to "act together." We are like-minded. The other is part of us. When we sense difference, when our goals or ends are not the same, we will not be with the others. We will protect ourselves against them.

The negative aspect of willing is just as important as the positive aspect. There is nothing inherently "good" or 'bad" about either aspect. Growth and change result from the to-and-fro movement between what one is and what one has to become, between the self at any time seeking to maintain itself in a moving, changing stream of behavior.

We resist change within and from without. We also seek change within and without. In varying degrees of intensity each individual struggles in his own way to find momentary balance between his own inherently-dual nature and/or between his own directing and the will of others.

The tension which arises between the assertion of selfhood, wanting one's self at the center of experience, and denying the experience of others, or between denying one's self-expression and accepting the experience of others leaves one dissatisfied. Such feelings of discomfort, more or less intense, are what we shall refer to as feelings of guilt. The greater the need (the will) is to express difference, the more intense will the will-guilt struggle become.

The Will-Guilt Conflict

Not all will agree that individuals differ at birth in the quality of will they manifest throughout life. Most of us will agree, however, that a young child is in process of development and does not possess the relatively stable attitudes of an adult. In the first instance, the parents, particularly the mother, strive to change and fashion the infant according to their ideals. The infant is not merely a mass of plastic protoplasm to be shaped in accordance with maternal designs. It has a particular, albeit undisciplined, will of its own. The mother acts and the child reacts in light of its inner needs. The child identifies with the mother. Through identification with the demands of the parents, the child achieves security. The parents furnish an objective reality, the standards by which the child measures his worth. He idealizes them and by identification their ideals become his. There are times, however, when he realizes that he is not living up to the standards of his parents. The disappointment results in self-criticism, feelings of inferiority and guilt.

Parent and teachers are professional moralists examining the child's motives, pointing out his faults and counselling him on the correct path to follow. We witness an enormous amount of projection, which cannot but increase the load of guilt carried by the child or pupil. What happens is that parents (and other family members) and teachers project their motives on to the child who internalizes them and acquires a deepening sense of inferiority and guilt.

If, in the process of development, the child could project its own needs, the sense of guilt would be lessened. By projecting on to others, the child creates a reality, expressing his will outwardly. In this way, namely, through self-criticism of the others who fail to satisfy the needs of the child, a balance between feelings of guilt and worth-whileness is attained. The guilt in not meeting the demand of others is partially allayed by projecting it outward in the form of criticism of others, instead of its being retained inwardly where it becomes criticism of self, accompanied by feelings of inferiority, anxiety, frustration, and hostility. The child feels inferior because he idealizes those whom he respects or loves and is made to feel unworthy of their approval. He feels anxious because the support of those with whom he identifies is threatened by their difference from him. He is frustrated because he cannot express his differences. He becomes hostile since he hates those reponsible for denying self-expression.

The self-criticism induced by the disapproval of others does not necessarily have to remain internalized. It can become the stimulus for self-improvement. Guilt, that is to say, motivates will. Instead of merely feeling bad about one's inadequacy, the individual fights to improve himself. He does something about the situation. He projects, he struggles with the problem until a better balance is achieved through control over his impulses or through an altered external situation. The individual does what he wants to do, independent of what others think or say. This is the beginning of self-discipline but not the end.

Daring to act in light of one's differences, daring, that is, to be one's spontaneous self, often runs counter to prevailing values. Fear and guilt also follow too much assertion of selfhood. We need others. Guilt overpowers will just as at other times will overpowers guilt. Thus, "we spend our lives in learning how to live." The acceptance or rejection of one's self is a life-long process. The struggle is continuous and the balance attained only temporary. The nature of the will-guilt conflict can be clarified if we glance at the way in which it is resolved by different groups of individuals. In broad outline, we can observe three classes of individuals who handle the will-guilt conflict in different ways. The creative individual, the artist type, uses his tremendous drive positively for self-expression. He produces something, a painting, a poem, a composition, a successful business, a political party, a religion. The neurotic, who also possesses a powerful drive to be different, uses his will negatively, to be unproductive, to be self-repressive. He wants to do something but will not. His will is blocked by his guilt, whereas the creative type gets rid of his guilt over his extreme differences from others by producing something constructively which gives him self-approval. The neurotic refuses to recognize and denies that he *will not* do something and maintains that he *cannot*. He is then forced to justify himself in his own eyes and before others the reason why he cannot act. He builds all sorts of excuses, rationalizations, and defenses which do not really satisfy him. He refuses to accept himself, he fears to express his differences, and continues on his unhappy way of taking it out on himself. The creator's guilt (because of his difference from others) is worked out in objective effort. The neurotic's guilt is worked out in subjective excuses. The artist creates a reality, his world. The neurotic creates a subjective world of phantasy. The neurotic is a sick, perverted creator.

Most individuals are neither creative artists nor defeated neurotics. They are respectable, conventional folk in whom the urge to be different is not extreme. They accept, more or less, the conventional attitudes of the society in which they live. They make the contemporary ideologies their own without too much difficulty. Indeed, they want to identify with group values since this relieves them of the responsibility of struggling with the will-guilt problem. Their will is given content. They are told what to do or discover what may be done and, hence, do not have to wrestle too strenuously with their developing selves.

The creative type senses his difference from others and asserts his need to be different. He suffers keenly when he is blocked but is enraptured when he creates. He is his best critic. He is extremely self-disciplined. His own standards guide him. The neurotic denies his extreme differences from others and suffers without the compensatory joy of creation. He frets in his own bitter stew. He will not accept the standards of others and dares not create his own. He remains in conflict. The average individual rarely experiences the joy of consummate creation or the ineluctable misery of utter defeat. He shares with the majority the petty irritations and homely enjoyments of daily affairs. He expresses his not-too-great need to be different in hobbies, work, clothes, competitiveness, gossip, and social activities. His sense of inadequacy (guilt) is felt in a not-too-disquieting unfavorable comparison with others regarding income, job, social status, clothes, good looks, and intellectual ability. The passion of the creator and the pain of the neurotics are less intense in the lives of the respected and respectable citizen of the community.

This classification of types is, of course, logical. All individuals undergo, sometimes, and in certain respects, extremely intense experiences of joy and sorrow. A small number of individuals live on a more intense plane oftener and in more respects.

The pattern and content of the individual's will-guilt conflict is shaped by what happens in the home and the school, the two institutions which furnish so much of the content of the child's emotional experience. The "training of the will" determines the balance between one's positive and negative self. Infants and young children behave spontaneously. They will, but their willing is explosive and blind. Their feelings are not consciously directed. The child does not possess the relatively-stable attitudes and values of the adult and, hence, the content of his will and guilt is not well patterned. His feelings, criticisms, and expressions are fluid. Gradually, through the years, the child is moulded by those around him. The manifestations of his emotions become associated with his awareness of their consequences.

Parents want the child to acquire their ideals and values. The teacher, no less, but in a professionally disguised manner, projects his beliefs upon the pupil. In both cases there is *a demand* for improvement and a code of behavior, corresponding to the ways of the adult, is imposed. The sanctions for this demand take many forms such as love, punishment, bribes, comparison with others, marks and grades. The weapons, however diverse, are reducible to some form of praise and blame.

The child adopts the values of others as his own, either because he is afraid of punishment or because he seeks praise. The exercise of his own will, independent of the approval or disapproval of others, is made difficult. He is taught, that is, imposed upon by others, and cannot educate himself.

The criticism by parents and teachers becomes the self-criticism of the child. If the latter is not given an opportunity to fight back, that is, to project his self-criticism on to an outer reality, the self-criticism remains locked within the child and leads to feelings of inadequacy.

School authorities aggravate the burden of guilt imposed upon children by the home. By denying pupils sufficient opportunity to assert themselves, self-expression is crippled. Praise and blame, reward and punishment, become the criteria for behavior. Motivation for conduct is placed outside the will of the student and is controlled by the standards of others.[8] The child conducts himself in accordance with what he expects to receive from others. He learns to get around people, using the tricks he has learned from those who have manipulated him.

F. N.[8] Jessie Taft, "The Catch in Praise," *Child Study*, Feb. 1930.

Much of one's behavior as an adult is counterfeit because it does not express one's real self in its differences and spontaneity. We become stencilled stereotypes stamped with the "do's" and "don'ts" of authority. We live in two worlds, the one of socially-accepted standards to which we conform, and an inner world where we ineffectually indulge in luxurious phantasy, not always an innocuous form of self-expression.

To accept people as they are is the beginning of *their* self-discipline. To help others in self-guidance is the way to develop constructive personalities. The individual must be given the opportunity to criticize himself by discovering his own weakness. We will not accept criticism from others as easily as we will blame ourselves, and "when we blame ourselves we feel that no one else has the right to blame us."

The student must make the values of society his own. They must not be forced upon him but offered to him. In the very process of assimilating the values of his culture, the student exercises his positive will in his own way. In the final analysis, he learns by himself. If left to find his own way, more often than not, the student will exercise his own will in the desired direction as normally as a hungry child will eat food when hungry. Food is around to appease hunger. Similarly, community values are around for the child to accept, voluntarily, in order to gain the approval of others by being and acting like them.

A group of educators has stated: "The first task of education is to transmit to the young the values and virtues of the social order, that way of life which represents the vitality of the state and nation or of the civilization to which a people consciously belong."[9]

This observation is commonplace. What is significant is the way in which parents and teachers present the claims

F. N.[9] *The Education of a Teacher,* Published by the Committee on Teacher Education of the Association of Colleges and Universities of the State of New York, p. 2.

of society. They must believe in and live the attitude of self-determination (within limits, of course). Their task is to set favorable conditions for learning. They must permit themselves to be used by the child in his explorations and discoveries. By pointing out the consequences of this or that action, without praise or blame, the child is helped to recognize them and to assume the responsibility for his decisions. The decision must be that of the self and not camouflaged by the subtle devices of praise and blame.

The teacher who accepts this point of view is giving the student the opportunity of educating himself. Furthermore, the danger of transmitting to the young the false values and the vices of the social order, which represent the decadence of a nation, is partly met. The student will be free to accept the traditional if it seems useful, and to create new values when they appear desirable.

In this chapter we have presented the basic aspects of personality development which serve as background for the understanding of the learning process we are to describe. The learning process, however, is an integral part of the teaching process. What is the role of the teacher in the learning process? What is the function of the teacher, and what is the responsibility of the learner? I believe that unless the teacher is aware of the premises underlying his teaching efforts, and what his job and that of the students is, no *professional* teaching is possible. The following chapter is, therefore, devoted to exploring the questions, "What, precisely, is a teacher supposed to do in a classroom?" and "What are the responsibilities of the student?"

Chapter 5

The Function of the Instructor and the Responsibility of the Student

The purpose of this chapter is to explore the teacher's function with the hope that a new direction may be pointed. Since teaching practices throughout the country are so divergent, and since the form, content, and goal of education are so diversified, it will be difficult to reach an agreement of our premises. Nevertheless, the author is inescapably committed in this study to analyze his position. And since loyalties to local practices will be involved, a warmth of feeling is bound to be engendered.

It is a mistake to believe that most untrained people can engage in effective college teaching without professional teaching equipment. It is strange that training courses for teachers of primary and secondary schools are provided while almost no thought has been given to the professional training of college teachers. A prospective college teacher does his graduate work in his specialty, receives his advanced degree, submits his references or recommendations, is interviewed by someone in the college administration, and, if invited to join the college, it is assumed he is ready to teach. He has had no professional training in one of the most difficult and complex of all professions, the profession of teaching. He is apparently qualified to teach by having successfully demonstrated his ability as a scholar, and by reason of having a more or less agreeable "personality." He, the embryonic teacher, has little if any sense of what his function as a college teacher is, although he has been motivated by an interest —his subject, a regard for academic life, or an amorphous desire to "teach."

It is earnestly hoped that the following discussion will help to clarify what the teacher's function is,[1] or at least, to raise the important issues about which differences of opinion concerning teacher-function will be expressed. It is in this spirit that the point of view in this chapter is presented.

Function and Process in Teaching

One of the most obvious facts of life is that none of us can act as he pleases all of the time. We have to learn to accept limitations. Man lives in a world against which or with which he must fight. From birth until death he seeks adjustment, finds momentary balance, and is again in conflict.

There are many kinds of limitations which hamper man's growth and creativity. There are obstacles of time and space, limitations in talent and opportunity. We have to accept the organism we possess and the world in which it strives. In order to adjust to conflict, we must take into account what can't be helped, whether it is within ourselves or in the world about us. By accepting the given, we have a basis upon which to build the desirable. By submitting to the inevitable, we husband our strength to create the possible.

Adjustment is adjustment *to* something. Development is development of something. We do not live in a vacuum. Adjustment and development require a framework of refer-

F. N.[1] The concept of a limited function in a professional relationship has been clarified, and successfully applied, in the field of social case work, both in the professional education of social workers and in case work practice. One of the best statements is the collection of papers in the *Journal of Social Work Process*, Vol. I, No. 1, Nov. 1937. See also, Goldie, Basch, "One View of the Teaching of Case Work," *The Family*, Dec., 1939. The concept of a limited function has also proven helpful in the training of industrial counselors. See Carl Rogers, *Counseling and Psychotherapy*, 1942. Nathaniel Cantor, *Employee Counseling*, 1945.

ence. Part of that framework consists of limitations within ourselves and obstacles about ourselves. To ignore them is to court peril. In brief, certain given factors are present in everyone's life, which must be taken into account if anything is to be changed.

There are many problems which relate to the teacher's function. Teaching takes place in a particular college which has its own organization, publicly or privately administered. The selection of students, the standards and qualifications, the curriculum offerings and requirements, degrees, grades, personnel, physical equipment, and so on, are among the problems which will effect the function of the teacher. They are dealt with in this study only in so far as they limit the function of the teacher.

What distinguishes the teaching process from other types of human relations is the particular kind of limitations set up by the college as they are interpreted by a professionally-trained instructor. What the teacher and student do, the direction in which the movement takes place, will be limited by the particular services the college offers through its several courses.

That is the given, the stable, the known factor. Whatever the student wants to do and whatever the teacher may do must take place within a defined area, which the college has established as a course to aid the student in a particular field and by an individual instructor. Indeed, were this not so, teaching would become a glorified, chaotic "bull session" in which there would be neither form nor direction. The teacher would, otherwise, be ready to talk about anything and the student would never discover what he really wants nor how to go about getting it. This would have to be so because the student would not know what the teacher, as the representative of the college, stood for and, hence, could not be helped to discover his real interests.

If the teacher understands his function, he is protected against the demands of the student. He knows the limits within which he can help. In turn, the student, in confusion and conflict, will turn in any direction unless the path he must tread, if he wants to learn, is marked out by the instructor. Then only can he discover and decide if he wants to learn in that particular way.

Students will try, in many ways, to avoid facing the acceptance of the responsibility for their attitudes and interpretations with regard to the subject matter of the course. The teacher, who knows what he is about, helps the student to become responsible for his work. The teacher represents a particular kind of help, and the student presents a particular kind of interest. *These two limits give purpose and meaning to the activity of the instructor and student.* Throughout the learning process, whatever takes place occurs within these boundaries. In order to clarify the nature of this limitation, we turn to a brief analysis of the function of education, viewed generally and specifically.

When we speak of the "function" of education, we refer to its general goal or purpose. When reference is made to the "function" of the instructor, function is used in a specific technical sense, that of helping students in a professional, skilled manner to learn a particular content.

Education, General and Specific

Students are educated by the life they live. They learn much more away from the classroom than they do in the classroom. The family and community shape the basic character-traits of the individual. The college, as well as the elementary and high school, reflects and is integrated with the traditional values of community life. The school is only one of many kinds of institutions which educate. Its special virtue lies in its ability to *direct* learning. The goals of the college cannot depart too far from the accepted standards of traditional community values, else they will not be tolerated or supported.

At the same time, a democratic society is self-critical up to a point. A democratic society places its faith in directed education. It believes that its citizenry must be enlightened so that intelligent participation in the problems of the day is made possible. A democratic society resents arbitrary authoritarian standards. It believes that its values are not absolute or self-evident (other than its faith in the democratic way of life) but must be modified and reorganized so that all of its members have increased opportunity to participate in a life which brings them and others greater peace and happiness.

The curriculum of a college which is committed to this faith will consist of a program which centers on the implication of democracy for the modern world. The courses offered, however far apart in specific content, will acquire integration in the light of this purpose. Of course, calculus and chemistry or physics and physiology may be taught as the background for a professional or for a specific skill. In this case the student is interested in acquiring specialized technique for vocational or professional purposes. But when such courses are offered in a college of liberal arts and sciences, the assumption is that they are to be used to shape liberal attitudes, to develop critical habits of thought, to acquire the experimental attitude of mind, to see the significance of scientific method in the modern world.[2]

If this be not the case, one wonders why they (or any other subject) are offered in the college program. Undoubtedly, some courses are now included in the college program for no well-defined or clearly understood reasons. Others are included to provide a background for future vocational or professional training. This means either that there is dis-

F. N. [2] See Louis Heil, "Determining Objectives of Science Instruction for General Education," *The Edu. Record*, 23:94, Jan., 1942.

agreement over what the function of the college is, or that courses are simply added for one reason or another, without attempting to see their significance in terms of a definite theory of education. The problem of selecting what is to be offered in a liberal arts college is further complicated because of the accelerated accumulation of knowledge and the limitations of time.

The purpose of education is "to increase one's perception of the world about him." (William James) Caught in the maze of daily living, the individual wastes his energy and wearies his spirit running to and fro in blind alleys instead of pausing, lifting his head to survey the landscape about him.

We believe that the general function of a college of arts and sciences is to aid young men and women to acquire attitudes and insights which will help them to find their way in a terribly confused world, through participation with each other in meeting the problems common to all of them. This means that instructors must be pedagogues in the literal sense of the word.

The word pedagogue is derived from the Greek *paidagogos* (*pais*-boy and *ago*-to lead). When the small community of Athens developed into a large city, with its differentiated and complicated activities, its citizens were in danger of losing their community spirit. The sense of wholeness was being destroyed by the fragmentary experience of beholding only its parts. The children were losing sight of what Athens represented and what was happening to the City. The pedagogue was one who could take the child by the hand and go with him from place to place, exposing him to various experiences. He was prepared to answer the child's questions and to satisfy his curiosity concerning the *meaning* of this and that experience. The boy was helped to understand the community as a whole. The pedagogue neither assigned lessons, listened to recitations, nor gave grades, credits, degrees. He helped the boy to grasp the meaning of Athens so that he might renew his loyalties to the community and re-dedicate himself to its re-creation.

The modern teacher must become a pedagogue who will help the student integrate his fragmentary experience, and help him to see that 2 and 2, when put together, do not always equal 4 but may result in 0, or 1, or 22. Whatever course is offered in the college of arts must contribute to making clearer to the student the kind of world he is living in, the kind of person he is, the problems he and others have to face, ways of meeting these problems, the traps which he will be exposed to, the contending beliefs, faiths, and hopes of man extending in time and territory. The student must be helped to acquire a sense of wholeness in a world "rolling on its relentless way, blind to good and evil, reckless of destruction." The individual, shoved around in the harlequinade of modern life, breathless and footless, or sheltered in the shadow of some side-show, must be shown the stars which canopy the whole.

While individual students differ in the kinds of problems they bring to the classroom and while the colleges differ in the courses offered, the teaching process or method used by the instructors in any class will have the following common elements:

(1) the teacher will understand the dynamics of human behavior in its individual and social aspects;

(2) the teacher will be concerned primarily with understanding and not judging the individual;[3]

(3) the teacher will keep at the center of the teaching process the importance of the student's problems and feelings, not his own;

(4) the teacher will clearly recognize that he can offer help only within the subject matter of the course, as it relates to the function of the college;

F. N.[3] The problem of evaluating the quality of the student's work which has to meet the *scholastic* standards of the college does rot conflict with the non-judgmental attitude of the instructor during the class sessions.

(5) most important of all, the teacher will realize that
     constructive effort must come from the positive
     or active forces within the individual student.

These factors will be recognized in all courses. The
way in which they will be applied, however, will vary in
light of the particular problems brought up in a specific
class. The teaching process is characterized by common
elements, but it becomes differentiated in terms of particular
students and particular situations.

The student's self, as that of the instructor, is a dynamic,
ever-changing one. One can never accurately know in
advance what one's needs are going to be, nor whether the
help that is offered is going to be accepted and to what degree. That is unpredictable. The teacher's responsibility
is not for the student's personal development as such but
for developing the meaning of the particular course. That is
what he is in the class for. That is his service. The interpretation of the data in light of its meanings to the student is
the factor which the teacher can consciously control.

This seems to contradict the position that the development of the student should be central in the teaching process.
But the apparent contradiction is resolved if one bears in
mind the general goal of education and its specific objectives.
The college student, as a whole human being, comes to college
to be helped in a better understanding of himself and society.
The instructors, in their several courses, are limited. They
must confine themselves to and deal with a specific subject
matter. In so far as the student shows interest in, or has his
interest awakened and enlivened by a special subject, he can
be helped to develop or modify his understanding and attitudes *with reference to that limited course*. Attitudes are
not shaped in a vacuum. They are acquired by facing and
working through specific problems. If the teacher sticks to
his speciality, the possibility of development is established
since a new, unique experience is made possible for the

student. Change and growth, by-products important enough to be considered almost equal to the translation of the limited subject matter, ocur.   To function in a limited way, through the specific course as it is related to the problem of the student in that course, while keeping in one's *background* the goal of general education, requires the highest kind of professional teaching skill. .· (The description of this process constitutes Part II of this study.)

The Personality of the Teacher[4]

The teacher, we have stated, must be fortified by a knowledge of, and an insight into, personality development as well as by professional skill.   Some day it will be realized that no one should be certified to teach in a college unless one has received professional training in the teaching process — and we do not mean the kind *of training generally given in state teachers' colleges.*[5]

Most of us live through childhood, adolescent, and adult experiences without realizing what little "guidance" we receive or give.   In our relationship with our parents, sisters, brothers, friends, teachers, and, later, with husband or wife and children, we exploit and are exploited by each other. We use each other in order to dominate or to befriend.   Rarely are we ready to stand by and permit ourselves to be used by the other person in precisely the way *that* person wants to be helped.   We are taken advantage of in order to satisfy the other's emotional needs.   In turn, we use others to satisfy our tensions and anxieties.   We are afraid of the new, hidden and powerful forces of creation, which threaten our own established habits and the conventions of society.

The positive creative forces of individuals which express their differences from those about them must be channelized

F. N.[4]   In Chapter Four this matter was discussed generally.   Here we comment on personality development from the point of view of the teacher's self.   In Part II the dynamics of growth will be discussed from the point of view of the student's self.

F. N.[5]   Carson W. Ryan, *Mental Health Through Education*, 1938.

into the encrusted bed of tradition. We fluctuate between attitudes of blame and praise in our intimate contacts with each other where emotional ties are strongest. We have to preserve whatever we have at stake and maintain our self-regard or the respect of others. Hence, we shuttle between dominating, excusing, or yielding to others. We wish to control or want to be loved. Rarely, in these deep contacts, does one stand aside and accept others just as they are. We are driven to create in our own image. It strikes one, if and when it does, as shocking and amazing how rarely a child or adult is permitted an effective margin of genuine self-determination. It is difficult, wholeheartedly and unaffectedly, to accept those who differ from us.[6]

Teachers share these inevitable needs to dominate or to be well thought of, to be approved of. There are not many individuals willing to assume the responsibility of genuine self-discipline so that they become *relatively* immune to the judgments of others and are willing to let others think, feel, and act in ways relatively different from their own. Such inner steel strength is acquired through painful self-discipline and professional training.[7]

When students and instructors meet in the classroom, they become objects of each other's will. Students want to have their way, and the instructor wants to have his way. The instructor who brings to the classroom a set of disciplined attitudes based upon insight into human relations recognizes

F. N.[6] Lawson F. Lowrey, "Competitions and the Conflict over Difference," *Mental Hygiene,* 12:316-330, April, 1928; F. Allen, "The Dilemma of Growth," *Arch. of Neur. and Psych.* 37:859, 1937.

F. N.[7] Percival M. Symonds, "The Value of Adjustment of Prospective Teachers," *Mental Hygiene,* 25:568-575, Oct., 1941 L. H. Meek, "Preparation of Teachers for the Emotional Guidance of Children," *American Journal of Orthopsychiatry,* 9:494; July, 1939; E. H. Roso, "The Classroom as the Setting for a Fulfillment of a Function," *idem,* 9:477. Superintendent Harry A. Wann of the school department in Morris County, N. Y., writes, "The training program for the teacher should include courses in mental hygiene, psychiatry, and social-case work techniques, such as are now part of the training of social case workers," "Mental Growth Through Education," *Mental Hygiene,* 25:21, Jan., 1941.

this conflict. He knows and feels his own responses and has learned to control them. He will permit students to develop at their own individual tempo and on their own level. He is not interested in becoming popular or in avoiding negative criticism. He is interested in understanding and accepting the differences expressed by the students. By recognizing the right of each student to be different from every other student and by *communicating* that feeling to them, he frees them to express themselves with regard to their honest reactions to the subject matter. Unless students are free to express their emotionally-sincere reactions to the subject matter of the course, movement toward genuine growth and reconstruction of their attitudes simply cannot take place.

The skilled instructor will not exploit the students for the release of his own tensions. The clasroom will not be used by him as a clinic to solve his emotional difficulties (which often remain unrecognized by the instructor). He will refrain from *imposing* his point of view upon students, always keeping in mind the tendency each one has to dominate, to be "right." He will not be sarcastic or exhibitionistic. He will not ridicule or "talk down" to students nor "baby" them. He will recognize the dignity and inevitable differences in capacity of every individual student. Aware of his own ceaseless struggle to dominate or submit, he will appreciate similar conflict in others and permit them a large degree of self-determination.

The instructor in any case will be interested in watching the reactions of the students to the data he presents to see what is happening to their attiudes which are being shaped by that course. If his authority is to be exercised, it will not be imposed arbitrarily but used professionally, as a necessary factor in helping the student meet the obligations of the classroom and the course. The spirit will not be "I'll show you who's boss here" but, "I am responsible to see to it that such and such conditions must be observed. There is nothing else I can do about it. It has to be this way according to my responsibility to the college."

The instructor who is clear about his professional teaching-self will not only permit but welcome differences in student attitude, differences in methods of expressing the attitudes, differences in the tempo of learning, and in ways of learning. (This will be discussed in Chapter Twelve).

Faculty members agree *intellectually* that all individuals differ in many respects. To translate this into a dynamic "give and take" relationship with students is another and more difficult matter. The tendency is in the other direction, that of viewing student accomplishment in the light of standards held by the instructor. It is the teacher's view of what constitutes the "right" interpretation of data, of the amount of work which students ought to do, of how rapidly they should move, of how much they should know, which constitutes the standard of work and accomplishment.

Most of us will agree that interpretations in the social sciences are not true or false. There is room for difference of opinion. But does this hold true for the physical and natural sciences?

I believe that this statement holds true even in the physical science courses. What is the "correct" interpretation of an experiment in the physics or chemistry laboratory? The answer depends on the problem. If, for example, the problem is limited to the determination of heat expansion of a certain metal or to the volume and pressure of a specific gas in the demonstration of Boyle's Law, then the facts are or are not as described. But if the frame of reference is, as I believe it should be in a college of arts, the nature of scientific method, the student's ideas as to what is involved are of paramount importance. The student is trying to come to grips with the procedure involved in defining a problem, setting up hypotheses to guide inquiry, proceeding to the inquiry, getting and testing the data in the light of a hypothesis, and reaching a tentatively-held conclusion which has a certain degree of probability, subject to change when new data appear. To acquire this attitude requires a long time.

The natural and physical sciences are splendid disciplines by means of which students can acquire the scientific attitude of mind, a very important attitude. Why should students who are receiving a liberal arts education and not becoming professional chemists or physicists retain the thousands of technical fact of these sciences? These facts should be used, accurately and rigidly, to illustrate what an experimental approach to problems signifies. It may require one or more courses over several years to have the scientific attitude reach down into the core of the student's living problems. We can speak of our own teaching experience over a number of years, which is that fewer than five out of a hundred students ever learn what the scientific attitude is from courses in science. For that matter, some university "scientists" reflect a mind as rooted as the Rock of Gibraltar. The data of everyday living make as much of an impression on them as the ceaseless ebb and flow of the Atlantic make upon Gibraltar. In time, of course, Gibraltar will be worn down but life is short.[8]

The Function of the Teacher

The task of the instructor has been implied throughout this chapter. By way of summary, we wish to state explicitly what his function is. The college determines the philosophy of education, the content of the curriculum, the selection of students, and the conditions for receiving credit.

The instructor, who is the representative of the college in a particular course, is charged with implementing that educational policy. That is the given, the known. It is

F. N.[8] A teacher of biology for fifteen years remarked in serious discussion regarding the unemployed, "There's one solution. Sterilize every unemployed who can work and hasn't found a job." He is charged with teaching scientific method to the hundredᵣ of students who "pass" through his classes.

the only stable factor, the only focus which defines the direction from which the learning process can proceed in the given course. The student comes to class. What will happen to any particular individual by way of genuine growth cannot be predicted in advance. It will depend upon (1) the student's discovering for himself *in the process of learning* what he *really* wants out of that course and (2) the skill with which the instructor utilizes and meets the *real* needs of the student. (These two factors are, of course, closely interrelated).

What takes place between instructor and student provides the dynamic conditions which will be used by the student in his own way. Whatever genuine learning takes place occurs when the help offered by the teacher, elucidating the meanings of the data, is accepted willingly by the student as an aid toward making the meanings his own. The instructor provides the aid; he cannot guarantee the willingness of the student to do something about learning. He can free the student from fear of authority, lowered self-esteem, the feeling of insignificance; he can release him to express himself, to show his differences, his disagreements, and he can help him to acquire a sense of determining for himself just what the course means to him. He can communicate to the students that it is their course and have them answer the question, "What shall we, the students, do about it?" Just as the instructor should make clear to them what his function is, so the students must be helped to define for themselves how they are to meet the responsibilities which entering the courses imposes upon them.

The Responsibility of the Student

Long before the student enters public school, certain basic attitudes have been shaped. The attitude toward authority is of particular significance with regard to the classroom situation. Every child learns rather early that there are external forces which can control him. In intimate contact with parents the child learns to submit to their authority, and avoid punishment. His brothers and sisters, or schoolmates and playmates, teach him, or compel him by force of numbers to do as they are doing. If he wants to get along, the opinion of the majority must prevail. In addition, being like others gives one a sense of reassurance. Contrariwise, being different is accompanied by a sense of fear and guilt, just as observing certain differences in others which have particular significance for the observer, brings a sense of fear, irritation, and hostility.

As the child passes through the grade school and high school, his previous attitudes toward authority are reinforced by classroom experiences. Now it is the parental-surrogate, in the form of the teacher, who wills authority, and classmates who represent the force of numbers. The teacher is older. He or she knows more. He knows, students hear too often, what is good for you. "Just listen to your teacher and do what he tells you." The student *just* listens to the teacher and does what he is supposed to do through the fear of examinations, fear of disapproval of teacher and parents, fear of grades, and the ridicule, if he fails. He fears making a fool of himself, and seeks anonymity by becoming lost in the group or in the assigned lesson. By giving back what had been assigned to him, nothing is lost and nothing essentially gained except being let alone.

The inference is not to be drawn that the authority of teachers or numbers is not desirable. It is — up to a point. Where such authority results in depriving the student of desirable self-expression, the point has been passed. What is "desirable" cannot be stated in a formula. It depends upon the particular situation and the particular individual's needs at the time.

The majority of primary and secondary schools emphasizes the academic curriculum. There are so many pages of text to be covered in a given number of hours. The child's emotional development, if attention is given to it at all, remains secondary. There is little appreciation of the fact that early school experience is primarily a heightened emotional period in which one's attitudes with regard to self-esteem, competition, rivalry, jealousy, hostility, confidence, humility, co-öperativeness, aggression, and the like, are being shaped and reshaped. The adjustments always carry important *feelings* of failures or success.

The pre-adolescent and adolescent find themselves in high school. How little the average high school teachers appreciate the nature of the real problems of their pupils! The teachers want "to train the mind," fill it with ideas and facts by means of lessons to be "learned." The pupils "take it," and return it. Their curiosities, confusions, imaginations, loves, and hates, with regard to themselves, their parents and others, belong in a world almost totally ignored by the school. Their real problems remain more or less concealed.

These high school graduates enter the freshman year of college in a haze. More authority, more "training of the mind," more facts and ideas, more lessons to be learned. College is high school piled higher and thicker. The physical surroundings of the college classrooms support the psychological atmosphere of the high school. There is the teacher's desk, the blackboards, the rigid rows of seats. The teacher enters. The lesson begins. What is the student supposed to do? The only thing he knows under the circumstances. Out come the nice new notebooks and pencils, and college education begins.

Under such a program, the responsibility of the student is to take notes, cover the readings, or laboratory experiment, and demonstrate that he has "successfully" done so. If he receives a passing grade, it is supposed by intructor and student that the latter's responsibility has been discharged.

This pattern of learning does not permit the student to participate in his own development. It is the pressure of authority, the pressure of grade competition, which forces him to conform. There is not positive participation on the part of the student. There results a split in his self. His real problems engage his private attention, and the external pressure of keeping up with the standards of the college force him to do the public superficial work required by others.

The professional teacher can help the student to define for himself a different kind of self-responsibility and the way it is to be discharged. The skilled teacher, aware of the attitudes the students bring to the classroom, can help to re-shape and re-organize them. This awareness will express itself in the *way* the class sessions are conducted, in the kind of assignments given, in the material selected for discussion, and in the degree to which students are successfully encouraged to participate *meaningfully, not verbally,* in the course.

The instructor should make clear what he has to offer the students, and what he will require of them. This does not mean that the students will grasp at once, or at all, the techniques and procedure of the instructor. Indeed they may not quite *understand* the nature of the responsibilities they are required to assume. It is enough, and even better, if they are, or become, responsible without realizing it. If they are led to participate in their own education, if they feel the instructor will sincerely accept what they think and feel about the subject matter, the students will genuinely respect each other's differences. Conflict of opinion will be expected with regard to each other's views and that of the instructor, and, therefore, there will be freedom to express one's difference.

The scaffold of ideas, around which this study is built, has been set up. The reader is now acquainted with the educational, sociological, and psychological ideas of the author and with his views on the function of the instructor and the responsibility of the student. We now proceed to describe the kind of learning-teaching which takes place in such a frame of reference.

Chapter 6

The Physical Setting

For the past several years, we offered courses listed in the college catalogue under the titles of "Culture and Human Behavior" and "Crime in Society." Each of these classes met for fifty minutes three times a week, the former for one semester, and the latter throughout the year.

The class in "Culture and Human Behavior" numbered around twenty-five students and the class in "Crime in Society" approximately forty students. The rooms assigned for both courses were typical of the average college classroom. The instructor's desk fronted parallel rows of seats. For the course in "Culture and Human Behavior," we arranged to have the place of meeting changed to a seminar room where several tables were placed alongside each other surrounded by chairs, all of which formed a circle. Each of us could observe the others. No seats were assigned. The students and instructor sat where they pleased. Smoking was permitted. The basic book material used was James Plant's volume, *Personality and the Cultural Pattern*. A supplementary list of books and articles, from which the students were asked to select a certain number for study during the course, was given to them at the beginning of the course. They were informed that they would be held responsible for whatever material they selected.

Unfortunately, due to physical limitations, it was not possible to transfer the class in "Crime in Society" to a seminar room. The forty students met in the typical college classroom.[1]

It was still possible to do something to dispel the teacher-pupil atmosphere of the high school. The teacher's desk was either pushed to a corner of the room or concealed by the wraps of the students. We did not want it around. It was a symbol of the kind of authority we considered undesirable. The young ladies in the class occupied the back rows and the men straddled the seats of the front rows so that, at least, two large groups faced each other.

Sometimes the instructor sat in one of the seats or stood at the side in a corner. This occurred from time to time when the discussion by the students was at its height. The writer tried to efface his presence and not give the students the chance to turn in his direction, expecting him to support them in their statements or to assume the burden of discussion. When discussion ceased or wandered or reached an impasse, he arose or turned to face the group in order to redirect the discussion.[2]

The *manner* in which the instructor handles the material of the course and relates himself to the students lies peculiarly in the realm of art. It depends largely upon the individual skill of the teacher. We do not believe it is possible to define or precisely to formulate how any one instructor should relate himself to the content of the course or the

F. N.[1] To meet this problem of a relatively large registration we tried to find a fair basis for selecting a limited number of students, not exceeding twenty-five. Difficulties of an administrative nature arose, which involved the registering for courses in advance. The only fair solution, it seems, is to provide several sections for the classes which have a large registration.

F. N.[2] The text used in the course in "Crime in Society" was the writer's *Crime and Society*. A printed supplementary bibliography was placed in the hands of each student at the opening meeting, and assignments were made. Each student was permitted wide selection in the choice of materials to be studied but was held responsible for the material selected.

members of the class. The class situations must be met as they arise, from day to day and from moment to moment. The direction a discussion is going to take can hardly be foretold. The imagination, sensitivity, and alertness of instructor and students, as they play on each other, and on the material, affect the relationship in ways too subtle to be expressed adequately by lame language.

Knowledge of what the instructor is supposed to do, and a *general* statement of what is involved in the learning process is possible. This volume purports to deal with that. *The precise way* in which this knowledge is to be applied by the instructor, and the precise way in which students learn, cannot, we believe, in our present state of knowledge, (or, possibly ever) be caught by words. We can make an analysis of general, common factors in teaching and learning. This constitutes the knowledge-content. The actual process of teaching and learning cannot by its very nature be translated into language without distorting what occurs. The processes of teaching and learning, in their qualitative uniqueness, differ for each individual. In brief, we can *describe* the process. We thereby obtain knowledge of its content but still fall short of catching the actuality.

The "Data"

In each of the classes we had arranged to have a student-stenographer present who recorded verbatim the entire discussion throughout the course. The students of each group were not aware of this, merely viewing the stenographer as one of the group. The shorthand notes, which were transcribed immediately after the class session, served several purposes. We used them to discover wherein we had failed in technique, to spot matters which escaped us, and to reveal errors in our procedure. They helped us to evaluate the progress of each student and the class as a whole. They were also used as illustrative material for this study.

There is one limitation of the material to which the attention of the reader is called. This qualification is implied in the above discussion of process and content. The most meaningful aspect of the classroom experience is the most difficult to communicate. We refer to the atmosphere of the class meetings. The author must accept the danger that the reader will interpret the account of the students' remarks, as well as his own, in a somewhat different context than that in which they occurred. No kind of written record can quite give the reader the nuances among the several students and between the students and instructor. Any written record, obviously, will fail to carry over the way in which a discussion is handled. Pitch of voice, the pressure or hesitancy behind the statement, facial or bodily gestures, looks of boredom, annoyance, hostility or friendliness — such matters cannot easily be captured by a stenographer who is busily engaged in recording *what* is said. Yet, these, and similar happenings, are very often the most telling indicia of what is happening to the student, to the instructor, and to the relations between them. Great skill is involved in both sensing and interpreting the meaning of the non-verbal behavior of the students as well as the grave danger of misinterpreting the meaning. In the final analysis, the validity of the interpretation of such factors will be proportionate to the knowledge and skill of the observer. We see no other way of using these valuable clues.[3] The understanding of what takes place both on the level of verbal and non-verbal behavior provides the instructor with his control over the process.

In addition to the verbatim report of the class discussions, use is made of the reports of students. In all classes students were held responsible for handing in a written report at the beginning of each week. This report consisted of the

F. N.[3] The question of evaluating the material is further discussed in Chapter Fourteen.

student's reaction to the class discussion of the past week and his reaction to the material assigned for the coming week. My experience with each class has been similar. It requires several weeks for the students to realize that the usual report on readings, which they have been accustomed to hand in in the usual high school and college course, is not what is wanted. Such reports usually indicate not much more than that the students have some ability to read or write the English language. It is *their* reactions to class discussion and assigned readings which is required. Reactions cannot be labelled good or bad, true or false, or be marked A, B, C, D, or F. One's reactions are just what they are. The problem, if any, is, fearlessly, to assume the responsibility for them. If students are helped to feel that there is little to fear from a non-inquisitorial instructor, and that their sincere reactions will be respected and accepted just as they are, then there is a much greater likelihood of genuine participation on the students' part.

One other source of material should be mentioned. Many of the students requested an individual conference with the instructor. During, or at the close of such interviews we recorded the substance of the discussion, as well as our interpretation of what took place. While most of these notes will not appear in this study, they have aided us in understanding some of the problems of the individual students. These interviews plus the weekly reports of all of the students served as the basis for directing discussion in the classroom. They also served as indices of the particular student's movement in relation to the subject-matter of the course.

One final statement should be made before we turn directly to the description of the work. The quotations of the students' work which occur throughout the succeeding chapters are merely *excerpts* from interviews, weekly or final reports. Sometimes, merely one or two sentences are selected from a report. Occasionally we quote in full a paragraph or two. We believe this procedure is justified since *we are interested not so much in evaluating* what *the student learned, as in illustrating how learning occurs.* As a rule, therefore, only sentences and paragraphs which illustrate this are selected. Of course, in certain instances, how one learns and what one learns are so integrally expressed by the student that no selection of the one without the other is possible.

The reader is asked to bear in mind throughout the following chapters that this study is concerned with the *process* of learning rather than with *what* the students learn. Since some readers will nevertheless want to have evidence of the changes in attitude which took place, excerpts from final student papers are included in Chapter Fourteen.

Chapter 7

Resistance

It is a truism that each of us must make adjustments to the world (and within ourselves). We have to accept limitations and to accomodate ourselves to realities. The organism resists change but must be disciplined to accept it. What role does the teacher play in this process?

All teachers would agree on the objectives, viz., that one must learn to bend one's will to others or to situations; that discipline in overcoming resistance is a condition of growth. Teachers differ, however, in the method of reaching that goal. In the current, traditional methods of instruction, it is supposed that the child acquires discipline by accommodating himself to the teacher. A different view, maintained in this study, is that the student acquires discipline by overcoming himself.

In the traditional type of instruction, the teacher dominates the student. The instructor is not very tolerant toward the differences and peculiarities of the students. The standards of the school or of the teacher are applied in the belief and expectation that they will be accepted by the students. They do dominate and control activity, but negatively, by way of student submission or self-effacement. The pupils, experiencing the external pressure, fight against it, not with it.

Many, if not most, students develop this pattern of fighting the standards of the instructor without being aware of it. They learn negatively, in that they are forced to learn and do not willingly participate. In a word, students, like the rest of us, resist changing themselves. They struggle against the imposition of a foreign will. This can be observed in the traditional pattern of instruction on all levels of education.

The public elementary and high schools and colleges generally project what they consider to be the proper way of learning, which is uniform for all students. Subject matter is standardized, hours and credits are assigned for various subjects, lectures, recitations, and examinations are given, and standardized results are expected. Children quickly learn how to react to this projection with a minimum amount of participation on their part. A few students of every large class stand out. The others seek shelter in the group. The hours, days, weeks, and months pass. An examination is announced. There is a feverish, scrambling activity the night before the examination. The given answers are memorized. The words are arranged. The questions are answered, and the student is at peace in the comforting pattern of the class until the next examination. He is sustained and secure in the patterned routine of the classroom, where he can withdraw safely and do nothing other than what he wishes since essentially nothing is required of him by the teacher except to sit and apparently listen or sometimes write and occasionally answer a direct question. If these are the requirements which the teacher projects, they are usually felt as an external pressure which must be conformed to — sufficiently to "get by." Positive participation is the exception, and negative conformance the rule.

This is the kind of general learning pattern students have acquired. This pattern of external pressure by the school and college systems must be altered. The students must be challenged, not coerced, so that they willingly and creatively participate in doing something for and to themselves. Unless they are *skillfully* opposed, they have nothing to struggle against other than the blind weight of external pressure. They must be given the opportunity to struggle *with* opposition and not against it.

The struggle can in no case be avoided but it can be directed into constructive effort, which will have positive value for one's growth. The opposition of the instructor must be applied professionally not arbitrarily. (This is discussed in detail in Chapter Eleven). He does not seek to break the will of the student, to force him by subtle or overt threats to do what is required, but guides him in his efforts to change. The student will follow the instructor's lead and challenge if he senses that the teacher respects, understands, and accepts him. Certain of this regard of the instructor, the student is fortified in his own struggle to overcome the obstacles set up by the material and the teacher.

The following description of the opening session of a class illustrates the initial effort in altering the attitudes toward learning which the students bring to class. The verbatim report of the first meeting of the class in *Personality and Culture* follows.

Hereafter the class in *Personality and Culture* will be referred to by the symbol "PC" and the class in *Crime and Society* by the symbol "CS." The names of the students have been altered. The letter "I" refers to the instructor, the writer.

First Meeting of PC

(When I entered the room the students were seated around the tables. I seated myself and looked around. For about one minute nothing was said by anyone. The students glanced at me and at each other, some apparently wondering and puzzled at the silence.)

I: I suppose all of you would like to know what this course has to deal with.

(Notebooks were being opened and pencils poised.) First, it will help all of us to know what you expect. Miss Melville, what do you expect from this course?

Melville: Why, I don't know what you mean. I registered for this course. It's the course in *Personality and Culture,* isn't it?

I: Yes, this is the course. I'm wondering what you expect to get out of it.

Melville: I came to this class because I wanted to take personality problems and learn about people.

I: And you think you can learn about people in this course?

Melville: Why, yes.

I: I wonder if that is possible. Mr. Lyons, what do you expect to find here?

Lyons: I thought I should have a little of Prof. Cantor before I left college.

I: How can I help you?

Lyons: To be frank, I want a good grade. (Laughter)

I: It's certainly legitimate to want a grade. Perhaps there are other values to the course.

Lyon: I was being facetious.

I: What do you really want?

Lyons: I thought it would be interesting to hear many points of view.

I: I take it you intend to listen and not to talk.

Rolfe: (A student of mine in a former class.) He'll be disappointed. It's not your way of teaching; you are here to guide us along.

(Turning to another student, I raised my head instead of repeating the same question.)

Hortense: (A former student.) I heard the course was very good, and I appreciate how your other course, criminology, was conducted, and I liked it even though I wasn't at **home** in it.

I: It's possible you won't be at home in this course.

Hortense: I don't know.

Rolfe: I heard the course is good.

I: Would you care to explain what you mean by that?

Priestly: I understand that Plant is very good and that we'll get different points of view.

Redfield: A year ago I planned my schedule. I seek a broad university background. At the time I read the catalog, I liked the description of the course.

I: What do you think the course might give you?

Redfield: I work for the YWCA and I thought this course would help me.

I: I hope so, but you may be disappointed in not getting what you like.

Mackenzie: I heard the course was different from anything before.

I: What do you look for?

Mackenzie: I don't know.

I: What would you like to find?

Mackenzie: I don't know.

Murdock: I heard the course was interesting, and I'm interested in people.

I: How will this course help you in that interest?

Murdock: I don't know.

Fields: Offhand, I couldn't say, but I expect to find out a bit more about the dynamics of culture than I did in sociology.

Curran: I'm taking this course because I'm interested in the subject matter.

Rolfe: (A former student.) In criminology last year something very interesting happened. It was the first time in my three years at college I worked on my own because I wanted to and not because I had to. I am interested in your new approach that really can't be explained.

I: My question is, what do you expect out of *this* course?

Rolfe: I don't know.

Moran: I don't know.

I: What would you like to find here?

Moran: I'd like to know more about people.

I: I don't know what any of you will get out of this course. Some of you may get what you expect, and some of you may get more than you expect, and perhaps a few of you will get very little. That happens sometimes. This course will deal with the volume, *Personality and the Cultural Pattern* as the basic text for our discussions. Our procedure will be as follows: There are eighteen chapters in the book. Each Monday, unless otherwise stated, each one of you will be expected to submit your comments on the chapter assigned for the week. It is expected that you will present your own reactions, whatever they are, and not the point of view of the author. Naturally, each one of us will have different points of view. Some of us will like the material; others will disagree and be annoyed. Still others will be impatient with the procedure in the classroom. Since we are different people, it is altogether natural to expect disagreement. Are there any questions?

Mackenzie: How long must the papers be?

I: I don't quite know how to answer that. I suppose it depends upon what you have to say.

Curran: Do you want us to take notes in class?

I: It is up to you to get the material we shall deal with in whatever way you think best. Are there any further questions or comments? Very well, we'll proceed.

We are to deal with personality and culture. They are both very difficult concepts and I, for one, am not sure just what they mean. Students in this field do not agree, and I would like to hear from you what you think personality is. Anyone may talk and may interrupt at any time.

Lyons: Personality would be the person as a whole.

Lawton: It is the dynamics of integration of behavior patterns. It includes all the reactions of the person.

Lyons: The individual personality is described and defined for the convenience which the psychologist uses and further than that is a figment of the imagination.

Fields: There is an old definition in psychology, do you agree, that the personality is the sum total of all the personality traits. Do you agree that it is adequate enough? I have a feeling that the traits are integrated definitely.

Lawton: The sum total is not right.

Fields: That definition is not adequate.

Curran: How could the personality be the sum total of all the traits? A person won't exhibit all the traits at one time.

Lawton: I didn't say that.

Curran: A person's personality is constantly changing. Personality is very dynamic.

Rolfe: Personality is the result of what the person wants to do and what culture prescribes, and the personality is the result of the conflict.

I: Does anyone notice anything about the people who spoke?

Answer: All boys.

Rolfe: May we draw the conclusion that boys are naturally more aggressive? You seem to want to draw a conclusion.

I: I did not want any conclusion. It just struck me as an interesting fact.

Melville: (One of the women students). When a definition of personality is required, people make a stab at it, but they really don't understand. I think personality is an integration of all our behavior patterns.

I: Suppose your grandmother was eighty years old. You came home and said, "Grandmother, I learned that our personality is an integration of all our behavior patterns."

Melville: She would probably ask, "What does it mean, 'integration of behavior patterns'," and I would say, "It is within ourselves, what we exhibit and what we really feel."

I: Is everyone satisfied? (No one spoke.   I remained silent.)

Curran: Perhaps they don't agree with the definition?

Melville: I want to know what other people think.

Lyons: That is only part of the definition.   Plant's book is also on culture which adds another complication to the problem of personality.

Lawton: It would be interesting to hear how to enhance the individual's adjustment by working on him or his culture and personality.

Fields: (Turning to instructor.)   Are you hinting that personality is indefinable and that you can only get certain ideas of it by observing the many kinds of activities that people indulge in, because there are so many ways that personality may be motivated?   A person's personality cannot remain the same for any length of time because it is constantly changing and cannot be definitely defined.

I: Am I hinting all that?

Fields: If I hint that, how much would that be worth?

I: You are the best judge of that.

Fields: I just got the idea and want to know what it's worth. That is why I want to finish this course.   *You* have several times finished this course and I would like to know what you think.

I: Perhaps that is unimportant compared to what you think.

Fields: We are to have some ideas when the course is finished?

I: I think you can answer that question better than I can.

Fields: It depends, I just got the idea, and I seriously wanted to know what the point was worth.

I: I don't think that it makes any difference what I think about it.   What's important is what you think about it.

Fields: Well, if it's right, it is important.   I don't know whether I am right.   I need experience.

I: Well, maybe you will have some experience.

Fields: Then, for experience we would complete the course.

Rolfe: Isn't Mr. Fields asserting a very common personality trait in wanting your approval?

(I glanced inquiringly at Fields. Rolfe turned toward Fields). You want Prof. Cantor's approval on what you said, otherwise what you said doesn't mean anything to you.

Fields: If it's right, it means something.

Rolfe: What difference does that make?

I: What do you care what I think about it?

Fields: You are supposed to have a better idea of the problem. The idea I gave was my own, and I wanted to see how it conformed with yours.

I: I have difficulties with this problem, too, and I am not at all certain that my statements would be acceptable.

Fields: I wouldn't have accepted your own statement.

I: Would you agree with me?

Fields: If I had the background to draw from, then I would be absolutely certain of the validity of the statement.

I: Why not get the background?

Fields: I merely wanted comparisons.

I: Then you would not trust your own background on the validity of concepts?

Fields: No, the validity of any concept depends upon the way it is arrived at. You have taken a longer time to learn what you know than I have.

I: And I may be dead wrong?

Fields: That's right.

I: So you rely upon your own ideas.

Fields: You certainly get more out of living with people than with yourself. And I want to be with you for a semester.

I: Why don't you wait for a semester?

Fields: You really get a preview about everything.

Rolfe: You don't learn anything about anything except

from yourself. It is mystical. Take a travelling salesman;
he has never had a course on personality, and he'll deal with
problems because he is accustomed to them.

Curran: I have some conclusions as a result of whatever
study I have made, gathering up the facts I have heard and
read. I would like to hear your comment. I may change my
thoughts, or go your full way. I would like to hear you
comment, or your opinions.

I: Why do you want definitions at all now?

Curran: We want to know what we are talking about.
Some people think that people have a good personality or a
bad personality, but they do not know just what personality
is. They are dumbfounded when you ask them for a definition. I take a scientific approach.

I: And you are not dumbfounded?

Curran: Personality is the integration of the traits of an
individual.

I: Are you quite satisfied with that?

Curran: Past experience has taught me that I may be wrong.
And this is probably the best place to find out.

West: Everybody wants a definition of personality but it
doesn't really mean much. The people in this course really
want to understand.

I: Are you distinguishing between a definition and an understanding of the definition?

West: Yes. I don't think you can say that anybody has
a bad or a good personality?

Lawton: We learn by doing. What we have been defining
is the term of personality, which has no meaning at all to us
in understanding what personality is. We have to learn by
experience.

A re-examination of this material illustrates the nature
of the movement which the instructor hoped to direct. Aware
of the essential fact that most of the students came to the
classroom bringing their customary attitude of leaning back,

awaiting the lecture of the instructor, the authority who is to tell them what is what, the teacher avoids lecturing.

To be sure, a certain kind of guidance takes place. I believe in education and hold to a certain philosophy of education. I am interested in students and have some appreciation for the confusion, difficulty, and pain involved in genuine growth. Sympathy is not enough. This must be accompanied by an understanding of the particular type of emotional experience the student is having and of my function in dealing with it. I offer to help, but I leave to the student a large degree of freedom of choice as to what he or she wants to do with this offer.

Interestingly enough, the students enter the classroom prepared to listen to the instructor as a rule, in a negative way. Their general attitude may be expressed as follows.

"Here we are. Talk to us and we'll do what we're supposed to do. Only please let us alone. Don't pick on us, don't ask any embarrassing questions. Just talk, we'll take notes. Let us know when the exam comes around, we'll do a bit of cramming, go through our notes of your answers and we'll pass. Only please don't bother us. We don't know the stuff. That's what you're here for. Tell us."

Their general school experience has been of this sort. They were handled by their teachers as youngsters into whose minds information was to be poured.. The whole previous setting tended to prevent their participation in their education. They were asked or compelled to *unite* with what was required of them by way of subject-matter.

In this opening session, emphasis is placed on difference. The attempt is made to have the students express themselves; the instructor refuses to accept their withdrawal. They are helped to sense their differences from the instructor so that they have something to say themselves. This experience during the opening meeting is characterized both by the strangeness and fear of any new experience and by the unexpected reactions of the instructor. The students are somewhat annoyed and do not quite know what to make of it. Why should they be asked what they expect of the course? How should they know? It's not their course. They want something from the instructors, or from the subject-matter. They want to get something or other. But they haven't been prepared to give of themselves in order to genuinely acquire something *for* themselves. They do not realize that it is *not* the instructor's course but their own to do with what they will (within certain limits).

Four of the twenty-eight students (Fields, Rolfe, Curran, and Lawton), it will be observed, carried most of the discussion during the opening session, eight others spoke several times, and the remaining members, more than half of the class, did not volunteer to comment overtly at this time. Whatever the reasons, a minority of the students felt sufficiently moved to express their differences. Others may have questioned themselves, thereby turning their conflict inwardly, and so stimulating themselves to further effort. Still others may have hardly extended themselves at all. They felt no need to do much, if anything, about an experience which did not vitally concern them. (The different ways in which students use the instructor and the subject matter are discussed in Chapter Twelve).

The opportunity for change has been given. If they want to take advantage of this they can. They cannot, however, rest upon the wholeness of the classroom setting. The feeling of secure anonymity in the classroom setting, where the instructor assumes all of the responsibility, is gone. Their accustomed pattern of being taught and learning under pressure has been broken up. Henceforth, whatever is learned must include *their* participation.

The students are not permitted to retain their old selves by withdrawing. By depriving the student of the instructor's support, separation from the accustomed teacher-student pattern in which the teacher assumed almost all of the responsibility is experienced. Movement toward some kind of re-organization of the self is initiated. This movement leads to new needs, new threats by opposing forces of other members of the class. When the student's self loses the support of the classroom environment, anxiety, further withdrawal, submission, or aggression occurs. One's self is then moved to get rid of the tension and to seek its comforting wholeness and balance once again by doing something to oneself. The tensions can also be relieved by sincere agreement, in which case one assimilates what one needs from another (the other is like him) or feels that the other sincerely accepts his point of view.

The pattern of resting upon the instructor and externally conforming with the classroom requirements is, in some cases, not easily changed. The following reactions of students to the first chapters in the text in CS is illustrative of this statement:

"I'm afraid I had no tremendous reaction to this chapter, I thought it was interesting. I did not experience any opposition to any of the statements made. I don't see how a novice in the field could have such an opposition when he knows next to nothing about the field. You are the authority."

(Robert.)

"Until I can spout forth authentic knowledge of my own, I am quite contented to survive at the fount of another's wisdom. I am willing to be led." *(Selig.)*

"The material in this chapter is simply a definition of crime, criminals, and criminal justice." *(Goddard.)*

"I think Professor Cantor did well in asking so many enlightening questions, but, as a criminologist-lawyer, he would have done essentially better to answer these questions immediately and not leave his students in the dark." *(Kareff.)*

Several papers consisting of reactions to the first chapters in the text in PC follow.

"I have read this chapter carefully. The ideas about 'personality' are traced. I feel I must accept those views as I accept 2 and 2 makes 4." (West.)

"I am inclined to agree with Dr. Plant's point of view. However, I have felt the same after studying over texts and attending lecture courses. I try to look at it objectively and realize that the manner in which the material is presented influences me considerably." (Sims.)

The PC class had met for the tenth time. Two students had as yet not spoken during the month. The following comments occurred at the opening of the class between these students and myself.

I: Miss Moran, what is your responsibility to this course?

Moran: To learn about personality and culture.

I: How does one go about doing it?

Moran: Isn't this course supposed to teach you this?

I: What's your role?

Moran: I'm supposed to learn.

I: How?

Moran: Listening to other people.

I: Miss Mackenzie, what do you think your responsibility is?

Mackenzie: To get as much as I can out of you and the class.

I: Aren't you part of the class?

Mackenzie: Yes.

I: Perhaps you have something to give to the class.

Mackenzie: I don't feel I have anything to contribute.

Both of these students as well as the writers of the previous excerpts are not permitted to withdraw. So, instead, they adopt the device of *submitting* to the accustomed requirements of the usual classroom and assignments. In effect they are saying, "If I give in, I'll be left alone and won't be hurt." In the course of time, through my refusal to allow them to withdraw or to submit, movement and change occurs as is shown by the subsequent reactions which are cited on pp. 231, 121, 124, 226, 227.

The professional teacher who appreciates the traditional pattern of learning acquired by students in the elementary, secondary, and higher education, must guard himself against supporting it. He must help the student to meet a new kind of learning experience, one in which the student actively participates. The instructor does not demand effort or common interest. By confronting the student with his own difference, he wonders and inquires what they, the students, would like to do about the problems which arise.

It is as if he said, "Here is a problem. We are meeting in this class to try and find out what this problem means and how we are to go about handling it. It is your problem as well as mine. Together we'll try to explore it. You will be confused and uncomfortable for awhile. I realize that you would rather not go to the trouble and discomfort of finding the answers for yourselves but would much rather that I, as an authority, present you with neat, well-defined answers which you can record. That is, of course, what you have been accustomed to in the past. I'm quite sure, however, that you will not learn very much that way. A much better procedure would be for you to tell me what you think and feel about the problem. Make it part of your own vital experience. Try to see what it means to you. Until you succeed in doing that, nothing I *say* will have very much meaning for *you*. Don't be afraid or timid in expressing yourself. I'll appreciate your difficulties. I fully realize that there is room for honest difference of opinion. There are many ways of looking at this problem. I would ask you and expect you to be responsible for whatever stand you take. You will have to support your position and, if you do not succeed, then some other point of view will have to be accepted. You won't like that. No one likes to feel that he is wrong and none of us likes to be disturbed. That however, is the way it is. We can't learn unless we struggle with ourselves in order to remake ourselves. I certainly will not fight against you and I hope you won't fight against me. Let's all struggle with this problem and see what happens to us."

The opposition of the instructor, if offered in this spirit, will, in most cases, be accepted by the students in the same spirit. Sensing his understanding and having his support, they will be encouraged to struggle with themselves in achieving an altered and meaningful re-organization in points of view.

We next turn to a more detailed description of the nature of this struggle through which students pass in order to experience genuine change in point of view.

Chapter 8

Ambivalence

In Chapter Four we spoke of the duality of the self and of the conflict involved in finding balances between being dependent upon and being independent of others. "We want to have our cake and eat it, too." Until a decision is reached, we are torn between conflicting desires. There are many everyday occurrences which demonstrate the reality of the opposing tendencies of a self (in addition to the conflict of the dependent-independent balance). We accompany a dear friend or a loved one to the railroad station to see him off. We are glad to go with him — and still, find the separation, as the train pulls out, painful. Or, while walking, one observes an acquaintance or friend a few feet away whom one would like to greet, yet one turns aside or crosses the street.

Again, we are engaged in friendly conversation; the time has long passed since "goodbye" should have been uttered. Yet one grabs for stray items to cover up the embarrassment over not being able simply to say goodbye. When the situation becomes too obvious to be covered up by idle talk, even then a straightforward "goodbye" is difficult to utter. There is a compromise settling of the conflict between wanting to be with and away from a friend. "Well, so long, I'll be seeing you," or "See you later," or "Goodbye, drop in again sometime."

Leaving a place one enjoys, graduating from school, getting to write an unwritten promised letter or a class assignment — these and hundreds of other familiar experiences reflect the conflicting feelings one experiences between wanting and not wanting. These opposing tendencies give content to the term "ambivalence" as we use it.

There are many ways in which the individual tries to conceal this recurrent conflict in order to avoid making a decision, since any decision which is made will leave another strong desire unsatisfied. If the conflict continues without any decision being made, one becomes increasingly restless. If the matter is vital, a neurosis may be the end product. And the function of the neurosis is to save one from having to face and make a decision. A neurosis conceals, but does not resolve, a conflict.

One can take a drink, rationalize, or try to avoid thinking about the problem. There are also many ways that are used to reach a decision. One may experience fear, anger, frustration, or guilt. A rush of emotion may accompany the awareness that whatever one does, something else which one also wants will remain unsatisfied. There will be a separation between one aspect of the will and its object or desire. Fear, anger, annoyance, frustration, or guilt may motivate one in the final decision, as well as recur after the decision is made because the decision was not made otherwise. The conflict is resolved one way or another, if at all, under the pressure of feeling which weights the balance to one side.

The *way* in which the student resolves his conflicts arising out of the learning experience is important. The instructor is not selling a bill of goods and, therefore, is not a high pressure salesman who seeks to talk the student into buying something. Nor is the instructor a minister pleading for the student to turn over a new leaf and embrace his faith and ideals. The teacher is (or should be) in the classroom in the interest of the student and should want to help him make his own decisions. The student will not grow unless he learns to resolve his own conflicting emotions and assume responsibility for his decisions.

The following material is taken from a class session held during the second month of PC. I had been unable up to this time to get the student voluntarily to participate in class discussion. It seemed to me, during this session, that she was making an effort to express herself. Twice she opened and then closed her mouth. There was a lull in the class discussion. I turned to her :

I: Miss Peters, didn't you want to say something?

Peters: Why, yes, but . . . but . . . (There was silence for a few seconds.)

I: I'm sure what you say will be important.

Peters: Well, I haven't got the fine language of Plant. I don't think I could make myself clear.

I: About what?

Peters: I'm bothered about the differences between security and adequacy.

I: I can well understand that. The distinction is not easy to see.

(There was no response. Many of the students continued to shift their gaze from the student to me. The uncomfortable silence continued for about a half a minute. The student was blushing furiously.)

I: I'll help if I can. What seems to be the difficulty?

Peters: I guess I'm just afraid to talk.

I: Why not simply try to express yourself in your own words? Your language is just as important to us all as is Plant's.

Peters: Oh, I'll just say a lot of silly things.

I: If you consider something important, it can't be silly. Your opinion is just as important to us as is that of Plant. I'm not sure that I agree with his distinction.

Peters: Well, I think a person could do a lot of things and still not have self-confidence. Isn't that so?

I: Indeed, that is so, Miss Peters.

In some way Miss Peters was struck by the important distinction which Plant made. Something vital enough occurred to her which she wanted to express, and yet she feared exposing herself to the judgment of the other students. She wanted to talk but was afraid to. If she had not been moved to talk, she would not have experienced fear. But if she had not talked and she did want to, she would have been angry with herself. It is interesting to note that after this discussion, which continued for about ten minutes, Miss Peters participated more and more in subsequent class discussions.

In an early paper, commenting on the class discussion, another student in PC wrote:

"The class seems to put a great deal of pressure on me. I feel confused but also that I am beginning to see a little light. I also feel that some of the ideas I express in class are futile, or better, are not being approved of by you. With this amount of uncertainty, not only in content, but also in the manner of conducting the class, I feel very uncomfortable. There is some feeling on my part that perhaps I talk too much in class. This causes me discomfort, and yet I feel forced to express myself." *(Bowers.)*

Miss Murdock, previously referred to, wrote:

"Do you remember that first day this semester before I'd definitely decided which course to take and I came to your class to see what it was like? Frankly speaking, that class made me very uncomfortable. It centered in class discussion, a type of thing in which some people seem to blossom out and expand and which I enjoy listening to, but have never participated in very much. My first impulse was to hurry over to the Registrar's office and enroll in Dr. ——'s nice, safe lecture course, as I had originally planned. Somehow, I could not. The subject matter of the course, which seemed to touch upon something so practical and vitally interesting and yet so elusive, so aroused my curiosity that I was compelled to stay, although I didn't want to."

"Something has happened to me in the past two sessions. I feel angry and stupid about not taking part in the class discussion. I have experienced a greater feeling of uncertainty and insecurity about myself. But, at the same time, I have a desire to find out why. In my last paper, I said I didn't feel I had anything to add to the class discussion. I do feel I want to ask some questions, but I experience what Plant calls a 'panicky-anxiety state' which blots out anything I think about. I hope the feeling will pass away.

"Isn't there something wrong in trying to see into things of this sort? Can't people accept what they have, what they get, without questioning the whys and wherefores? When the questioning begins, unhappiness begins. A little faith wouldn't hurt any of us; we are too searching. Why not be satisfied with what there is? Still, I confess, it is satisfying to find out how false many of our views have been. At the same time my feeling of security is shaken. I find myself trying to defend myself against what Plant says although he is very convincing. It's all very disturbing." *(Mackenzie.)*

Instead of being timid or afraid some students feel more or less helpless while at the same time wanting to do something themselves. As one student in PC states:

"Frankly, your approach to our class has been very different from any others I have experienced. I believe that your procedure tends to stimulate thinking more than the usual classroom procedure. However, I personally feel that an introduction into the subject should acquaint us more readily with the scope of the course. I fully appreciate that it is our course and that each of us has our part in it, but I don't know where to begin. The class conversation seems to me to be floundering and presents a discouraging outlook."

(Katz.)

Other students in CS expressed themselves as follows:

"In 1937, when I first entered the University, you gave a fireside talk to the entering freshmen in the Blue Room of Norton Hall. You asked us a very disconcerting question, "Why are you here?" I didn't say a word. I just listened. I did not come back to the school the following year — I've spent three years out, ever since graduating high school. I still don't know what you meant that night, and to find out is one of the reasons I am taking this course. I want to find the answer to that question, but, right now, I find the class one of confusion, embarrassment, and bewilderment." *(Caldwell.)*

"Our class discussion has been helpful, and I heartily approve of open discussion rather than a boring lecture in which I personally could share no part. I like the chance to voice my opinion. But my difficulty is that I walk out of class twice as confused as when I walk in." *(Ball)*

"I suppose there is a point to all this introductory confusion. I wish I knew what it was. Can't you tell us? Really, it's awfully disheartening to sit down in a classroom and listen to everyone talking in what seems to be circles to you. The trouble is I can't seem to get any conclusions. If someone said, 'Is criminology a science or isn't it?' I wouldn't know what to say or where to begin. I'm bothered because I feel I'm missing something in the discussions. Won't you clear this up at our next meeting?

"So far as I'm concerned, all the elaborate notes I've been taking the past week can go down the drain like so much dirty dishwater. For, to put it mildly, I am confused — inexorably so. Every assumption I had about crime and criminals seems to be false." *(Kuhn.)*

"Should someone ask me again, 'When is a murderer a criminal?' I'd be glad to slay myself just to find the actual answer—if there is one. What's wrong in your telling us just what the definition of a criminal and crime is?" *(Morse.)*

"Do you recall the latest song hit, 'Where do I go from here?' If I listen to any more discussion and read any more of the text, I'm quite positive that I'll take the wrong road and never get anywhere. When I entered the criminology class in September, I expected to learn a little something about the subject. It's now early October and all that I've learned could be put in the left eyeball of a cat. I sincerely feel that any more confusion will soon lead to chaos. I wish I knew what the course was all about. Isn't it your job to straighten us out?" *(MacGuire.)*

"It appears to me that confusion is still dominating over clarity in the subject of criminology. I may be entirely wrong, but it appears to me that all we have found out so far, in three weeks of school, twelve sessions, is the meaning of crime, criminals, and criminal justice. I enjoy this new (to me) method of teaching but it appears that we are progressing too slowly, and that we are not going to accomplish very much in the short time we have unless you squelch a lot of the aimless discussion and help us understand the material."

(Rush.)

"I like the idea of discussion very much. The only fault is that most of the students aren't talking in the same frame of reference. The discussions are opinionated. We need more guidance." *(Selig.)*

The central idea in the above comments is, "Although we like what's taking place and want to do something about clearing up the ideas, we can't do it. We're confused and we need your help." The students are demanding that I take over their responsibility of struggling with the formulation of some of the basic problems in the course.

Sometimes the classroom experience initiates movement which gives rise to a sense of guilt or hostility instead of fear or dependence.

"The reading of Plant, in my experience, has been akin to the sensation of a series of flashlight bulbs popping one after the other. Unlike other courses, this one refuses to roll smoothly and effortlessly over the heads of the class members. Whether invited or not, it enters into them and forces action of some kind. You're forced to think about yourself and it isn't comfortable.

"For quite a while, in regard to this course, (PC), I have been possessed of a feeling of guilt. These feelings come and go. The guilt is present, possibly, because of the fact that the subject matter is so important to me and revealing in a personal way. It can be so directly applied to myself that I sense my shortcomings and it makes me uneasy. I feel that I want to do something about it but don't know what." *(Hortense.)*

"I think I must have the trait of complexity (discussed by Plant in the text) for it seems to me I do nothing but silently talk to myself and put myself at arm's length to get a better view. I give myself advice and reprimand myself. I try to prevent my emotions from controlling me by forced logical thinking — and suffer from it by being forced to think about it. I get very angry with myself for indulging in wishful thinking." *(Murdock.)*

"On thinking over the classes of the past week or two, I find that I have a kind of hostility toward you — not when you "pick" on me, but when you pick on Miss Moran who happens to be my best friend, though I know it is probably good for her. That must show something about me; what, I don't know." *(Mackenzie.)*

Students Moran and MacKenzie were non-speakers in the classroom. I had tried without success to have them participate in discussion. I would ask, "I wonder, Miss Moran, how that strikes you?" or "Miss MacKenzie, would you like to comment on that point?" The responses were usually monosyllabic or a word or two. Miss Mackenzie's hostility is to be expected. She reaches the point where, at least, she is no longer indifferent. She has sufficient courage to express her hostility, although it is accompanied by fear at her daring. She uses the common protective device of justifying her personal resentment toward me by attributing it to the treatment of her friend, Miss Moran, (part of her resentment is probably due to this, since she is closely identified with Miss Moran). She dares to take me to task, but, at the same time, she is afraid of her attitude. She softens her criticism by stating, "it is probably good for her" and "that must show something about me." Miss MacKenzie is unable to accept her own feelings of hostility. She denies they are her own and, because of her fear and lack of self-assurance, has to justify them through Miss Moran.

"What have I done in this paper other than echo Plant? I just wanted to reveal that I have said, in effect, little better than nothing. I feel I could do a better job, but the element of time interferes. It is a certain guilt that forces me to write this. My standard has been hit by it, and no one else knows my own standard better than I." *(West.)*

"In this last hour that I've been trying to write this paper, I've been terribly conscious of the fact that I want to write a paper, yet I know it will be mostly bluff, because the first paragraph is all I can really say I can understand in the chapter. I don't get it — so help me, but this is the way I resolved a problem I had, so this paper is more of a confession of a problem than a paper on culture and personality, which leaves me with the guilty feeling of not writing a paper for class. All I can say in my defense (I have to defend my position) is that I tried to understand it, to no avail. I wrote one side of a page, but threw it away — too much bluff for my conscience—so that's about all I can say. I feel better for not having bluffed a paper, but I feel badly for not turning in a paper on the material in the chapter." *(Bird.)*

"Riding downtown to the trial" (The class in CS was attending a trial in the supreme court where the defendant "———" was being tried on a first-degree murder charge.) "this issue (insanity viewed from the legal and psychological point of view) was answered during a three-man, two-girl bull session. I didn't give them any satisfaction by telling them so, but I'm afraid they have convinced me. I'm not, however, abandoning ship completely. I still believe there is some logic in my argument and that, at least part of it is correct." *(Morse.)*

In these last six excerpts, the students are fighting their negative attitudes. They acquire a sense of guilt about some attitude and want to do something else. They distrust their own negative resistance but, as yet, do not know how to move in a positive direction.

The students find themselves in a strange setting. Repeatedly they remark in their comments, only a few of which have been cited in this study, on the strangeness of this new type of class meeting. They are given the opportunity to make the class their own, which it is. Yet they find it difficult to meet this new situation. For most of them, this is, indeed, a unique experience. They find themselves in the presence of what appears to them to be an "authority" and yet no authoritative demands are made. In accordance with their previous experience, they expect to be told what to do and how to do it. Instead, they are invited to take the initiative. For many of them, this is their first experience of being confronted by an authority who either does not know all of the answers or who refrains from giving them.

The students have not had any similar previous experience which would prepare them to meet this kind of teacher-student relationship. It is not surprising, therefore, that confusion arises. They are given a large share of the responsibility in exploring the course, which they find difficult to accept. They wish to express themselves but are not quite sure that their differences will be accepted. They are not accustomed to questioning authority — in the presence of authority, yet they are expected to and invited to do just that.

It is to be expected that their feelings will be ambivalent in the early weeks of the course. During the first few weeks, the students who are more sure of themselves take the initiative. A few others cautiously feel their way, wondering how far they can go in expressing their difference. Gradually, as they discover that such differences are unaffectedly and sincerely accepted, student opinion becomes more pronounced. Others, previously silent, now participate. A point is soon reached where the class members not only question but begin to criticize and make demands. The following chapter on "Projection" will illustrate this movement.

Chapter 9

Projection

An individual who refuses to reorganize his attitudes will reject any experience which threatens the self as previously organized. We label this rejection "projection." It is not easy to alter attitudes, especially about matters with which one is vitally concerned. The need for having one's views accepted by others is part of the need to be considered important. Each of us wants to stand for something, and we want others to agree with our ideas. If they disagree, we seek to convert them by persuasion or argument. If talk doesn't help, we, sometimes, use blind authority to gain our point and, upon occasion, even brute force.

Another way of stating this is to say that the individual wants to bend the will of another to his will. The more intensive and extensive the change one is called upon to make, the greater will be the annoyance and discomfort one will experience. In order to avoid such inner conflict, which results when our settled ways of feeling, acting, or thinking are interfered with and threatened, we do one of several things. We refuse to attend to the challenge or avoid it or modify it so that it fits in with our established habits. We may also meet the challenge of change by reaffirming our position. Whichever alternative is employed, what we are doing, essentially, is asserting ourselves. We are projecting our negative will: in effect, we are saying, "This is the way I am and this is exactly the way I am going to remain. I will not be different."

An individual who wants to have his way "will simply not listen" or "will not discuss the matter." If he does "listen," he will, most likely, hear what he wants to hear and not what the speaker intends. The members of an audience or the readers of a book generally hear or take from the speaker or author that which fits in with their previously held opinions. Frequently, we resist change by overtly reasserting our position, when it is questioned or attacked. Finally, although we may speak the *words,* which apparently reflect a change in point of view, we, nevertheless, may remain basically unconvinced. Talk is cheap and, often, tricky. It conceals a stubbornness of heart as often as it reveals a change of mind.

These processes can be observed in the classroom, as in all human relations. Following the initial reaction of confusion and ambivalence, many students, over a period of time, seek to resolve the relative annoyances they experience by giving expression to the way *they* feel about the problems which have been raised. They enter the class with certain notions or opinions. At the very outset their opinions are questioned. They become uneasy. No one welcomes an inner struggle or enjoys confusion and tension. The instructor could lecture or argue or dominate (or even punish) the students. This would be more welcome than asking them to re-examine their positions since it would remove the intrapersonal struggle of the self and substitute for it a fight *against* the will of another.

The skillful instructor realizes that students resist change. If they do change, it will come about by the student struggling *with his* ambivalences, not by fighting against the alien will of another. By permitting the students to express their honest differences of opinion, and welcoming such expression, their participation in learning is encouraged. A re-affirmation of student attitudes (projection) resolves the initial disturbance. It is as if they said, "This new stuff and the questions you raise are all very interesting, but this is what *we* stand for." The professional instructor, in spirit, would rejoin, "If that's the way you feel about it, that's the way you feel about it. There is certainly room for your point of view and I respect it. I wonder whether there is any merit at all in a different point of view such as so and so's."

Now, what occurs? The students have projected their differences. There is no *contest* of wills. There is no spirit of, "I'm right, you're wrong — no, you're wrong, I'm right." Their differences have been accepted. They are *asked* whether they would care to entertain a different point of view or whether *they* would like to re-examine their present positions. A new disturbance is set up, directed not against the instructor who has tentatively accepted their differences, but toward themselves. The conflict is internalized and cannot be directed against the instructor who has not opposed them. This new movement may subsequently stimulate a positive willingness to change, to learn.

The negative side of the student's will to remain as he is has not been directly challenged. He has been allowed to project his difference, his independence, and to express his negative will. Now his other positive, constructive, creative self is appealed to. A swing in the opposite direction from projection, that is, toward identification, (discussed in the next chapter) usually occurs.

The following excerpts illustrate projection by the students. The reader will observe the freedom with which the members of the class criticize the material or the instructor and express their own attitudes. They have reached a point where they no longer are afraid to express their difference since they are confident that their differences from the instructor will be accepted and respected.

"I think it is intimated that both the positive and classical schools are unable consistently to apply their theories to the protection of society; in fact, I doubt if the author is convinced that punishment can protect society at all. And this I challenge. Jerome Hall, in a note in his article on the modern penal code, complains that the Positivists are too eager to accept any new theory offered. I believe you are guilty of this, too." *(Thorn.)*

"I find that a great deal of this chapter is rehash. It has added nothing to what I already know." *(MacDowell.)*

"I have a criticism to make of this chapter. The discussion of the material is too abstract. The matter of definition doesn't seem to end. Concentrating on this sort of intangible procedure seems to me to be tedious and confusing."
(Tylor.)

A few months after this was written, Mr. Tylor handed in the following comment:

"In *my* opinion, this chapter, especially the section on social responsibility and treatment, belongs under the first section of the book on Perspectives. It seems to me that the historical development of criminal law, what it was and how it changed, and how it lags behind the scientific view of human conduct and how to treat anti-social behavior, are facts that caused needless confusion earlier in the course. The class discussions were often colored with value judgments reflecting the very religious and social mores that the present criminal law is built upon. If this section was understood first, the conflicts in the points of view and what our present course is advocating in the way of understanding and treating criminal behavior, would have been more sharply defined and a clearer picture with historical perspective would have been obtained. The first section, of course, did point out the nature of criminology as the study of a social problem, but the origin and growth of criminal law was not in my estimation, brought out with sufficient emphasis." *(Tylor.)*

Mr. Tylor had reached the point where, through his own efforts and development, he had understood what had previously been confused. He has re-organized his thinking. Want-

ing again to assert his independence from the instructor, he
expresses the belief that his understanding of the issues would
have been simplified by giving him the answers at the beginning of the course. He does not realize that several months
of his struggling with the ideas had been necessary to gain this
appreciation.

Miss Grinnel expresses this same idea when she writes:

"I noticed, as I was reading this book, (Sanford Bates,
Prisons and Beyond) that many of my *reactions,* which I
was noting down, had become stereotyped. About halfway
through, I realized that I was attending particularly to those
old familiar friends which I had noted and reacted upon a
dozen times before — such things as personnel problems, ab-
normal environment of the prison, etc. . . . Perhaps this is
an indication of a lazy manner of taking the material presented, or perhaps it is a healthy sign that a large number of
these really vital problems connected with criminology have
really became a part of my thinking, affecting my experience and my attitudes. In other words, I am wondering
whether a certain amount of the material is becoming 'stale'
for me because of repeated readings of essentially the same
ideas, or perhaps it is not so much that it is 'stale' as that I
have absorbed it well enough that genuine reactions are limited by the familiarity of the material. I feel that the latter is
the case." *(Grinnel.)*

The above comment reflects the student's lack of interest in the material dealt with at the time. Reactions are
"stereotyped." Attention is given in a "lazy manner" to "old
familiar friends." Student Grinnel made the above remarks
toward the end of the course. This illustrates the dynamic
interplay between projection and identification. During
the first few weeks, students will not really participate in
struggling with their confusions. They want to remain as
they are and not be bothered with assimilating different
points of view. Later, after having gradually accepted other

ways of thinking and feeling about some of the ideas (identification), they again project their own (modified) point of view, usually without realizing that a change has taken place. Thus, for example, student Bird writes in two different papers, during the same period student Grinnel wrote the above:

"For the last few class sessions, I have been astounded beyond words at the lack of interest on the part of most students and on my part. I've tried to discover the reason — it's getting too much like an ordinary class. There has been a letdown from the intense interest that fired the class the first semester. Perhaps it's the material or perhaps it's the way it's presented in the text — I don't know.

"You put in italics the statement about crime not being merely individual, but also the product of society, as if it were a new fact. It seems to me that we mulled that problem over last semester, and that it need not be stressed so emphatically. However, as I mentioned before, we did discuss this problem in a previous chapter — perhaps it would have been better to have placed this section in a previous part of the book — it would have clarified our discussion of this problem and made us see it without all the hodge-podge we went through to arrive at it." (Bird.)

Similarly, Miss Blake comments:

"If the last chapter had been presented as the introductory chapter, I am sure we would have had a more solid foundation of what this course had stood for and would have saved lots of time. This chapter had more power than the rest of the book. I think the sentence that said 'criminal behavior is the response of individuals living in a specific culture,' seemed to be the essence of our problems, dealing with crime, criminals, and criminal justice." (Blake.)

True, the sentence quoted by Student Blake represents the quintessence of the volume, but it could not have been extracted by her without a tremendous amount of squeezing out of the pages of the book to collect the distilled drops of significance into a satisfactory drink. If, in accordance with the students' judgment, the latter "clarifying" chapters were placed at the beginning of the book, I believe there would be neither confusion nor understanding on the part of the student. Before problems are investigated or answered, they must be recognized. The following five excerpts illustrate how the students failed to recognize the problems dealt with.

"In order for anyone to know anything about the field, one must know so much of everything else that, at this point, I fail to see how we are going to complete the course and know anything about the subject." *(Sievert.)*

"It matters not to me what procedure or method the police may employ in their efforts to solve a crime, or in getting information, providing they prove effective. If a man or woman is unfortunate or stupid enough to get entangled in an enterprise outside the law, he deserves all that he receives in the way of harsh treatment. The 'third-degree' has proven, in many cases, to be the only language some persons respond to." *(Morse.)*

"Your criticism of the district attorney's office and the political set-up means you believe in complete social reforms — Yes, that's lovely, but a reformer is only a dreamer. It's impossible to change the selfish attitude of 'I'm going to take care of myself' to the feeling that everyone else is important. I can't see the organized political game refusing to swindle people. To me, this would be fantastic change." *(McGuire.)*

" 'In God We Trust' — on a cash basis. This statement (in the text, *Crime and Society*) is definitely antagonistic to me. Even though this is supposed to be a supremely modern period with mass production and technical advancement, I still believe that Christianity and its teachings have a definite, important place. I defy anyone who sincerely believes this statement." *(Robert.)*

"To be quite frank, I have to say that, although I read the whole chapter on Crime, Law, and Society, it didn't mean anything to me. You stressed the fact that different patterns of society changed in the last few centuries, and that it gave rise to new disorders, and that our criminal law is the same as it was centuries ago, not changed to meet the new problems. You continue to say that the kinds of disputes which the criminal law of today regulates come out of the kinds of rules developed in England a hundred years ago, and that we must conclude that the present administration of criminal justice is partly shaped by the inheritance of a traditional technique. Then there is an elaborate description of how the church dominated the Middle Ages with its ecclesiastical courts, etc. Following was a presentation of different age cultures.

"Although I am not sure whether I understood correctly the material in this chapter, I'd like to give one opinion. Why should there be a change in the criminal law? Aren't all things based on 'good' or 'evil'? If taking one's property was an evil in the early centuries, just as it is now, I don't see why the criminal code should be altered. By that I mean as long as there are things to take, as long as man craves revenge for things, punishment will be dealt out. People were, are, and will be subject to sin, and that is one good reason for holding on to the traditional criminal laws."

(Karpf.)

Miss Sievert remains confused. She cannot crystalize specific problems because she feels she doesn't know enough. Mr. Morse remains unregenerate. He doesn't care at all about procedures or methods employed by the police. If anybody gets caught, he deserves what he gets. Mr. McGuire tells me that my criticism of the district attorney's office and the political set-up mean I believe in "complete social reforms." That is what my criticism means to Mr. McGuire, not to the author.

As a matter of fact, the text in question reads, "We face an imponderable problem. How shall we permit discretion (to the prosecuting attorney) and at the same time limit the tyrannical and corrupt use to which it may be put? The general answer is the one given whenever the issue of discretion arises. Entrust discretion to conscientious and able administrators. The extent of the discretion should be matched by the competence and character of the public servant." There is nothing indicated anywhere in the chapter about "complete social reforms."

Miss Roberts permits her strong religious ties not only to obstruct her understanding of what was said, but to distort the context of the statement, " 'In God We Trust' — on a cash basis."

The text reads, "An almost completely new basis for human society confronts us. The Cathedral of Chartres, lovingly erected to the greater glory of God, with its incomparably beautiful stained glass and sculptured masterpieces and twin spires pointing to Heaven, is today a museum place for vacationists rather than a haven for the pious laden with the burden of sin. We, instead, possess the Empire State Building and its observation tower from which we proudly gaze down upon the Metropolis of the World and admire the handiwork of man. Instead of the Catholic Synthesis we find a world knit together by finance-capitalism. 'In God We Trust' — on a cash basis."

Mr. Karpf writes frankly that the chapter "didn't mean anything to me" and then proceeds to tell what it did mean to him. He's not quite sure whether he understands correctly the material, but, nevertheless, he is positive in his statement that "people were, are, and will be the subject of sin, etc."

These five students resist doing something to themselves. Instead they project their present attitudes. They do not want to accept any point of view which will require them to examine their present beliefs or feelings. That is uncomfortable. They are saying, in effect, "That is what you say. Well, this is what we say." And in having their say, they sometimes fail to understand, and, often, must pervert what the other says.

To avoid possible misunderstanding, it should be made clear that students are free, of course, not to accept the point of view of others. They are at liberty to disagree. Disagreement, however, is of two kinds. One can disagree after having allowed himself to understand or having sincerely tried to appreciate an opposing point of view. One can also disagree because one *refuses* to examine another position and persists, at all costs, in maintaining a former stand. It is the latter attitude to which the term projection applies, as it is used here.

Before leaving the discussion of projection and turning to the polar concept of identification, I should like to present one final excerpt, the only one in this chapter from the class in PC. The student's comments represent a clear cut illustration of projection.

"When Plant discusses the feelings of inferiority as being due to poverty, I am reminded of childhood feelings of my own. When I was a child, my family wasn't poverty-stricken, but still my father was paid a small salary which meant that I wasn't able to have the clothes and spending money that my friends had. I had then and still have a feeling of intense inferiority. I believe this may be at the bottom of my not being able to talk in class." *(May.)*

This student turns to the past to find justification for her not talking in class. Instead of doing something about the *present* difficulty, she avoids the problem by seeking explanations, a common device. She is saying, "I cannot because of what happened," instead of "I don't want to because I'm afraid." She is projecting, getting rid of her annoyance, justifying her attitude, instead of facing the problem, criticising herself, and bearing the discomfort involved in bringing herself to participation in the discussion.

Chapter 10

Identification

An individual who likes another person is identified with him. One may also be identified with objects, situations, or ideas; that is, one feels them to be a part of oneself. The feeling of identification is not static. It represents one phase of a dynamic relationship with other people or situations. In the process of adjusting ourselves to conflict, we assert ourselves (projection) or accept and assimilate other points of view or situations (identification).

The process of identification has a double aspect. On the one hand, others are accepted by an individual because they feel, think, or act in accordance with his own feeling of wholeness. The others are like him. On the other hand, one can *become* identified with another who represents, initially, a differing or different outlook. The other person's difference can be assimilated and become the center of one's reorganized feeling experience. The new organization is a yielding of oneself to another's whole or self. The other person's differences or projections are not opposed. There is a bond of common feeling, which not only permits but encourages one to become like the other without fear or opposition. The self does not fight to maintain its prior organization but positively seeks to satisfy a need through being drawn into or assimilating the differences of another, thereby undergoing change. The degree of identification varies, of course, from the unimportant agreement with another on the state of the weather to the intimate surrender of lovers to each other. When an individual identifies, he becomes like another, or likes another who is like him.

The movement from projection to identification indicates that a person is ready, able, and willing to surrender the comfortable security of his former wholeness, which has been disturbed or threatened by the differences shown by others. The difference, manifested by others with whom we subsequently identify, often creates tension. However, instead of projecting the fear, blame, anger, irritation, or anxiety which accompanies our awareness of difference, instead of getting rid of the feeling by casting it out (projection), we willingly bear the annoyance or pain. The common experience of not losing one's temper, but instead, controlling oneself and trying to understand the other person, is a case in point.

Compensation is found in the subsequent feelings of union and understanding which we receive from those with whom we identify. The urge for momentary satisfaction, through projection, which will permit the individual to remain unchanged and avoid the inner struggle of re-organizing part of himself, is inhibited. Instead, one receives from the other something which means enrichment to an expanding, governing self.

The process of identification is illustrated by the following report of a conference with a student and by the series of excerpts which follows it.

Mr. Bell approached me, at 11:30, after the close of the hour.

Bell: Can I make an appointment to see you in your office?

I: I'll be glad to see you. Will to-morrow at 11:30 suit you?

Bell: I'd rather see you today, now, if possible.

I: I believe I have an appointment at noon.

Bell: I'll only need about five minutes.

I: Very well. Suppose we meet at my office in five minutes.

I was struck by the tenseness in the student's manner. I had also noticed Mr. Bell had participated more fully in the discussion that morning than at any other time. This appeared to me to be significant in light of the fact that Mr. Bell had failed to hand in several reading assignments and had not handed in any of the previous seven assignments, the students' reactions to chapters in the basic text. I, therefore, felt inclined to grant Mr. Bell an immediate appointment.

Mr. Bell was waiting at my office door when I arrived a minute later. I invited him in and asked him to sit down. Immediately he said,

Bell: I suppose you know why I'm here?

I: I'm not sure.

Bell: Remember, you told us in class that you planned to see some of us pretty soon? Well, I thought I'd come before you called me.

I: Yes?

Bell: I'm slipping in my work. I got a job early in October working from 4:30 to 11:30 P. M. and I haven't been able to do my school work. You know that I haven't been doing my assignments in "crim," but I know the stuff.

I: What leads you to think you know the work?

Bell: Well, you saw how much I talked today. I talked more than any other student.

I: What makes you think that because you talked today you are meeting your responsibility to the course?

Bell: You mean I haven't covered the first seven chapters or handed in the three book reviews?

I: That was your responsibility, was it not?

Bell: Well, that's what I wanted to see you about. I want to find out where I stand.

I: I suppose you feel uncertain about whether you are doing satisfactory work?

Bell: I don't think I'm doing passing work. But I couldn't do those readings and hold my outside work. It pays me 80¢ an hour and I need the money.

I: I certainly realize how important that job is. It may be more important than your work at school and I can understand that. Perhaps, in fairness to yourself, you ought to resign from the course?

Bell: Not if you think I can pull through.

I: I don't know whether you can or not.

Bell: You mean it's up to me?

(Student straightened up and leaned forward eagerly. His whole manner changed.)

I: Yes, definitely.

Bell: I'll get all my back work in within a week, and have everything ready on time. I've made an adjustment between my outside job and classes and I'm sure, if I have a chance, I'll make good.

I: That remains to be seen. You have the chance.

Bell: Gee, thanks a lot, Professor Cantor. That's a load off my mind.

Mr. Bell felt guilty and insecure in the realization that he was not meeting his responsibilities and was not doing work of a "passing" quality. It bothered him to the point where he felt he must do something about it, not tomorrow, but "now." First, it is his job, not himself, which explains his failure to do the work. Then, although he hasn't done his work, he declares he "knows" it. I must, he feels, agree he felt this way since he proved it not only by talking in class but by talking more than any other student. This represents his projection. I recognize this projection, and project my different point of view back to him. It is now up to Mr. Bell to decide wheher he wants to fight back (project) or accept my difference and re-organize himself in accordance with my challenge. He accepts my difference and moves toward my direction. He identifies with me. The tension due to his guilt disappears. A new self, with regard to this situation, has been organized. He feels whole once again. "That's a load off my mind."

The following series of comments by students in CS were handed in during the fourth and fifth week of the course.

"It's funny — I can't think of a better word except un-canny — the way our discussion on the difference between meanings and knowledge of an experience clears up something I've been wanting to put into words for a long time. All the class meetings have been impressing me this way: things said don't apply only to criminology but to everything else.

"At first, I was completely lost and gave up hope of ever understanding the terms and definitions of crime and crimi-nals, and what the course was about. But I think I know now what I was confused about. I'm finding out just how much I don't know. The general set-up is damn interesting and I'm having a lot of fun." *(Caldwell.)*

"This chapter and our recent class discussions have made a start in clearing up the fog. For a long while I thought we were up against a stone wall. I can see now that things can be right and wrong from different points of view. You seem to offer many sides of the picture (as in the section on crimino-biology) and consistently straddle the fence. This, in my view, is very good because it leaves room in the student's mind for their own ideas." *(Howard.)*

"Finally, I see the light. I was much happier when I left class last Wednesday, for I feel for the first time I see the purpose of the past discussion, the concept of meaning in the sense we have been discussing it. It's really so simple, yet so huge, that — well, I can only say — I'm speechless!"

(Bird.)

"For the past weeks, in my reports, I stated I was com-pletely confused and in a fog. Well, the fog is beginning to lift. In the beginning of the course I felt we were rambling. It was not until I came to the section labeled The Reality of Social Events that I noticed the rambling seemed to disappear. I firmly believe that I learned more about the type of reasoning used in criminology in the last eight pages of this chapter, than I have in all the class discussions put together." (Dole.)

"I like the way the discussions clarify and supplement the material presented in the book. I notice that our discussions have been shorn of much of the aimless quibbling that characterized those of the first few weeks. The active participation of the intructor as a co-ordinator no longer leaves the class in a net, but rather, so it seems to me, stimulates the class." (Bacon.)

"I have never been so confused in any class as during the past month but I have never been as suddenly enlightened. Being intermittently plunged from darkness into light is, at times, discouraging, but the darkness has served to make the light more intense." (Leiser.)

"While at first the class discussions seemed irrelevant and unnecessary, I discovered that many points which confused me were becoming clear. Even though at first the method employed seemed like a complete waste of time, I believe I have gained more from hearing various opinions of the class than if the time had been spent in listening to a boring lecture and losing interest in the subject." (Sims.)

These excerpts are typical developments of a movement which occurs during the first four to six weeks. Upon entering the course, the students feel the strangeness characteristic of a new experience. They seek comfort in the traditional way, that is, they are ready to listen to a lecture and take notes. They discover, however, that there are no lectures. They are merely told what the course is to be about, what is expected of them by way of assigments, and then asked what it is they expect. The instructor accepts their initial statements and places the burden of discussion upon them. The meetings of the first week or two are characterized by a great deal of definition seeking. Students love definitions and want the instructors to give them so they can put them down and "have" them in black and white — on paper.

They are disappointed and annoyed at not getting anywhere. There are more questions and inquiries than definite statements and answers. The text-material and readings are not reviewed but questions are welcomed — for them to answer as best as they can. There are many embarrassing periods of silence during the early meetings during which it is hoped the instructor will take over. As a rule, the instructor waits for a lead from some interest of the student, and develops it into another series of problems rather than into definitive answers.

Different students react differently to both subject-matter and the instructor. (This is dealt with in Chapter Twelve). Generally, however, they feel their way rather insecurely. Some want to talk and do not. Others speak up and apologize in one form or another for what they say or for daring to talk. Still others start to speak with assurance but end their comments with a question. "Isn't that so?" "Don't you agree?" "At least, that's what Professor So-and-so says." A few are afraid or timid or aggressive as their comments, in reactions to the assigned material, indicate. This ambivalence is understood and accepted. There is a minimum of pressure exerted by the instructor to have the development of subject matter or students follow his pattern.

During the third and fourth weeks, the students feel more free to articulate their feelings. They are confused or discouraged and plainly say so. They are starting to project themselves upon the instructor as the previous chapter indicated. They make demands. They express their own points of view and their disagreements with the text and the manner of conducting the course. They have become active participants in the course. Without being forced to, they are given the opportunity to meet the difference presented by the instructor. He does not criticize them wholesale but accepts their criticism and confusions, and *asks* whether there may not be other ways of looking at the problems which are raised or the statements which are made.

Those students who are willing, able, and ready to learn react to this difference represented by the instructor, and assimilate it. They make it part of their own thinking, feeling, and willing. In so far, they become identified with the instructor who presents, at this point, something they themselves are ready for.

Thus, Mr. Caldwell finds out how much he doesn't know. He has been re-examining his confusion and has discovered its source. Mr. Howard is surrendering an "either — or" attitude. "Things can be right and wrong from different points of view." Mr. Bird had never before conceived of "meaning" as it was discussed in class. Mr. Dole states that he learned something about the "type of reasoning" used in criminology and that "the fog is beginning to lift." Mr. Bacon remarks that "our discussions have been shorn of much of the aimless quibbling that characterized those of the first few weeks." Mr. Leiser has never been so confused nor so suddenly enlightened. Miss Sims observes that the "irrelevant and unnecessary" class discussions were clearing up many points for her.

Miss Sims reacted to the first few chapters of the text in PC as follows:

"Perhaps I've seemed too dogmatic in my criticisms but I can't and won't apologize — it's purely and sincerely the way I feel. Plant is simply confusing a very simple issue. The individual is born into a culture and is influenced by it. The environment is one thing and the individual is affected by it. Why all the confusion and making a mountain out of a mole hill?"

Toward the end of the course Miss Sims wrote:

"How much time we would have saved last February in the first few meetings of the class, if we had known then that there are no personality problems alone. Personality problems are always culture-personality problems. Although, I had never realized it before reading this book, and also Miss Benedict's book plus the volume by Dollard, it is now definitely impressed in my mind that personality and culture are inter-related. It's all so obvious now that I wonder at my ever thinking differently."

Mr. Turner, who majored in the physical sciences, writes about the first part of Dr. Plant's text:

"I am of this opinion: The book is a technical one in its field and probably written for people with experience in the social sciences. In all frankness, I must say that the book is definitely not for me. With all due apologies to the author, I don't like the book. I don't get much out of it. There is no careful definition of terms and there is a sloppy use of language. I am greatly disappointed."

Toward the end of the course Mr. Turner writes:

"With every chapter I have read it seems as though a new world is continually developing in front of me. I am learning things now that once I took for granted as existing but did not know anything about and where I was at one time concerned with just personal matters and problems, I find now that in order to properly understand myself is a hell of a more difficult job than anyone would have thought at the beginning of the course. I am truly amazed."

Mr. Speck's comments on the first few chapters read:

"Plant's habit of bringing up questions and not answering them definitely annoys me. I suspect that he can't answer the questions because he doesn't know the answers. I think Plant ought to settle his own problems before he tries to settle them for the reader."

A few months later, Mr. Speck wrote as follows:

"The material in this chapter is enough to convince me that Plant knows what he's talking about. So he uses vague terminology once in a while. So he occasionally draws an invalid conclusion. That's true and there is no use denying it; but he also makes statements that are pregnant with meaning ' . . . while we build our house among others, it is so built that it will stand even if they go.' What essential insight is reflected in this statement! If everyone who reads Plant's book could see and understand the implications of this sentence, certainly they would have received more from this 'lesson in living' than they received from the rest of their four years of academic training.

"The change in my point of view toward Plant reminds me of the old Christian evangelical saying: He came to ridicule; he stayed to worship."

Most of the students are, of course, unaware of the fact that the confusion they experienced was the inevitable introduction to their learning. The instructor, by deliberately refraining from lecturing or supplying the answers, and by guiding the students through raising questions, helps them to understand their difficulties and to acquire other points of view.

The burden of untangling the knots is placed squarely upon the students, where it belongs. Each individual has to discover for himself what the discussion and subject matter are about. The discovery is, essentially, intra-personal. If, and when, change takes place, the student understands the previous questions and suggestions of the instructor. He has assimilated another way of looking at the problem, and agrees with the instructor. He is now identified with him.

These swings from projection to identification are, of course, not uniform for all students with regard to time, intensity, or focus. The movement toward or away from the instructor and subject-matter (or other members of the class) varies from hour to hour and with each student. As one student expressed it, it is "being intermittently plunged from darkness into light." The enthusiasm of one meeting may be followed by disinterest or day-dreaming in the next. Even during one hour of class discussion, the tension at the beginning of the hour may stimulate marked curiosity, which is satisfied, only to be followed by some new problem which again puzzles or annoys the student.

As the weeks pass, however, the intensity and area of projection, and identification increase. Horizons are extended and student participation is more active. Change in attitude is more pronounced. In a word, there is a much greater range of movement.

At the close of the first five or six week period, when the students have caught the spirit of the discussions and what the course is about, they begin to enjoy the meetings — too much. They feel that they understand the content and that the instructor understands them. From now on everything is going to sail smoothly. The skillful and sensitive instructor begins to notice at this time an increasing lack of participation on the part of the students. The periods of silence increase. Few students seem to have anything to say. The subject matter seems clear. It is during this period that special effort must be made by the instructor to stimulate student projection by, again, throwing the responsibility of the course on the students. Their dependence upon him must again be broken up. This leads us to a discussion of the activity of the teacher.

Chapter 11

The Activity of the Teacher

In ordinary contacts with each other we sometimes show consideration for others and, at other times, exploit them in order to work out our own needs. The teacher-student relationship, however, is not an ordinary one. The classroom provides a professional setting. The relationship between teacher and students is a professional one. The teacher who understands his function is in the classroom, not to use the student for the expression and satisfaction of his needs, but to help them. He knows his limits, he is aware of a definite goal, and he possesses some knowledge and skill about the process of arriving at it. The student may not quite understand what is taking place but the teacher's activity has to be disciplined in the classroom, as well as in individual conference.

The instructor's contribution includes not only knowledge of the specific subject-matter but an understanding of the learning process. He must watch what he says, and how he says it; he must understand when he should speak, and to whom. The activity of the instructor is a dynamic whole whose focus shifts as different problems emerge. For purposes of discussion, however, his contributions may be viewed from several points of view.

The Knowledge and Experience of the Teacher

The instructor, it may be assumed, possesses sound knowledge of the facts and problems in the subject he deals with.

The students have the right to look to him for information regarding questions they raise, to learn what developments are occurring not dealt with in their assigned readings. The instructor's superior knowledge and experience in dealing with the problems of the subject should be at the disposal of the students whenever they properly call upon him for such information. The instructor, obviously, should be able to discriminate when called upon among fact, opinion, and hypothesis in the subject matter of the course.

The discussion of problems, as discussion, is on an intellectualized basis. Concepts are dealt with. Students, especially at the beginning of a course, do not feel free to think aloud and to express themselves. They fear they do not know enough. They find it difficult to expose their ignorance as contrasted with the knowledge of the instructor. They rightly depend, at this stage, upon his superior knowledge, which should be utilized. What is not so simple, however, is the way the instructor uses his knowledge.

Knowledge consists, to a large extent, of a series of related symbols. Most of us acquire verbal symbols without ever having had the chance to observe the realities to which they refer. As a result we tend to identify the symbol as the reality and, hence, we talk about words instead of meanings, i.e., the reality for which it stands. The farther removed the symbol is from the living non-verbal context it describes, the more abstract it becomes. Thus, for example, mathematics or symbolic logic is not concerned with living contexts, with the truth or falsity of propositions or probability of *actual* occurrences, but with whether or not certain logical propositions are *implied*. It deals with whether or not certain propositions follow, not whether they are true or false.

The average student has been "educated by definition." He is exposed to and required to accept statements, symbols, long before he can understand what they refer to. The symbol becomes the reality. Therefore, when called upon to examine what the symbol really represents, he can find nothing but the symbol, which represents nothing but itself. His knowledge, in other words, consists largely of hollow, empty concepts.

An instructor who meets the expectation of the average student by opening the course with a series of definitions perpetuates the tradition of education by definition. The student has been *trained* to take down definitions. Once memorized, he feels he knows what the subject is about. As a matter of fact, the skilled instructor's first task is not only to avoid giving definitions but to help the student unlearn the related definitions he brings to the opening discussions in class.

The difficulty of completely understanding what one is talking about is, of course, never entirely overcome. Socrates was forced to drink hemlock, it will be recalled, because he merely asked: What is Justice, Truth, Beauty, Goodness, Virtue? He was corrupting the youth of Athens. He knew enough to raise the questions but wasn't quite sure of the answers. He was forever examining verbal symbols, articulated uncertainties. The road to genuine understanding (and to becoming unpopular) is by way of becoming clear about one's confusion instead of concealing it or having it covered up by verbal symbols.

Definitions, concepts, symbols are indispensable. The point is that the symbol must be clothed with the meaning given to it by the student. The student is not ready for a definition unless and until *he* has struggled with and felt the confusion and conflict which accompany defining one's attitude toward complexities of living in our modern society.

Indeed, learning may be said to consist of a continuous redefinition of meanings. This implies a continuous re-examination of the language one has been using. Through the laborious and exciting process, one discovers new insights, unsuspected refinements, and subtle distinctions in the use of language. This, in turn, results in the construction of more significant concepts. In brief, the time for unqualified definition of the meanings in one's life is reached when one is about to die.

So far as the definitions of a specific course are involved, the students are ready for them, if at all, only at the end of the course. At that time one better *understands* what one is *talking* about. If this be not so what purpose is there in "taking" the course?

The following comments in a PC discussion, the second week of the course, illustrate the false emphasis on symbols. The group had been struggling with a definition of "personality" and had not gotten very far. They were now asking for a definition of "culture."

Lawton: Plant defines culture as being the same as personality. Isn't culture more than just that?

I: What more is there?

Lawton: The whole environment. It is plain to see that there is a difference between personality and environment.

Fields: I think it will be just as difficult for us to define and talk about culture as it was to define personality last week. I think that, from our other courses in sociology, distinctions of some sort were made between culture and environment. Now, I don't see how any distinctions will hold.

Curran: I think the distinction between culture and environment is a matter of degree. The culture of a community is the environment in which a great number of people are affected. The environment is not the same for all and the difference makes a difference in their personalities.

Lawton: You mean there are cultures within a culture?

I: I wonder if all of you share my feeling that the discussion would be improved if we chose some specific concrete examples which would illustrate the distinctions you are trying to make. Suppose you draw examples from this particular room.

Curran: As a result of our culture every male in this room is dressed in a suit, and every female has a dress.

Chaplin: The very fact that we are here tells us something about our culture. The students and instructor in this room have come to this class because they want to get something out of it.

Hortense: The individuals here are necessary for culture but the environment is not.

West: If there were no students here, would there be an environment?

Chaplin: Can't you define culture as the total sum of the behavior of individuals?

West: Every individual has an individual culture. It would then be part of his personality and, so, personality and culture are identical.

Fields: Culture consists of certain conformities which may be educational, ethical, or religious and so on. You can't define environment in those terms.

Lyons: Aren't we getting away from specific examples of culture in this room?

Fields: I can't take any definite examples out of here.

I: Why not?

Fields: If we were all out of this room, there would still be an environment. The person might come in and find walls and tables. That is the environment. The person could do what he wanted. However, if two people came into this room there would be limitations placed on their activity. These people would have different sets and habit systems and by coming together would have created a certain type of culture. They would agree on certain things.

I: Are you making a distinction between physical and social environments?

Lawton: We have to distinguish between physical and social culture, and I think Plant is talking about physical culture which is the same as physical environment.

(At this point discussion ceased. In silence the students glanced at each other and turned to me. Some shrugged their shoulders, others moved about, annoyed and restless.)

I: We are trying to understand what is meant by culture just as we tried to understand what is meant by personality. We do not agree on the meaning of these terms. If we do not know the meaning of culture and personality, obviously we cannot discuss the relation between the two, which is the problem raised by Plant.

Fernold: I don't think any of us know what we are talking about. I know all this talk doesn't mean a thing to me.

Lyons: (A student majoring in Philosophy.) We should set up a definition, however arbitrary, and use it. We can improve upon it as we go along. That's the scientific approach.

Fernold: What Lyons says about scientific method doesn't get us very far. You don't learn from a definition. You're just using words.

Rolfe: But you've got to have a theory to investigate any science. If we haven't, we have to use induction, observation.

I: Go ahead, Mr. Rolfe.

Lyons: The trouble with this discussion is that there's no empirical content.

I: Mr. Rolfe, why don't you make your observations which you suggested? Mr. Lyons, why not supply the empirical content?

Rolfe: Well, there's one group of students that are doing the talking and one group that is quiet. That represents two different cultures.

Curran: Those that are quiet might be thinking about what's said. That doesn't mean their culture is different.

West: There could be as many definitions as there are people in the class, and each definition would mean something to each individual.   We should not try to form a definition but should try to understand it.

I: How would you start, Miss West?

West: We aren't used to being on our own.   If you were leading us, we could bring in our statements, but if we're left to begin we don't know how to.

I: What do you suggest?

West: I don't know where to go any more than anybody else does.

Curran: I'm in the dark.   What are we trying to do anyway?   Why doesn't someone just give a definition of culture in so many words and then we can start?

I: Something is wrong, that is obvious.

Lawton: In the ordinary class somebody gets up and makes a speech.   But this is progressive education.   Nobody learns anything.   (Laughter.)

I: This has been very dissatisfying, hasn't it?

Rolfe: All of us have conflicting concepts about personality and culture.

West: Everybody has different concepts about everything.

Fernold: Maybe we're trying to define something which defies definition.

Hortense: I don't see why we can't discuss what we mean by culture without having a definition.

I: Perhaps that is a wise suggestion.   Our time is up.   At our next meeting, you may want to follow Miss Hortense's suggestion.

All the students in this group had "passed" one or more psychology and sociology courses, where the concepts of personality and culture had been discussed time and again.   The above discussion reflects how little essential meaning was got from their previous courses.   The concepts "personality," "culture," and "environment" are thrown about without much regard for the realities which they are supposed to symbolize. The students find it difficult to leave the abstractions and look behind the words. As their instructor, it would be relatively simple for me to give them a working definition of culture. I could tell them that culture is made up of the entire activities of the individual and the society in which he lives. Anthropologically, that is a sound definition. Those who have studied ethnology, ethnography, prehistory and archaeology, linguistics, and physical anthropology, those, especially, who have engaged in field work, will *understand* that definition. They will appreciate its import and implications. They will have spent months endeavoring to untangle the difficulties involved in trying to see the relations between psychology, sociology, history, and anthropology, the dangers of jumping from one level of discourse to another, the problem in method, the rather arbitrary dividing lines between the several disciplines. They will be particularly aware of the problems which remain to be solved, the unsatisfactory state of the concepts in the several fields.

It is not to be expected that undergraduates will possess the insight into these difficulties such as a mature graduate student or specialist in the field is likely to have. This is not in issue. The point we wish to make is that whatever degree of understanding undergraduates reach in the use of concepts depends upon the extent to which they get behind the language and translate the words into meanings which they can grasp; then retranslating the meaning into concepts by themselves, and in their own way, they will really be said to have learned. The process must be their own; I do not believe that any statements or definitions which I might present in the early stages of a course do much to help them.

As the above discussion was being carried on, I realized the nature of the difficulty the group was having. Instead of using my knowledge directly, I tried to direct the discussion away from the abstract level to their own experiences from which they might generalize. Mr. Fields, in his own thinking, came close to an important distinction. I thought at that point, the distinction between physical and social environments could be made in those terms *and* that it would then have more meaning for the group. The students, however, reached a point where they were blocked and annoyed. I had to overcome the temptation to define culture for them at that moment. Instead, I indicated what the trouble was and reassured them that the effort to understand those terms was worthwhile and necessary before we could continue. Mr. Rolfe and Mr. Lyons seemed to sense the difficulty. I tried to encourage them to follow through. Miss West seemed to be on the right track, and I encouraged her. Miss Hortense, too, reached the point where she was willing to continue without a definition.

In the CS class, we had reached the topics of probation and parole. The value of these new techniques for the "individualization of treatment" are little understood even by the professional workers in the field. There is no agreement on the procedure or technique to be used in supervising the offender. In part, this is caused by lack of clarity in what the probation officer is supposed to do. In class, the question was raised as to what the function of the officer should be. This is a very complicated problem, which, I knew from past experience, could not be solved by students in the introductory course. Nevertheless, it is one of the important techniques in treatment and should be discussed. The individual student will get what he can out of the discussion. From my point of view, this was a class in criminology, not a course in social case work, and I felt it was of no particular significance whether the function of the parole officer was clearly understood.

In probation and in parole, as in all forms of social case work, one of the important aspects of the worker's function is to help the client face his own short comings or obstacles. This isn't so much a matter of knowledge as it is of feeling. It is a matter of establishing a worker-client rapport in which the client feels free to be himself, to express his real feelings. The members of the class, as was to be expected, were having difficulty in undertanding the nature of the officer's supervision. Of course, my *stating* in so many *words* what I considered his function to be would have meant very little to them. The problem was to find a way, if possible, by which the students would "see" for themselves what was involved in the function of the officer. The following situation presented such an opportunity.

During a discussion on parole supervision at the beginning of the hour (two weeks before the close of the first semester), I noticed that Mr. Bell was not paying attention to the discussion but was working on a written assignment due that hour. It was not my intention to "use" Mr. Bell, but to illustrate an important point. Miss Prentice had raised a question. I inquired,

What do you think about that, Mr. Bell?

Bell: I'm sorry, I wasn't paying attention. (He reddened and was decidedly uncomfortable.)

Other students then took up the analysis. The issue was the function of the parole officer. Most of the speakers maintained that his role was to talk with the parolee and point out his social attitudes which had gotten him into trouble. I raised the question whether knowledge of the parolee's faults helped him very much. Mr. Bell had been unusually active in the discussion, insisting that knowledge would certainly make a great difference.

Bell: The fact that we're getting knowledge of the problem of parole here in class certainly makes a difference in our attitudes toward parole.

I: Just what do you think is involved in getting knowledge? How do you get it, Mr. Bell?

Bell: By listening, I suppose.

I: Mr. Bell, you've spoken five or six times during the past ten minutes. I'm wondering about your sudden interest. Can you tell us what interests you so keenly?

Bell: Why, the function of the parole officer.

I: I wonder whether that's what really interested you during the past fifteen minutes?

Bell: Certainly, I don't know what you mean.

I: I may be mistaken, but perhaps you are interested in other matters, too?

Bell: I think I know what you mean if you aren't "down" on me.

I: I think you feel that I'm not "down" on you.

Bell: Well, you mean, I've been talking a lot because I want to vindicate myself in your eyes for not paying attention. Sure, that's right.

I: And it wasn't because of your particular interest in parole?

Bell: Right.

Mr. Bell was under considerable tension. During this exchange he squirmed about in his seat, shifting his position, turning and lowering his head, pulling his hands, and swallowing hard several times. Nevertheless, he was able to meet my challenge.

I: Now let's try to see whether we can use this incident to throw light on the function of the parole officer.

Prentice: What Mr. Bell was saying didn't matter much. It was the way he felt that made him talk. He had to square things with you. The parolee will be interested in what the parole officer has to say only if it touches some feelings that he has. That's the way he "gets" what the officer says.

From this point on, a lively discussion took place. A few students sensed the importance of the discussion, Most of them talked about the issue without insight. Generally, I think it unnecessary as well as unwise to direct discussion in classroom with regard to the personal attitudes of the members. I deliberately introduced it at this point primarily as an illustration for the class of the difference between what one says and why one speaks.

Mr. Bell certainly felt this distinction. He lived through the experience of discussing a problem which *apparently* interested him but which, in reality, was carried on, on a totally different level, that of getting rid of his guilt feelings, of justifying himself in my eyes. He would have entered the discussion no matter what the issue was, not because of any intrinsic interest in the subject-matter, but because of the personal tension for which he sought release. Mr. Bell knew his work was unsatisfactory. (See pp 140-143.)

In so far as some of the other members of the class *felt* what had occurred, they, too, had gotten the point. Such living experience can do more for making clear how language can be used by the parolee to conceal feelings and thoughts than could hours of explanation and discussion. The comments which followed support this statement.

McDowell: Isn't that what takes place here in the classroom? That's why you don't give us any answers. We don't understand the problems unless we're really interested.

I: How does that tie up with the function of the parole officer?

Green: The parole officer can talk until he's blue in the face. It won't help unless the parolee wants to become responsible for himself. Why, this class is the same thing. We won't understand the problems by your talking but by what we think about them. Gee, I get it now for the first time. That's just what we're doing. This is great stuff.

All of the students were tense. They were all glancing toward me. I deliberately withheld any comment. The half-minute of silence which followed was marked by an intensity which had not been previously experienced in our class discussions. I glanced about at the faces of the students. The classroom bell rang.

I: That is all. We meet the first Friday after the first of the year. Commissioner Moran of the parole department will be our guest that morning.

The Role of Opposition

Our general explanation and descriptions of human activity are couched in terms of traditional beliefs derived from the authority of the church, state, family, and school. Through the various avenues of communication we assimilate the non-rational values of our society. These beliefs are not irrational; they are non-rational. Values, as such, cannot be described as "good" or "bad" any more than the color red, as a color, is good or bad. Colors exist, so do values. Man, by his nature, is an evaluating creature. He believes what he believes. It is inevitable that he possess beliefs.

Science concerns itself with describing phenomena, attempting to reveal how certain events are systematically related. It has nothing whatsoever to do with passing judgment on the worthwhileness of certain beliefs. That is the province of ethical evaluation. Science can only describe. It cannot validate what we *ought* to believe or how we *should* act. It can, however, describe what follows from our beliefs and what must be done if we desire certain ends. Values are not scientific, but we can construct a science of values.

The confusion in our thinking about the complexities of human affairs is caused by mixing up, without often being aware of it, the "is" and the "ought." We tend to describe what takes place in terms of what should or ought to take place. We interpret or determine "facts" in light of ethical beliefs held in advance of our investigation. Hence, most often, we describe social phenomena in terms of "right" or "wrong." From the point of view of *description*, we must try to *understand* and not pass judgment. Once matters are understood, the heart's desire can be used to direct changes in any direction one chooses. Science and ethics must not be confused. In science events have a certain probability of "truth" not "goodness." Events are not described as being "bad" or "wrong" but as "false." Truth and error are on a different level than good or bad.

Students bring to the classroom their stereotyped "rights" and "wrongs," "goods" and "bads," their "either-or" views of social behavior. They tend to describe and interpret social events and individual behavior in terms of more or less fixed moral attitudes. They confuse the observation of premises and the nature of conditions with their moral judgments about them. One of the responsibilities of the instructor is to help them learn to look at society from the many different and conflicting points of view. They must be helped to acquire the scientific attitude of mind. As new facts and new interpretations arise, previous attitudes must be modified or qualified.

The naive ethical approach to social problems, which students bring to the college classroom, must be challenged. The superior knowledge, experience, and authority of the instructor are to be used in opposing the more or less fixed attitudes of the students. Students will be puzzled, annoyed, and confused at meeting this opposition. They will resent the exposure of their simple-mindedness, their ignorance, their hidden assumptions. They find these experiences disconcerting and upsetting. No one enjoys the experience of discovering one's cherished beliefs exposed, of recognizing how simple minded and downright foolish one's attitudes have been.

While the instructor is responsible for assuming this negative role he must be careful in his use of it. It is the *way* in which he opposes the points of view of the students that is important. His criticism of what students say and feel must not be so complete that the students are overwhelmed and reject completely what he has to offer. In the early meetings of the class, the criticism of their work must be partial and impersonal. An opportunity must be given to them for taking hold and correcting what has been criticized. In this way, the students become responsible and confident. They feel that something definite is being accomplished. As they become increasingly responsible and confident, the criticism of the instructor can be better handled by the students. The deeper the identification with the instructor, the more extensive can the projection or opposition or criticism of the instructor become in his relationship with them.

This can be stated in another way. If criticism of the student is partial and directed toward the subject-matter and not the student, that is, if it is objectified, the student does not feel that it is directed against him as an individual. Hence, he has no need to fight against it and cast it out. He does not have to defend himself. Later in the semester, as students and instructor get to know each other, both through classroom discussion and individual conference, and feel more free in their reactions to each other, the criticism of the instructor can be more severe and even directed at the student himself. Thus, for example, I took the chance of challenging Mr. Bell as I did, feeling that he was sufficiently identified with me to be able to "take it." (See pp. 160-161.)

The spirit of the criticism is better understood, and more readily accepted, because the student trusts the instructor. The responsibility which the student must assume is increased. His previous experience in changing gives him sufficient support to work through the heavier load which he is asked to assume. Periods of confusion are followed by better understanding. New horizons are revealed only to be followed by discouraging confusion in another or the same area.

Knowledge of Student's Work

We have stated that there are certain common elements in any teaching process. The teacher will be concerned primarily with understanding and not judging the student. He will keep at the center of the teaching process the importance of the student's problems and feelings, and not his own. The teacher will realize that constructive effort must come from the positive or active forces within the individual student.

In order to judge what is taking place, the instructor must keep in mind the student's discussion in class, in personal conference, and he must carefully scrutinize his written work. There is no one simple way of accomplishing this. The larger in size the class, the more difficult does this become. For myself, I have found the following procedure desirable.

At stated intervals, usually a week apart, all students are asked to hand in their written reactions to the material to be discussed during the week as well as their comments on the class discussion of the week. For some classes I have been able to have a stenographer record verbatim the entire discussion of every class session. When this was not possible, I have recorded what appeared significant in the class discussion immediately after the hour. Similarly, I have made it a practice to record significant comment after individual conferences and on class discussion. In this way, one can derive some idea of what seems to be happening to each student with regard to the course. This information is also invaluable in helping the instructor decide upon what the topics for discussion should be, what should be emphasized, and what should be reviewed or corrected. Furthermore, there are usually a few students who, for one reason or another, remain silent or rarely contribute to the discussion in class. Their written reactions or the notes on their individual conferences become the chief source of information about them.

The following comments illustrate how the instructor utilizes his knowledge of what students say and write. Miss Jacobs, a student majoring in psychology, writes:

"The view of personality which Plant gives is an entirely new one. As such, it has been hard for me to accept. For three years I have had personality presented to me from the point of view of behavioristic psychology and it is rather hard to unlearn all that I have learned. I cannot yet accept Plant's idea of data and findings." *(Jacobs.)*

"I admit that my point of view has been conditioned by traditional psychology. Dr. Plant's theses, as far as I'm concerned, have not been proven. I cannot accept them."

(Lawton.)

Miss Jacobs and Mr. Lawton were "majors" in psychology. Their comments were similar to the point of view expressed by three other students who were also majoring in psychology. As a result of these comments, I directed the discussion toward exploring with the class what Plant meant by these terms.

From papers in CS I received the following:

"According to this chapter and chapter four, the system of the administration of criminal justice is corrupt and unethical, to put it mildly. I have always felt that the United States was a pretty fine place in which to live, a place where most people could get a fair deal and this awakening to the procedure of the administration of justice is terribly disillusioning." *(Robert.)*

"Your description of the conditions existing in American prisons, the dishonesty in the bail system, the activities in the district attorney's office left me with a feeling of intense disillusionment." *(Lawrence.)*

"I think it terribly depressing to read about all these corrupt factors. It leaves you with a very bad taste."

(Sievert.)

"This chapter came as a shock to me. I never realized how incompetent and corrupt the police were."

(MacDowell.)

"These chapters were not inspiring reading. The facts unfold the sad tale of wanton official brutality, neglect, and deplorable inefficiency . . . the poor remaining in unspeakable filthy jails because of inability to meet the bail bond — fixed cases — the autocratic power of the D. A.

"I honestly do not like to assume a defeated attitude but, in light of what I read and my own limited personal acquaintance with similar conditions, what else is there left? I might, tomorrow, approach a big shot, try to make a connection. Who, then, am I, to complain about the system? I wish I could be wrong." (McGuire.)

The above remarks were typical of the reactions of the class to a description in the text of the inefficiency in the several agencies in the administration of criminal justice. I had presented data selected from statistical reports and crime commission surveys. I also tried to point out in the text that the personnel of the several agencies were probably as competent and integral as most professional groups. Apparently, the description of this material failed to convey to the reader what I had in mind. In any event, I felt the impressions the students received were false, because too one-sided. The next two class periods were, therefore, devoted to this issue. Students were asked to justify their generalizations in light of the facts. When I presented further data, they were willing to qualify their wholesale condemnations. Here the instructor learns about the attitudes of the students, recognizes an over-emphasis on certain points, and introduces further data so that more accurate impressions are gained.

We had spent an entire week discussing the subject of probation. I was not sure whether to pass on to the next topic. The following comments are taken from several papers.

"I still feel confused as to the subject of probation and do not feel as if I know very much about it." *(Sievert.)*

"In regard to the class discussion, I feel that you stymied the discussion by not analyzing what the word "adjustment" involves." *(Rush.)*

"The reading of the chapter on probation and the class discussion opened a new channel in my thinking. Never before had I been so aware of this problem — so vital and so urgent in society today. My ideas, however, are all in a jumble." *(Cochran.)*

"I just reread my paper (Mr. Bird's reactions to the class discussion) and it sounds as if the writer is in a muddle as to just what probation and its problems are. Well, I don't know what it's all about." *(Bird.)*

In light of this series of reactions, we devoted another meeting to the subject of probation.

The knowledge of what the students write and talk about is one of the criteria which determines what is to be discussed and how fast the class will move. This has to be weighed against the need to cover the basic material of the course. No hard and fast line can be drawn as to precisely what should be covered. Each time a course is given, some special topics are discussed, and more or less time is devoted to the different problems.

This knowledge also helps the instructor to check his impressions of the individual's work and progress. Students who fail to hand in their assignments on time, or at all, are called into conference where the attempt is made to discover not why they are failing, but what is to be done about the quality of work they are doing. The following conference illustrates this.

Mr. Robin was called to a conference with me. He had failed to hand in several previous assignments. He came 45 minutes late for the appointment. Another time was arranged and he was 10 minutes late.

Robin: What did you want to see me about?

I: I thought we might discuss your work in relation to the class. (Robin remained silent.)   How do you feel about the quality of work you are doing?

Robin: I'm very much interested in the course as you can tell by my discussions in class.

I: Apparently your interest doesn't extend to handing in the written assignments.

Robin: Oh, those.   The reason for that is simple.   I don't like to hand in papers written in my sloppy handwriting, I prefer typing them.

I: Yes, I find it much easier to read.   But I've received no typewritten papers.

Robin: I want to do good papers and haven't got 'round to complete them.

I: I believe they were all due weeks ago.

Robin: Well, you wouldn't want me just to hand in a paper for the sake of being on time if I haven't anything to say?

I: It may be that if you have nothing to say, the course isn't giving you enough, and you should resign from it.   That sometimes happens.

Robin: I don't want to do that, I'm getting lots out of the course.

I: What are you giving to it?

Robin: You mean the papers, again?

I: That is your responsibility.

Robin: I am interested in the course, but I carry three lab courses and am taking the course in flying.   The trips to and from the flying field take an awful lot of time, and I can't get around to writing the papers.

I: You mean typewriting the papers.

Robin: Well, that was the original reason I gave.

I: If you are too busy with others matters, I suppose the wise thing to do is to select what interests you most.   If you haven't time to carry out the responsibility of this class, perhap it's best that you drop it.

Robin: I don't want to drop out. (I said nothing during the next half minute of silence.) Suppose I accept whatever penalty goes with not handing in papers?

I: It isn't a matter of penalty, which should interest us, but whether you are doing the best kind of work of which you are capable.

Robin: Well, what do you want me to do?

I: That's up to you. What do you want to do?

Robin: What's the point of going through the motions and just handing in black scribbling on white paper — just to hand something in?

I: There isn't much point to that.

Robin: Well, I could do that like others are doing.

I: Perhaps some of the others who just hand in anything also aren't meeting their responsibility, doing their best work? I suppose, too, that what they do is irrelevant to our problem. (There was silence for about a minute.)

Robin: Will you do something for me, Dr. Cantor?

I: If I can.

Robin: I've been in a jam in my other work, too. I don't know what's the matter. I'm having trouble with my girl and my parents. Can you understand what I mean? (Tears started to appear.)

I: I appreciate something of the difficulties which must be involved. And in addition you have the problem of doing something about your work in criminology.

Robin: You're the only professor I feel like talking to.

I: What would you like me to do about helping you in your work in criminology?

Robin: Will you give me a week's time to think the whole matter over?

I: What is there to think about?

Robin: I want to decide what to do about the course.

I: Very well, suppose we meet a week from today at the same hour.

Robin: Thanks, I know it's my problem and I'll settle it.

Mr. Robin was not doing satisfactory work, he failed to hand in written assignments, and when he did participate in discussion I felt his remarks were perfunctory. He was late for both appointments. His first direct remark, "What did you want to see me about?" carried a defensive tone. His first defense for not handing in the assigned papers was his failure to typewrite them. The second justification was lack of time. (He gives himself away when I remark he meant "typewriting" instead of "writing" by stating, "Well, that was the original reason I gave.") The third reason was that writing papers is formal and worthless, "black scribbling on white paper." He was unwilling, as yet, to face the fact that he has tried to escape his responsibilitiy. My criticism gave him something to think about and feel about. He could not continue in the same way. Some new direction had to be defined one way or another, and he had to discover it for himself.

He was, apparently, dissatisfied with his work not only in CS but in his other courses. My holding him to account led him into another attitude. He suddenly dropped his slightly belligerent attitude, and asked me to help him out of a jam.

He wanted to talk about the backgrounds of his difficulty. It was a temptation to which I almost yielded since I felt that he would be immensely relieved if he could express what was troubling him. But by talking *about* what led up to his poor work would have been another way of avoiding doing something about it. I could offer my help to him only in so far as his difficulty was reflected in the kind of work he did in the CS course. I am not a therapist. My function is to deal with a student's difficulty only insofar as his work in CS is involved. My firm stand gave Mr. Robin a chance to come to grips with one definite obstacle if he would.

Sooner or later, the movement initiated by my criticism must have lead to a reorganization on Mr. Robin's part with reference to the course, or he would have to leave it. If he accepted and assimilated my difference, it meant he recognized the legitimacy of it, i.e., his positive self was criticizing his negative self (represented by my negative criticism.)

Two days after this conference, Mr. Robin handed in, at the regular time, his reactions to a long chapter in the text:

"The chapter makes clear the extensive disorganization and lack of effective policy in the treatment of prisoners. The problems involved in treatment are complicated and far from being solved. — Impressions not completed."

The last three words were hastily added in pencil. I had observed his writing this brief paper in class. Mr. Robin was again asked to see me. An appointment was made. He did not appear. I subsequently learned that he resigned from the college, having also been in difficulties with his other courses. (Some of the administrative officers of the college had tried to help Mr. Robin and had not succeeded. I do not know whether I would have helped him if I had permitted him to discuss his personal affairs with me. I feel, however, that that is not my function. I could, perhaps, have suggested, but failed to, that Mr. Robin make an appointment with the school psychiatrist.)

Balance Between Teacher and Student Activity

One of the great difficulties confronting a teacher is to learn to keep quiet in the classroom. By tradition and training, the average instructor is expected to carry on the business of the hour. It is commonly supposed that his job is to lecture. It is his course and his right to conduct it as he sees fit.

The point of view maintained in this study is that the course belongs to the students and that, to a large extent, they determine how it shall be conducted. The activity of the members in the class is certainly as important as the guidance of the instructor. The instructor who lectures deprives the students of their right actively to participate in their class. A lecturer assumes almost the entire responsibility for the course, leaving the students only with the opportunity of taking notes or day-dreaming or responding to his questions. The instructor who is aware of his function refrains from using students for displaying his knowledge. He permits himself to be used, in a professional way, by them.

It is often difficult to determine the balance between the activity of the students and that of the instructor. The following class discussion in PC was concerned with one of the main points in the first chapter in the text, "Changing Concepts of the Personality."

(I ask the reader's indulgence. I can well understand that by this time the reader will have become a little tired of the discussion of personality — as did the author during the class discussion. I think, however, that the point being made will be better appreciated if the reader is willing to go on in order to receive the accumulated effect of the material).

Dr. Plant indicates that the terms environment and personality are little more than general and specific modes of speaking of the same thing.

I: The central theme before us is the relation between one's personality and the culture in which one lives. It is no simple matter to understand these relations, but we can all try to see how well we grasp them.

Green: What are we to include in the concept of personality?

I: What do you think?

Green: I think we ought to discuss what personality is.

I: Yes.

Green: (Directing the remark to me.) Would you say one's attitudes are a result of one's personality?

I: I wonder what the class thinks of that?

The students in this class have "had" the traditional introductory course in psychology, and are acquainted with the concepts of "heredity" and "environment." This particular controversy is beset with terminological difficulties and freighted with traditional misinterpretations. Unless one struggles with this problem, it is unlikely that one ever realizes how words conceal the difficulties.

The instructor starts by limiting the discussion of the chapter to one of the important theses. Part of his activity is to focus discussion. Mr. Green asks the instructor to indicate what should be included in the concept. At this point I could make a five- or fifteen-minute speech on what I believe to be the fundamental unintelligibility of the heredity-environment controversy, thereby taking the students' class away from them. In return, they would receive, more or less, a few additional intellectual concepts, the implications of which would not be clear, since they had not been assimilated by the students' own struggle to get behind the words. Instead, the responsibility is passed back to the student so as to permit him to carry on.

His reply is merely a restatement of the question with no discussion. I agree we ought to discuss what personality is by merely answering "yes" to his statement, hoping to encourage him to continue. He does, but continues to depend upon me, asking my support. Would I agree with him that one's attitudes are a result of one's personality? Here again, was an opening for the instructor to take the matter away from the student and lecture a bit. Instead, anyone in the group is invited to comment. The discussion continued.
Laurel: In psychology, we learned personality is the result of the interaction between the organism and the environment.

At this point there was silence. The students in the class turned to the instructor. I was tempted to make a speech. I checked the impulse, feeling it was desirable for the students to become more active.

I: Is everybody satisfied with the statement made by Miss Laurel?

Frank: A baby is born without experience but has some kind of personality.

Bristol: We know nothing about a baby's experience.

Frank: You can't say there is any definite time of developing personality. Everybody has some kind of temperament and personality grows out of temperament.

At this point I felt the discussion was about to become muddled and said:

I: Perhaps it will be wise to restate the precise issue?

Willard: We want to see the relationship of personality to the family, church, school, and so on.

I: Suppose, Mr. Willard, you start.

Willard: I don't know how to begin the discussion.

Kryle: You've got to start somewhere. Let's put down a few statements that we'll all agree with.

I: Suppose you do that.

Kryle: I don't think I can.

Caldwell: Do we have to have a definition of personality? I don't think we do.

Green: I'm not asking for a definition. All I want to know is what are we going to work with now.

Frank: Suppose we call the individual's personality the way he behaves?

Laurel: Why not the way he wants to behave?

Lark: There's something I'm not quite clear about. Personality is not an isolated thing. We are often personality acting in a society. You can't isolate personality from society.

Sievert: But the personality makes the culture.

Ziegler: The culture or environment influences the personality.

Frank: Both statements are correct.

Laurel: I believe society is an entity in itself.

Gerber: Aren't we putting the cart before the horse? For me personality is nothing that you have or possess. You are a personality just as the personality of a dog is, let's say, dogality.

Again, I felt the issue, viz, the heredity-environment issue, was being lost sight of, so I remarked:

I: What are the relations between personality and environment?

Gerber: Oh, there still is an environment.

Kryle: To me it is obvious that we are in a room, and that this classroom and discussion affects each of us.

Laurel: Personality, then, is a function of the environment.

Bristol: I think we are arguing over terminology. There is a terrible lot of confusion now.

I noted that the hour was about to draw to a close. I remarked:

I: Perhaps the difficulty is terminological. Maybe we ought to drop the words heredity and environment because there are no such things. We can discuss that, if you like, at our next meeting.

The class is still left with the problem of groping with it. The instructor gave no answers, but merely guided the discussion. A hint as to the possible difficulty is given at the close of the period in order to lessen the confusion. In succeeding classes the students, through their own dicussion and exploration, seemed to agree that the dichotomy of heredity-environment were not entities, but ways of looking at human behavior for purposes of analysis and discussion.

"This chapter seems to help me understand a little better the preceding chapters, and also it shows me more and more how complicated life really is. I had never realized so clearly that the personality and the environment are so closely tied up. I also am beginning to get a new meaning to the word personality. I can't explain this but I do know it isn't the exact defined thing I had always thought it to be. Being more personal, I never realized that my life could mean anything or in any way affect my surroundings, except to my immediate family. Definitions certainly don't begin to catch what a person is really like." *(Kryle.)*

"After reading over the first sentence of the second paragraph on page 252, 'We have come to suspect that there is no line of sharp demarcation between the personality and the cultural pattern in which we live,' — I had to smile. The first two weeks of class were spent debating about this question, and its truth and conviction, NOW, it can't be denied. Looking back at the first weeks makes me feel foolish." *(Caldwell.)*

There are times when the instructor must definitely play the leading role, especially when the class as a whole seems bored, negative, or disinterested. Such lulls in class interest are to be expected.

During the first semester there is a feeling of insecurity and a lack of confidence in meeting the strange situation of the classroom. The students are uncomfortable because they do not quite know how to meet the responsibilities attached to the course. The burden of discussing the material and reporting on it, with no definite rules to guide them, is not easy to assume. As the weeks pass, they experience slight changes in themselves. They discover their own individual way of doing the assigned work. Their attitudes change. They become a bit more sure of themselves. The fear of change gradually disappears. They become identified with the instructor, assimilating new points of view by their own active participation in the process.

The relationship between students and instructor does not remain static. As the weeks pass it becomes more complicated than at the commencement of the course. Students and instructor have agreed and disagreed. Attitudes have developed, and disagreements have arisen. The initial excitement and strangeness of the early sessions have given way to patterned expectations of responding to each other. In brief, one knows more or less what to expect. In fact, the classes become a bit tiresome.

The identification with and the dependence upon the new points of view leads, periodically, to an opposing reaction. When one assimilates something new, there is a tendency to retreat and to protect the self from too great a change. The self again wants to become independent of the other. The swing from identification and dependence to ego-independence and self-expression, takes place within areas of varying sizes as well as of different tempos. It may be observed during class sessions, from week to week, and over entire semester periods.

During these periods of silence and lack of interest in the task at hand, the skilled instructor must become active by way of helping the student to *self-criticism and self-guidance*. I do not mean that the teacher is to threaten or to scold. He recognizes that a stage has been reached where the students feel threatened by being deprived of their independence, having become too much like the other. They defend themselves against such invasion of self-hood by becoming negative, by refusing to participate in discussion, or by handing in perfunctory reactions to the assignments.

By quietly and directly calling attention to the altered level of discussion and character of the work, and leaving them with the responsibility of what to do about it, the instructor once again calls upon the positive and constructive self of the individual. In other words, the need for self-expression and independence of the student is precisely what is, again, being invoked by the instructor. It is as if he said, "I understand and appreciate that you're a bit fed up on me, and the work you've been doing. That's to be expected. Go ahead and show me why you're fed up." In some such manner a new creative movement on the part of the group is aroused. The following description of a class period illustrates this.

Following the week-end in which one of the important basketball games of the season and the annual Junior Dance were held, the students in CS gathered in class on a rainy Monday morning. This was a few weeks after the second semester had started. During several preceding weeks, I had observed a decided change in tone of discussion and in the spirit of the written reports. The bell rang, the class was in session, and no one spoke.

I: We are ready for dicussion, comment or questions. (No one spoke.) I'm sure the chapter must have raised questions in your minds. The material is certainly not very clear.

Still no one spoke. Few students looked at me directly. Some slouched in their seats, others glanced through the windows. One or two were drawing pictures. A few others were aimlessly turning the pages of the textbook. I waited another minute. No one spoke.

I: What seems to be the trouble?

MacGuire: Nothing's the matter. The stuff (sic) was clear so far as I'm concerned and there's nothing to discuss.

Sievert: The material was factual, historical, and there's nothing to argue about.

I: If there is nothing to discuss, either something must be wrong with the way the chapter is written or else many of you have not read the material over this crowded week-end of activities. I wonder how many of you are not prepared. Will you raise your hands, please?

Two-thirds of the class raised hands.

I: Well, I suppose it's asking a great deal to expect criminology to compete with the Junior Prom and the basketball game. On the other hand, this chapter was assigned for today. No one can force your interest, and no one should force it. For the past several weeks many of you, it seems, have not been really interested in the assignments or in the class discussion. If you're not interested, that is not to be held against you. There are many things which we are more interested in than others. It seems to me, however, that so long as you remain in this course, you are obliged to do the work which goes along with it. I could give you an examination on the text this Friday, and so force you to do the reading. I think all of us would consider that undignified. One doesn't force responsible adults into a fake acceptance of their responsibilities. On the other hand, it is my duty to judge and report on whether each of you will have satisfactorily completed this course. Obviously, I cannot certify to that unless you do satisfactory work. I would rather ask each of you to decide for yourselves what is to be done in our subsequent meetings. It is easily understandable that some of you may find the classes and material uninteresting. It is your unquestioned privilege to resign from the course. I see no reason why anyone should be necessarily interested in this work at this point. You may have gotten all you think you can get, and may have given all you are capable of. If so, this is the time to turn to other things. You will have to decide whether you are capable of learning and giving more. I'm sure you all agree with me that each one of you is the best judge of whether you are doing the best work of which you are capable. That is the standard which, for the time being, we should employ. The question I'd like to leave with you is, "Are you honestly doing the kind of work which satisfies you?" Each of you must answer for yourself. My own feeling is that many of you can do much better work than you've been doing. Are there any comments?

There were none at the time. The remainder of the hour was passed in rather dull discussion. I have not yet excused a class before the regular time. It seems to me, however, that upon occasion, when the group will not participate it would be well to adjourn until the next regular meeting. It might even become necessary to repeat this procedure several times. It would be an exceptional group that would persist in its refusal to take over the discussion. In such unusual event, the instructor would be justified, I believe, in refusing to pass any of the members, or in failing those who will not assume the responsibilities.

The subsequent class meeting was lively. Three students who had not participated in class discussions before entered into it. Several students remarked as they handed in their papers, "Thank you for the Monday speech." "That talk last time helped me snap out of it."

The criticism I made would have to be reacted to. For the students who really want to give and get more out of the course, this direct activity of the instructor initiates new and positive movement. Others feel it to be a personal attack and, in fear, will resent it, particularly when it is a sound criticism. In any case, it is the instructor's function to become more *active* in stimulating discussion during periods when students appear to be doing unsatisfactory work.

The unacceptable work of the students may be caused among other factors, by confusion, or by lack of interest. Student lack of interest may also be, and often is, occasioned by the fact that the semester (first or second) is drawing to a close. That is to say, the students feel they have gotten all that they can receive from the course. Subsequent meetings, they feel, and, sometimes, rightly so, are repetitious. Ideally, in light of the psychology of learning, the classes should close at this point. Unfortunately, the requirements of matching hours of credits with clock hours prevent this. Perhaps some procedure could be worked out which would allow students to leave a course at stated intervals such as at two-thirds of the course, and to receive two-thirds of the credit. This suggestion is not so far-fetched. It is a modified form of the practice which permits students to drop out of a course at the end of one semester and yet receive credit for the first part of the course or permits them to enter a year course during the second semester.

At the beginning of the course, the instructor is more active or responsible than the students in order to lessen confusion, and to give form and direction to the discussion. As the students take hold and begin to understand what is required of them, development on their part occurs. During this period, the instructor assumes less responsibility for the direction of the class. The members of the class are permitted to move forward at their own tempo. Periods are reached when interest lags and students are not curious. Students who are not troubled are not ready to receive help. At these times, the instructor again assumes a more direct role in order to present the students with obstacles with which they can contend, if they will, in order to continue their development.

Chapter 12

The Student's Will-to-Learn

The learning process is an undivided, continuous experience. For purpose of analysis, however, it may be viewed from at least three different points of view. (1) The instructor provides certain control over the procedure with regard to time, place, and content. (2) We can look at the learning experience in light of the relationship between the instructor and students; the ways in which teacher and student adapt themselves to what is being taught and learned. (3) The students, however, also establish the limits within which learning takes place.

In previous chapters we have discussed (1) the function and the activity of the instructor as well as (2) the relationships between him and the group. In this chapter we deal primarily with (3) the activities of the students, the learners. The learning needs of every student vary. Each student will use the material in a different way and will respond to the subject matter in accordance with his own needs.

That there are individual differences in learning has been recognized in theory as often as it has been denied in practice. Learning is a private individual matter. Each one utilizes opportunity and experience in light of one's unique capacities and interests. You can lead a student to a class room or a text book, but you can't make him learn unless he wants to or wills to learn.

The liberal arts college, we have assumed, presents the opportunity for the student "to acquire" a certain amount of factual knowledge which will aid him in understanding himself, his activity, his relationship to others, the nature of the world, and his place in it. In order to take advantage of this opportunity, something must happen to the student's self. It is not enough, indeed, it is of least significance, that one memorizes "data" or glibly employs a technical vocabulary. Deeper changes in the organization of the self must take place before factual knowledge can be truly "acquired."

Intellectual capacity is certainly a condition precedent to doing college work. It is taken for granted. It is the capacity to use that intellect with intelligence, sensitivity, and responsibility which alters the structure of the self. Many students successfully practice the ritual of lecture-recitation-examination-marks without more than a superficial notion of what any of it means in their living experience. To learn means to change.

Change ranges from adding a few facts to one's intellectual equipment to a radical reconstruction in the behavior of the personality. The greater the growth of the self, the deeper are the changes in one's ideas, emotions, and impulses, and the developing self becomes more integrated and more willing to accept responsibility for new kinds of decisions.

Bits of knowledge are, relatively, easily picked up by the college student with average intellectual equipment. Students differ markedly, however, in their willingness and capacity to struggle with the implications of the data and to assume responsibility for the difference in their behavior which necessarily follows. Some students react positively to suggestion and criticisms. They are eager, curious, and ready to learn. They move forward to meet the challenge of the instructor. Others seek ways and means of avoiding responsibility. They are altogether dependent upon the instructor. They want to be told what to do, and when to do it. They will mechanically conform to requirements and do only what is required of them. Still others want to have their way altogether. They are argumentative, aggressive, and manifest an "you've-got-to-show-me" attitude.

Of course, there are no definite types of learners. Each student has his own peculiar ways of reacting to the subject-matter of the course. So long as the student is developing, the peculiar way of learning presented by each individual is, within certain limits, accepted. The speed and quality of learning will differ for every individual. The different ways of learning and of reacting to the subject-matter are illustrated by the material in this chapter.

Differences in Learning

The following comments are taken from papers written toward the end of the first week in the PC class.

"I have previously thought much about the organism and the environment. I realized vaguely that the two are inseparable. One does not have to know much physiology and psychology to realize that. And, I have known that the individual acts on environment and the environment acts on the individual — that there is always interaction — that there is no organism without environment — and no individual distinct from environment. This sounds like a jumble of ideas — but that is just the point. — it has been a jumble to me. The organism concept helped me out a little. I think that the course and the book are going to help a lot because they will help me orient my ideas and discard a lot of them.

"I don't want to give my opinion of the class discussion yet. It is too soon. All I will say now is that I was discouraged with the first two sessions. I tried to kid myself with thinking that I would not get anything out of the discussions because there did not seem to be any direction or purpose. I finally got honest with myself and realized that I was confused and my ideas unformulated. I thought I knew more than I do. I wanted to drop the course after the first session, but I guess that I will be glad that I stuck with it instead of running away from it, because I thought I knew more than I did and because I saw at the start that a lot of my pet ideas were not going to hold water in all probability."

(*Frank.*)

"It's my one fault with Plant, and I don't think it's a lazy man's criticism so much as it is the criticism of disliking unanswerables—relatives rather than black and whites,—confused groping where there should be certainty; probably partly the result of a culture pattern and (probably more) partly because it creates some insecurity. — And that one fault is that he so often hints at something which, if explored, leads to some painful mental states, and I'm soon lost in a welter of unanswerable implications. But I wouldn't have it any different." (*Lark.*)

"I find in the classroom discussions that I feel what we are dealing with but still have some difficulty in trying to verbalize the feeling. At the point in the study or actual living process of the classroom experience, I feel like a fellow who had climbed a high mountain in the morning and reaching the top finds himself surrounded by low hanging clouds and mist so thick that to glance in any direction shows nothing. Yet standing at the top with the mountain at your feet you feel quite secure that you won't just fall but have at least something solid to stand on. It is uncomfortable because you cannot seem to see anything except the fog. Yet at any moment you expect some sort of light to burst through so that you can do something besides look at the mist and feel damp." (*Lyons.*)

"Afer reading the first chapter and listening to the class discussion, I begin to realize that I will have to give a lot of thought to the problems in order to grasp them. Previously, I had studied all the sciences where the facts were to be memorized. The student's thoughts were not prerequisite. The course is forcing me to use my own reasoning and logic which, up to this time, I now realize, was stagnant." *(Leiser.)*

"Until Thursday morning, Li'l Abner's 'It's amuzing but confusing' expressed my feelings of the course. I read the chapter and only slightly understood what Plant was trying to say and what we were discussing in class. This morning, however, I got into a discussion with W.R. and J.G. which lasted about three hours. I feel that now I have a better understanding of the material. We'll see." *(Bird.)*

"Note: This first paragraph is purely unnecessary, but it makes me feel better.

"I should like, first of all, to make a brief comment on the class discussion in general. While I am in complete accord with the method employed in conducting the class, I must confess dissatisfaction with the results and the progress. I am fully aware that results and progress are arbitrary things and can be measured only by the use of a predetermined standard, which can be one of many. From certain points of view, there has probably been much progress. From my own personal point of view, most of the class time has been a waste, having been devoted largely to quibbling over irrelevant points or statements made, without any apparent thought behind them. I find myself becoming a little less tolerant over the constant quibbling over points which to me seem obvious; and I strongly object to the stream of words which, to me, show no evidence of having been carefully thought out. Not that I object to thinking aloud when an idea has formed but not clearly, but I do object to a lot of talking which to me seems thoughtless. I don't think I am in any way different or superior to the other members of the class, although the fact that I am a few years older than most of them may make some difference, but since I do not subject the class to a lot of thoughtless prattling on my part, I in turn expect the same from the class. In short (and the above paragraph can be put into one short sentence) I should like each member of the class to think about three factors before opening his mouth to say something; 1st — think about what he is going to say; 2nd — decide whether a little more thought won't clear it up; and 3rd — make sure that it is relevant (and thereby constructive) to the material under discussion.

"The question, it occurs to me now, has been made clear by the discussion today. If I had followed my own advice in the first paragraph, I should have cleared the question without wasting the class' time." *(Lark.)*

At the close of the semester in the PC course several visitors were present. They asked the group to tell them what the course was about. No student was able satisfactorily to articulate the content of the course. One student wrote at the end of the week:

"Dr. Plant writes an excellent recapitulation of his previous chapters here — one which is skillfully inclusive. It was almost startling to me that the class, including myself, was unable to put into words what had taken place during the semester either from our own experience or that of the book. I felt that we should have been able to express the tone of the book if nothing else. Did we not understand what had taken place, and did we take refuge in that lack of understanding by saying that we couldn't express it? In other words were we faking? I felt that I could say something but found it difficult to use words which would clearly indicate what I was trying to express — the meaning that I attached to the words seemed to have so many connotations that they would be sure to lack clarity and incisiveness. This has disturbed me a great deal and I have spent much time in trying to find out what or where lies the difficulty. Perhaps I haven't a grasp of the meanings — yet I feel that I have, and so will begin to attempt to find some medium of expression of what I am trying to say. I realize that this is not an easy task but yet I feel that there must be a way, and that it is an absolute necessity that we find it. However I am not sure about this." *(Lyons.)*

The writers of the above comments show a positive attitude toward learning. They are willing to approach the material to see what is in store for them. They want to get help. They are eager and curious while, at the same time, questioning and flexible in their attitudes. They feel uncomfortable, but they do want to learn.

The writers of the comments which follow reflect an opposite spirit. They have to differ with the content of or with the way the class discussion is being conducted, or with what the author of the text writes. They carry a chip on the shoulder. They start with being argumentative rather than being receptive.

The material is not approached in the spirit of "I wonder what I can learn from this" but, "Something's the matter with the material (or the author or the class discussion)." A defensive tone is apparent. Something is wrong, not with them, but with what is offered to them. I should like to present three sets of excerpts which illustrate these contrasting attitudes.

"I don't think I have ever read a more muddled piece of writing than Plant's Chapter 4. I'm sure I haven't the vaguest notion what the Chapter is about. I do not like divisions and subdivisions, anyway. The title is 'The Structure of Personality,' and then follows much about inherent things and all the categories that come under it. I haven't been able to digest the Chapter, the class discussions don't seem organized or related to the organization of the Chapter — I have the feeling that we're getting nowhere fast, and also that we're moving too rapidly to cover a great many things."
(Bristol.)

In contrast to the above comment by Miss Bristol the following reaction to the same chapter reflects a different spirit on the part of Miss O'Malley:

"In Chapter 4 of Plant's 'Personality and the Cultural Pattern,' I am being told that alertness, complexity, pliability, temperament, and cadence are inherent structural elements. It seems a matter of unlearning, with explanations, many of the things which I have so carefully learned in the last few years. It is becoming evident now that these traits are not intangibles, but are simply labeled aspects of structure and its functioning and, as such, are necessarily inherent. It really seems to simplify the whole matter to realize that alertness is merely a matter of thresholds, that these other four elements also seem to have structural bases although to me at least they are less obvious than those of alertness. The tie-up between alertness and thresholds may be especially evident to me because of my experimental investigation of thresholds in Psychology 205-6. At any rate, personality is becoming much more clear and concrete for me through the presentation of the material in Chapter 4. I look forward to the succeeding chapters." *(O'Malley.)*

The two excerpts which follow are a striking example of the differences in learning attitude shown by Mr. Rush and Mr. Turner. They both refer to the same chapter.

"In my opinion, Plant's chapter on the church is one of the most vague and weak in the book. It's opinionated and I see no reason to accept his opinions rather than anyone else's."   *(Rush.)*

"In direct reversal of opinion that I expressed for Dr. Plant and his Chapter 15, I feel that now in this chapter he has treated the subject of the Church in the only way in which it can be treated. This discourse is perhaps the most delicate of any discussion in the book and the author is very wise when he says that words trick us; that we are unable to express adequately with words the problems involved here. I have been terribly disturbed by these problems and eager to obtain the help I think Dr. Plant offers." *(Turner.)*

Several members of the class selected "Crime and Justice" by Sheldon Glueck as part of their supplementary reading. Here are two reactions.

"As Sheldon Glueck ranted on, lamenting first this needed remedy and then that abuse, I had to sit back and really sympathize with the poor soul. So many things wrong and so few right, or are there any right at all? He didn't say. He writes like a very unhappy man." *(Morse.)*

"Glueck's book was, to me, one of the most inspiring and thought-providing documents I've ever read for Criminology. Not only are the attitudes we've been developing all year expressed, but they are argued for and against. Despite the black realities, you feel encouraged because we are facing matters as they are and trying to find out how to overcome the defects in the administration of criminal justice." *(May.)*

During the first week or two of the course the students, unaccustomed to accepting responsibility for their own creative efforts in dealing with assigned material and in participating in class discussion, show some annoyance. They have been in the habit of outlining or reviewing assigned readings. Instead, they are told in these classes that their own reactions to and interpretations of the material are expected. That the students should be irritated because they find this procedure troublesome is to be expected. The following remarks present the reactions of two students to this requirement. The first student is definitely negative and wants to fight against assuming self-responsibility. The second student also questions the procedure but in quite a different spirit.

"The questions asked in class are artificial—brought up just for the sake of avoiding lulls in the discussion. I don't find any desire to discuss things in class. Also, I don't know whether this is the place to say it or not, but I think this paper writing is silly unless you feel there is something you have to say not said in class. But to have to write a paper, when both

class proceedings and book reading exhausts all you are interested in saying or asking, seems a little out of keeping
with the manner in which the course is conducted. It seems
pointless." *(Bristol.)*

"I'm at a loss as to just what to write this time. I think
it's a waste of time merely to recapitulate everything that
was said in class or review the chapter. Any questions I had
on this chapter have been cleared up in class; what questions
I still have will be answered in later chapters, so it's prema-
ture to bring them up now. I'm in complete accord with
Plant; certainly his logic and method, if clearly understood,
leave little room for disagreement; one is at least forced to
support old beliefs and accept his line of reasoning. I'm
trying to be as critical of Plant as I can, for there is certainly
no point in merely agreeing with him because it may prove
expedient to do so, but I am frank to admit that, as far as
I'm concerned, his reasoning has been sound and what questions I have had, have all been cleared up by a clearer understanding of just what he's saying, either through a more
careful review of the chapter or through class discussion.
Would that some other writers in the field of Sociology were
as lucid in their writings.

"I had begun to fear that the study of Sociology could
never be phrased in terms familiar to anyone but a lexicog-
rapher. If you will permit my saying so, and it isn't my
business to question on your procedure, I cannot see the point
of writing these weekly papers. The questions I have on a
chapter are cleared up before I write the paper, so I'm without ammunition. Perhaps my stand is wrong, but so long as
I think Plant is sound I have little to say. When a point of
disagreement is reached, however, I shan't hesitate to say
so. My point is this: I would prefer being critical in class
and having my questions cleared up rather than asking them
on paper. If, on the other hand, your purpose is to gain an
idea of our understanding of Plant, which can't be gained

otherwise because of the size of the class, then you want a critical review of the chapter. I would like to know whether we are writing these papers because you want some information or because we want some. In all likelihood, I'm missing the point. The fault, if any, probably lies with me." *(Lark.)*

Mr. Lark objects, as does Miss Bristol, to what is requested. But Lark is seeking enlightenment. He is disturbed, he expresses himself directly both as to his agreement and disagreement. "This," he is in effect saying, "is what I think and that is what you apparently think. If you have no objection to my raising the question I'd like to find out just what is expected."

Miss Bristol definitely states that the questions in class are "artificial" and the paper writing is "silly." These contrasting attitudes of the two students, it is interesting to observe, are reflected in their class discussion and papers throughout the term. One learns positively, the other through differing with what is expected. One fights with the responsibilities of the class, the other against them. Both, in time, gain some understanding, but in different ways.

The following remarks are taken from the CS class. We were dealing with the various theories underlying the treatment of prisoners.

"From class discussions, I drew the conclusion that some of my classmates would send our criminals to an athletic club or the Y.M.C.A. to serve out their prison terms.

"I don't agree with them. If a judge, after taking other matters, and all the angles into consideration still finds it expedient to send a man to prison, I believe he should be made to suffer the punishment society has planned for him.

"Let us look, for a moment, at the policies of the new reform. They advocate gymnasiums, methods of relaxation, self-government, and some even go so far as to advocate no prisons at all. They are attempting to make prison life as near like our normal life as possible. What for?" (Morse.)

This was written by Mr. Morse toward the close of the second month's work in Criminology. One could read the above and conclude that it does not reflect a negative attitude, an unwillingness to learn except negatively. Mr. Morse's position, it might be maintained, can be supported, and the student's attitude can, with equal validity, be considered a positive one.

No student in the "class discussion" even hinted that criminals should be sent to "athletic clubs" or "Y.M.C.A.'s" This is Mr. Morse's interpretation of the point raised in class, viz., that prison programs should be meaningful from the viewpoint of the inmate's rehabilitation.

In the light of Mr. Morse's *need to oppose* he distorts (not deliberately) the context and the data. In order to illustrate the negative attitude toward learning which characerizes this student, I should like to present excerpts from six of his papers written previously to the one from which the above comment is taken. (Notice his comments on pages 123, 126, 135, 193.)

The six papers show Mr. Morse's reactions to reading assignments dealing with (1) "The Field of Criminology," (2) "Methods of Approach," (3) "The Police," (4) "The Prosecution," (5) "The Court," and (6) "Probation." The excerpt selected is characteristic of the spirit in which the entire paper was written.

1. "If I continue to read any more of the text, I'm quite positive I'll never get anywhere. When I entered the course, I expected to learn a little something about the subject. All that I've learned to date could be put in my vest pocket. I found instead of a criminology course one in logic. Any more confusion will lead to chaos."

2. "You made the statement in class, "Perhaps the confusion some of you feel will gradually disappear." I think

this is absurd. If I don't understand the subject at the beginning of a course, and thereby lay a good foundation I'll never understand it and get a respectable grade. Frankly, I feel like resigning from the course."

3. "I'm with the police one hundred per cent. It matters not to me what procedure or methods the police may employ in their efforts to solve a crime or in getting information, so long as they prove effective. If a man or woman is unfortunate or stupid enough to get entangled in an enterprise outside the law, he deserves all that he receives in the way of harsh treatment. The "third degree" has proven to be the only language some persons respond to."

4. "On the whole this chapter was not boring. Hope there are more similar to it."

5. "You want a perfect court system? I think that's foolish. Because it's a Utopia. You can't do away with corrupt court politics, untrained judges, and crooked juries."

6. "It is strange to me that society should be so sympathetic, generous, and forgiving to criminals. First, society expends time, money, and effort in an attempt to provide a livable prison system and then concocts a still more formidable practice — a comparatively new theory — probation.

"Riding downtown to the trial, five students were trying to convince me I was wrong. I didn't give them any satisfaction by telling them so, but I'm afraid they have convinced me. I'm not, however, abandoning ship. I still believe there's logic in my argument."

Mr. Morse is a chronic complainant. He writes that he has learned nothing. He feels that it is absurd that his confusion will disappear. He feels like resigning the course. Those who get caught should be given "the works." He doesn't say the chapter was interesting, but, it was "not boring." "You can't do away" with corrupt court politics. Society "concocts" a new theory, probation. The reader is asked to note the negative forms of expression he uses; "noth-

ing," "absurd," "resigning," "not boring," "you can't" and
finally, the derisive expression, "concocts."

No matter what the content happens to be, Mr. Morse
feels it necessary to oppose someone or some point of view. He
fights against surrendering attitudes with which he entered
the course. He wards off the possibility of change. As he
himself states it, "I didn't give them any satisfaction by
telling them so, but I'm afraid they have convinced me—
However—I still believe there's logic in my argument."

The point being made is not that Morse (or any student)
is expected to share the attitude of anyone else, or that he
should adopt a "progressive" point of view. Any student
should feel free to differ with the entire group and the instructor. It is the spirit or the attitude behind the difference
—or agreement—which is significant. One can differ with
a majority point of view in a positive sense. That is, one
views the material or data and interprets it, and reaches a conclusion not shared by others. There is room for an honest
difference of opinion. If, however, there is a psychological
need to be non-conforming (what that need symbolizes is another matter), it is not the data but the individual that is
responsible for the position taken. It is no simple matter to
decide what role one's needs play, as against the logic of the
data, in reaching a conclusion.

Granting, however, that everyone tends to select the
data which support one's position, there are decided differences in the degree of projection different individuals employ.
Students who learn negatively try to twist the data so that
their present attitudes are least disturbed. They wish to
preserve their difference and will challenge anything which
threatens its surrender. The problem of the self, and not the
consideration of the material, or the attitudes of others, is
central in their learning. Some students throw the burden
of learning upon the instructor, or other students, or upon
the content of the course. They do not have a positive will

to learn, and, at the same time, they are afraid to express their own negative attitudes. There is an apparent lack of interest shown in the classroom discussion and in the comment upon assigned material. These students do what they are told to do, no more and no less. They attend class, and silently sit through the discussions, rarely participating. Their papers, which are handed in when due, contain superficial comment or consist of a lame repetition of the ideas expressed in the readings. They do not seem to identify themselves with the course. They are withdrawn. The illustrations of this point, which follow, are taken from papers in CS.

"The chapter makes clear the extensive disorganization of lack of effective policy in the treatment of prisoners. The problems involved in treatment are complicated and far from being solved." *(Bacon.)*

"I have read the chapter and do not find anything that I do not understand, that cannot be cleared up by you during Friday's class." *(Lawrence.)*

"I cannot find anything in particular in this chapter to put my fingers on and say that it is wrong. This is principally true because the material in the chapter is not stated as facts but as debatable points such as the hypothesis to explain crime. This debatable material makes a subject like criminology different, for usually the Bus. Ad. subjects as economics or accounting, are matter of fact." *(Robert.)*

"I have heard many stories of the relation of the church and the law, and this chapter bears out some of these tales about the corruption that existed. I also found it interesting to see how the law started. I often wondered how feuds originated. I regret that this is all I can write but it just doesn't register.

"I was asked the other day in class a question which to me meant that the professor was wondering why I have little to say in class. I feel that when I can contribute to the discussion, I will, but when I have nothing worthwhile to add,

I had better be a listener rather than talk just to make myself heard. I've never been in a class like this and am still trying to adjust to it." *(Marsh.)*

"One feature of class procedure is the way some of our classmates seem to get going and talk all around a point as if they knew the whole inside of everything. I think those students should be squelched and those, who, perhaps, know as much or more but can't express themselves in as thoroughly a sociological manner, be urged to join in the discussion."

(Howard.)

"I really cannot find anything that I can say should be improved. I like very much the method we are now using in class, for we progress along the study as quickly or as slowly as we will, not as someone else would have us." *(Cochran.)*

"This chapter is very interesting historically and, therefore, it is difficult to comment on things that happened years ago. We can see, though, that we have been improving gradually as time goes on, but that we still have a great deal of room for improvement." *(Rooney.)*

Some students have to differ, others fear to express themselves. It is important to distinguish between those who withdraw and are afraid to expose themselves, and those who are simply not interested in what is going on, or who prefer mulling things over in their own minds before expressing themselves. In other words, not all students who fail to speak in class or react neutrally to the assignments should be considered timid or afraid. The attitude behind the apparent lack of participation indicates whether the student is timid, disinterested, or wise.

Over a period of time, during which the student's series of papers are read, and observations of the way in which the student speaks or reacts, when called upon, are made, the instructor is able, I believe, to make a reasonably sound judgment as to who are the timid souls. This judgment can be fortified — and I have usually found it to be the case — by individual conferences with the students. They are, as a rule, the timid members of the class. They fear the disapproval of the instructor or other students. They dare not face competition. They fear being found out. They gain protection by remaining silent in discussion and by refusing to criticize the material they read. Through submission, by mechanically accepting the routine requirements of the course, or by withdrawal, they protect themselves against change. Blaming others for talking too much is one way of defending oneself for remaining silent and allaying feelings of guilt.

It is usually from this timid group of students that I get such questions as, "How long must my paper be?" "When must they be handed in?" "Do I have to read that book?" They are the ones, who, when asked directly whether a difficult and complicated point is clear, lamely, reply, "Yes, now I see the point" and when (upon occasion), are asked to explain it, redden and stammer in quasi-panic. Often, I have made it a special point to glance at several students in this group, without calling upon any one individual, remarking, "Perhaps some one has a further comment or criticism to make? The question isn't simple and there certainly is room for difference of opinion." More often than not, the students quickly shift their line of vision as soon as our eyes meet, seeking comfort in the relative anonymity of numbers.

It is important that every student develops understanding of the subject-matter and struggles with the problem of assuming responsibility in his learning process. It is meaningless to set up "average" standards against which the growth of any individual student is to be measured. No two students learn the same way. Every individual will take out of the course what he feels he wants or needs and will put into it whatever effort his capacities and willingness to learn allow. The instructor who is aware of these differences in learning will permit different students to use him, and the

material of the course, in their own unique ways. As long
as the student is sincerely trying to do something with himself and struggling to learn, he should be permitted to move
at his own speed and on his own level.

The different attitudes in learning are revealed by the
different ways in which students use the subject-matter of
the course. The remainder of this chapter will illustrate difference in "catching on," the depth and quality of understanding reached by students.

Different Levels in Learning

To learn, we have said, means to change. If taken literally, it is a truism that a living personality is forever learning, since it is continuously changing. No one's self is rigidly stable. The personalty is subject to changes in the environment and changes within oneself.

The important question is, how extensive are the changes
one undergoes? How crucial are the experiences, "inner"
or "outer," for the development of personality. The significant problem in education relates to the focus of change,
the intensity, and extensity of change. What part of the
student's personality is being affected by the classroom and
study experiences as such? The further question is, what
changes brought about by the classroom experiences affect
other aspects of the student's personality?

The instructor can be directly effective only in the
classroom and in conferences, and only if the student wants
to learn or discovers meaning for himself in that experience.
Education can be effective, learning will take place, in the
degree to which the student is ready to learn.

The position can be taken that the changes in the growth
of the self initiated in the college classroom are narrowly
limited. Familiarity with the problems of criminology or
economics or history or anthropology will not help the student to solve the problem of earning a livelihood, nor help

him successfully to untangle the conflicts of family life, nor find greater peace within himself. There are many more important difficulties in one's life than the question raised in a college course.

This objection is a serious one and will be considered in detail in our last chapter. For the present, we reply that a change going on in one area of a personality isn't isolated. It can extend itself into other aspects of the self. It all depends upon the quality of the change, its focus, its meaning to the individual. We thus find ourselves returning to the matter of the different levels in learning which the rest of this chapter will illustrate.

There are three groups of excerpts which follow. The first series reflect the superficial intellectual level upon which the students in question remain. The second series represent the thinking of those students who follow through intellectually the *implications* of the data they deal with. The third group not only see the conceptual implications of the material but also apply it in a way that involves more of their total self.

Series I.

The following comments were taken from a series of papers written by Mr. Kareff over a period of six weeks. (The italics are mine.)

"From my first reactions to the book *Crime and Society,* and discussions in class, *I have concluded* that criminology is the science that deals with the investigation and study of crime and criminals . . . A crime is an act punishable by law in the interests of the community . . . When a criminal intention is present, the person is said to be actuated by malice . . . The detection, arrest, trial, conviction, and punishment of the criminal should be certain, speedy, just, and adequate, both in the interests of the criminal and of society."

*   *   *

"In the book, *Crime and Society,* I *found* that a science consists of the systematic collection of related facts. I think the term is correctly used, in this light, to denote the results of these criminological inquiries into the phenomena of nature which can be pursued by means of observation, experiment, and reasoning."

*   *   *

"The chapter on *The Police* was enlightening as to the status of the efficiency and ability of police today in coping with modern crime developments. The officer of today must be physically fit and generally intelligent. It was a surprise to learn that a private citizen has the power to arrest anyone who has committed a misdemeanor or a felony."

*   *   *

"After reading the chapter on *The Court, I have concluded* that there is no definable uniformity in the procedure of the various state courts in the United States. A large number of judges in the courts obtain that high office because of political pull . . . The purpose of the trial is to decide whether the accused is guilty or innocent of the crime charged. The jury is a number of men, selected according to legal rule, and sworn to inquire into and decide on the facts in the case."

*   *   *

"From the chapter on *Imprisonment, we see* that the chief purposes of punishment are now regarded as the protection of society and the reformation of the criminal so far as this is possible. There are certain methods of punishment in use in the United States such as whipping, fines, imprisonment, the death penalty, etc. These methods of punishment are largely traditional . . . "

*   *   *

"In probation, the offender's sentence is deferred or suspended; he is released on honor during good behavior. I *discovered* that the court suspends punishment in the hope and belief that the offender will mend his ways in the future

... The probation officer is expected to follow the case up and render such advice, encouragement and assistance as may be possible."

Mr. Kareff selects statements from the several chapters and repeats them without even, in most cases, changing the language of the text. Mr. Kareff "finds" and "concludes," and "sees," and "discovers" nothing which is not precisely stated in the text.

The following series covering reactions to the same material comes from Mr. Goden.

"The text is very interesting, and I find it easy to read. I enjoy sitting and reading the book in my spare time, not as a text but as a novel. The first chapter of the book was well written and well placed in the chapter *(sic)*. The chapter was like a football coach's speech before sending his team out to play. By this I mean, I'm waiting eagerly to get further into the course so I may express my views as to my idea of capital punishment."

* * *

"I don't think it is possible to criticize the chapter nor the method by which the course is taught. It's the way I would conduct the course if I was smart."

* * *

"In this chapter, *Is Criminology a Science*, you have brought forth the invalidity of environment in relation to delinquency, I have as my background only one year of psychology and therefore am limited to that field in relation to Criminology. Dr. —— says that environment plays an important part in the foundation of a normal person while you state the opposite."

* * *

"To me it is not possible to use common sense in working scientifically and therefore appreciate the fact that, in this course, I'll get a chance to think. I would like to suggest that we spend a period of discussing the effects of environment upon criminals and youths."

* * *

"This chapter was very clear. It raised one question in my mind. In the various statistical records of broken-home delinquents was the greater percentage in homes where the father was gone or mother?"

* * *

"I found this chapter fairly comprehendable. Of course, as per usual, there were a few difficulties that arose, but most of them you settled in class."

* * *

"We all admit that the present day probation system has been advanced greatly since its first introduction into this country. But, we have to admit that it is far from perfect. After reading this chapter, I agree that something must be done."

Mr. Goden, it seems to me, simply does not possess the average capacity of a college student (whatever the reasons) to do much with ideas to which he is exposed. Far from discovering new ideas or integrating those presented, he does not have the ability even clearly to express ideas which he garbles from the text.

Series II.

The following sets of contrasting comments illustrate the superficial, intellectual acceptance of ideas by some students and thinking through the *implications* of the ideas by others.

"The ultimate goal of the present criminal law is to protect society from the violators of its laws. The development of probation and parole have increased the effectiveness of the treatment phase of the criminal law. Physical and technical changes of imprisonment, probation, and parole are necessary in the relations between officers and offenders. The repression of emotional life in the prison is, indeed, an obstacle to correctional administration. For re-adaptation of offenders to non-criminal behavior in our normal world, it is necessary to gain the co-operation of the prisoner by noncoercive means. It is not too difficult to foresee a better and more effective administration of a modern and corrective criminal law." *(Koenig.)*

"This chapter appears to summarize attitudes toward crime, criminals, and criminal justice which have been developed throughout the year. The relation of punishment and of treatment to the basic issue of the protection of society, with treatment coming out on top, except with so-called incorrigible criminals, and the serious limitations to rehabilitation which the prison systems, institutonalized as a system of punishment, is described. And the conflicts inevitably resulting from this dual function are again brought into focus. For myself, I am convinced that the interests of society as a whole are best served by treatment and rehabilitation of the criminal and that it is toward this end that effort in the fields of criminology and penology should be directed. But as I indicated in a recent paper, instead of nicely resolving the problem as far as I am concerned, it rather provoked a new one, as yet barely touched upon in class. That is the question of whether we know enough about human behavior, about changing attitudes, about rehabilitation, treatment, and the other neatly generalized expressions, to justify our undertaking a program of reform, or are we embarking upon a sea of troubles in a theoretical ship with no, or at least, an adequate anchor of empirical data. (Pardon the metaphor, but I think it indicates what I mean.) Admitting that the chapter is cautiously and moderately written, nevertheless, I think that treament is assumed to be far superior in most cases, and consequently this problem becomes vital. *(Grinnel.)*

Mr. Koenig does nothing to the ideas presented. He accepts and repeats what he reads. Miss Grinnel, on the other hand, is not willing to accept what is stated, without further qualifications. New problems arise as she reads. Do "we know enough about human behavior — to justify our undertaking a program of reform?" This question had not been discussed up to this time either in the text or in the class. It is one of the most important issues in the field of penology. Miss Grinnel read beween the lines. She explores the implications and the assumptions of the material and raises very pertinent questions.

Mr. Dole, reporting on his reactions to a volume by Beccaria, *Crime and Punishment* (1764), a landmark in the development of the criminal law, writes as follows:

"I can see why people called Beccaria crazy. This man was a couple of hundred years too soon. Who knows, in years to come one of us may be looked at as crazy because we had some ideas. I would say this man was a master genius. He knew what was right and wrote about it. I have never read a book of this sort in my life but am willing to state that this book did a lot to influence changes in criminal treatment right up to this present day. Although I am unfamiliar with the present day penal code I can plainly see a lot of Don'ts in these essays, that were told to me by my family, teachers, friends, and of course, our splendid law-enforcing body." *(Dole.)*

Compare the above with what Mr. Green found in Beccaria's brochure.

"This book left me with the impression that its author was primarily interested in democracy and secondarily in criminology. I somehow had the feeling that the field in which he wrote was important only in so far as it provided a medium for the exposition of his belief in the equality of man and the rights of men. Most of his ideas, and certainly his most important ones, in their relation to crime and punishment, hinge upon the theme of equal rights for all men before the law. My guess is that Beccaria, influenced by the ideas of the Age of Enlightenment, carried their spirit over into the criminal law field. Both the trial and the punishment of the noble-man should be not unlike the trial and the punishment of the lowest member of society, according to Beccaria. It would seem that today criminal procedure, which it must be under-stood, was vital and urgent in his day, represents but a minor problem if, indeed, it is at all pertinent, in our present setup for the administration of criminal justice. With the per-spective given us by Time, we can now see that in his desire for democracy in criminal *procedure,* Beccaria overlooked the possibilities of the effective treatment of the criminal. In a democracy the individual even as a prisoner, is entitled to the protection of his rights and opportunities." *(Green.)*

Mr. Green relates what he read to his sense of history and to his awareness of the nature of democracy. He offers an interpretation (and a correct one) of the general influ-ence of culture upon Beccaria's ideas.

The class had been assigned a chapter called, "From Pun-ishment to Treatment." This material describes the shift in theory and practice from punishing people for the crime they have committed to treating offenders in order to prevent future criminal behavior. Here are several comments which illustrate the different intellectual levels of understanding of the several students.

"I realize that it is a problem to know what to do with the criminals and the ultimate aim is to prevent further crime, and also that individualized treatment is the only way to treat because each case is so entirely different in its causes and so forth, but I still believe that prisoners should be pun-ished for their anti-social behavior. I was absolutely amazed at the statement that 95% of all the inmates will be returned to society at the expiration of the average sentence of two or three years. I probably am wrong, but I can't see where the loss of one's liberty is enough of a punishment. Why should prisoners who have deliberately done wrong, especially repeaters, get too much consideration? If they do, what will be the reward for fair play in life?" *(Blake.)*

"At the close of this chapter, I find that I am completely baffled as to how all these fine reforms are going to work. The material in this chapter is very clearly stated. I realize that this report is very factual and contains material directly from the chapter. However, I do feel that in order to understand what we are doing today in our criminal code, and what improvements should be made, we must know the factual material stated in this chapter." *(Edwards.)*

"Crime is not merely the act of an individual. It is also the product of society. You, therefore, conclude that it is not fair or just to punish the individual! I dislike to appear the typical layman, yet I am afraid I am not scientifically minded as I cannot appreciate this statement. To me it conveys the meaning 'each dear criminal is the unfortunate victim of circumstances." *(Morse.)*

"I was rather surprised to note how recently and how frequently statements have been made and resolutions adopted by leading criminologists, or at least persons interested in criminology, embodying ideas which I have learned to consider antiquated and inadequate. It seems so neat and so reasonable to say that the protection of society can better be obtained by treating rather than punishing the offender. It appears obvious that the high rate of recidivism and the great number of first offenders should convince many of the Classicists and the conscious or unconscious exponents of that school, that punishment does not effectively protect society by deterring either those who have felt its effects or those who contemplate crime for the first time. Also, when I read that the majority of people still believed in retaliation, it hardly seemed possible. But the more I thought about the attitude of these groups, the more I understood their feelings. On the basis of logic and reason, and armed with the long-time view of things, I can hardly agree with them; but trying to ferret out some of my own immediate reactions to certain criminals helped me at least to understand the attitudes of the majority. It was not too difficult for me to recall several specific crimes, both before the criminology course, so horrible from a moralistic point of view that my first reactions were to think of all the terrible things that should happen to such an inhuman criminal. When my first reaction becomes an immediate desire to 'treat' such an offender, to take him in hand as one with a disease, and try to restore his balance in relation to society, then I may hope that my alleged positivistic ideas are more than an intellectual veneer."   (Leiser.)

Miss Blake and Mr. Morse read material which, perhaps, for the first time in their experience leads them to examine their attitudes with regard to the treatment of prisoners. Miss Blake momentarily accepts the logic of the position of a point of view with which she differs. "I realize that it is a problem to know what to do with the criminals . . . etc.," "but I still believe that prisoners should be punished . . . etc." "I probably am wrong, but I can't see where the loss of one's liberty is enough of a punishment." Mr. Morse dislikes "to appear the typical layman," "yet I am afraid I am not scientifically minded." To him the material assigned means, "Each dear criminal is the unfortunate victim of circumstances."

At this point, we are not illustrating the content of the students' reactions but the focus. Students Blake and Morse read the ideas and begin to react to the ideas read. Student Leiser meets the ideas, and she thinks about the ideas and develops her own reflections to the point where she realizes that her understanding of the positivist position is "intellectual veneer."

As a final illustration, the summary statements of two students, which refer to the same material, neatly summarize the distinction I have been trying to make between those who read the words and those who want to think about them.

"It seems to me that with this chapter, we have gotten away from confusing definitions and have really entered the body of our course. Now everything is clear."

(Southern.)

"The material in this chapter is more factual than that of the previous chapters and as such was much less thought-provoking and, hence, less exciting. It is simply a presentation of material on policemen and there was little in the chapter to puzzle the reader. I hope succeeding chapters raise questions rather than describe material." (Gilbert.)

Mr. Southern is satisfied when the thinking is done for him. "Everything is clear" when the ideas are arranged and delivered in neat paragraphs. Miss Gilbert states she wants to participate and not merely be given facts.

Series III

The next series of excerpts indicate how some students put more of themselves into the material and, therefore, receive more than intellectual data.

"It is now Friday evening. I have completed a discussion on Criminology, which was my first other than with members of my class. Present were a lawyer, his wife and my parents. I started on different reformations and the chance for change in the future. Surprisingly enough, they were not unaware of the needs of Criminology to fit modern patterns, but they also presented another picture concerning limitations, which I found to be most annoying and which made me feel that I must be less dogmatic. Of course, certain of the facts that they presented had been touched upon in class, and only gave me a more valid picture of conditions that are existing and which prove to be obstacles in the way of reform.

"This was one of the most exciting evenings that I ever spent. I am writing this in bed, but I just had to tell you about it, so please excuse the pencil. I doubt if my description is adequate, but for the first time I felt that I did stand for progressive thought, and felt that I could talk some about Criminology, although I know that there is so much more to know.

"The discussion this evening made me feel about the subject more closely. I can now see your point in spending so much time the first semester on Frames of Reference because it takes an awfully long time to get a group of people to speak about a certain thing on the same level as you are talking. I found this jumping around and confusing issues made a lot of trouble. It seems that whenever you talk about anything you ought to be sure the person with whom you are talking and the speaker should be on common ground. I never realized this so much as tonight." (Sievert.)

"It certainly seems as if we do get our share of problems in this course, no matter what field you enter. Troubles, troubles, and more troubles which we must combat in one way or the other, — for we cannot merely dismiss them with a nod of the head. These conditions exist. There are so many different angles to any one problem. It becomes a very confusing circle. It struck me how this same kind of confusion exists with regard to problems outside of our course. If you try to understand your family conflicts and look at them from different points of view it becomes terribly confusing. You're not so sure any more that you're right. And then if you try to understand social and economic questions, there are so many ways of looking at them that it tires you out. Problems aren't so simple for me as they used to be." (Ziegler.)

"Criminology three times a week has been knocking my criminal-belief-pins from under me. Reading *Youth in the Toils* climaxed this inner revolution. It is I, and people like me — obviously there are too many — who, knowing nothing about criminology and our penal system, even in a satisfactory common-sense way, are, as a result, preventing necessary measures from replacing the old traditional ones now in use in the majority of our courts and penal institutions.

"Honest to God, my blood boiled when I read the chapters on detention of delinquents in the Tombs. The whole system is so glaringly wrong and is so popularly believed to be right, that I'm convinced that here is one of life's greatest paradoxes. We are supposed to be highly civilized and highly educated. But the way we are allowing our fellow beings to be treated, because they commit something we call a crime, is not even funny. It's pathetic. I'd like to do something about it." *(Caldwell.)*

"— I don't know just how to go on with this paper. I think I understand what you mean by social work treatment of prisoners but I can't get rid of the feeling that I'm only issuing words. All I can say is that I wish I had experience in working in prison and with offenders so that I could be certain that I'm not just using words.

"The idea I got was that case workers really help a man cure himself by making him think out his own problems. What a job! If the prisoners are anything like some of us in this class, and I imagine they are, I can see what a job the case worker might have. Most of us bluff a great deal of the time and try to shirk out of our responsibilities by pushing our work on to others. We don't know ourselves well, let alone trying to help others. And we are the ones who may be going to the School of Social Work and then do case work in prisons or reformatories. All I can say is that something important has got to take place in us before we can try to help others. I'd like to know what and how it is to take place. It's really very annoying." *(Green.)*

The four students, all in the course in criminology, derive different values from the content and discussion which set up movement in the development of different aspects of their personality. Miss Sievert gains insight into the common error of people trying to communicate without first being clear as to the issue. Miss Ziegler is struck by the complexity of human relations, the different points of view with which one can approach any social problem. The different approaches to a single problem in criminology, Miss Ziegler realizes, is merely one illustration of how all social problems are to be approached by examining many points of view which give a better perspective and increased understanding.

The acceptance of difference is certainly not easy. "Problems aren't so simple for me as they used to be." Mr. Caldwell's awareness of the present treatment of delinquents is not merely intellectual. He has been undergoing an "inner revolution" and wants "to do something about it!" Mr. Green senses that there is much more to the actual process of treating delinquents and helping others than he gets from the brief description of the treatment of prisoners which is found in the text. The ideas there stimulate him to an evaluation of himself and he becomes annoyed. "I'd like to know what and how it is to take place."

The significance of such changes on the part of the students who approach the material with something more than intellectual curiosity is not being considered at the moment. The excerpts do illustrate, it seems to me, the different reactions set up in the several students. They possess, for one reason or another, different needs, the answer to which, in a measure is found in their activity in this course. To use the common phrase, they get out of the course what they are willing to put into it.

In illustrating the different levels in learning, we have up to this point, deliberately selected comments from the papers in the CS course, the content of which is not so intimately tied up with one's more personal problems. In the PC class, where the subject matter is more directly related to the student's personal experience, it is relatively easy to illustrate the levels in learning. On the other hand, even in this course, some students find it difficult, in the early weeks, to get beyond the stage of language and manipulation. Later in the course, almost every student gets beyond the "cold knowledge" stage. (This point will be developed in the next chapter.) How meaningful the student finds the material, how far beyond the knowledge level he reaches, depends chiefly upon the student. However, since we are concerned with showing different levels in learning, we may select students' reactions to the same material at any given stage of the learning process.

"It would be best, perhaps, to state my own position to the subject now under discussion. For five years I have attended college, four of these as an undergraduate, and the fifth as a graduate student. My education, in the main, has consisted of the physical sciences. Therefore, I have had to learn that a thing is or is not so, that there is no middle ground.

"Now I find myself concerned with a subject which is abstract and which can be defined using any criteria anyone chooses. Personality cannot be dealt with in generalities. If it can't be accurately defined, it can't be dealt with scientifically." *(Turner.)*

"I have previously thought much about the organism and the environment. I realized vaguely that the two are inseparable. I have known that the individual acts on the environment and the environment acts on the individual—that there is always interaction — that there is no organism without environment— and no individual personality apart from the environment. Personality is the product of the interaction. This sounds like a jumble of ideas — but that is just

the point — it has been a jumble to me.   These are the ideas
I got in psychology course and they never were really clear."
(Frank.)

"Previously, I had majored in the biological sciences
where the truth was there to be memorized, and thought
by the student was no prerequisite.   After reading the first
few chapters and listening to the class discussions, I begin to
realize that I'll have to give a lot of thought to the problems.
This course forces me to use my reasoning and logic which
to date was stagnant."   *(Leiser.)*

"I don't know whether it is the fact that the material
of the past weeks is so new to me or so difficult for me, but I
seem to have a hard time finding something to talk or write
about.   I read the text and find that I agree with all the
author says."   *(Carr.)*

These four students' comments show that, for the time
being, they have not gone far in translating the ideas into
their own non-intellectual experience.   Contrast the above
comments with the following reactions to the same material.

"I got such a wonderful feeling tonight out of reading
this chapter that I hardly know where to begin.   I now can
honestly say I'm getting something besides language out of
college.   Probably this doesn't make much sense but I'm
so enthusiastic over the chapter that I just can't put down
what I mean."

"Plant's statement 'security is not simply absence of insecurity' struck home.   Personally, I've never been very insecure for any lengthy period of time, yet I've never had
very much security.   This caused me to build up a protective shell which I still have.   I know it's there and I've been
trying to do something about it.

"As I explained before, the status-preserving wall that
each person builds up to separate the ego from the environment of fear is what I have as everybody has.   Sometimes it
tends to disappear which I think is taking place partially

right now. That's why this paper is the mess it is." *(Bird.)*

"The thought occurred to me that this status-preserving mechanism is tied up with the sense of inadequacy. We are afraid that if people know us as we really are and not as we want them to think we are, that we will be rejected and will consequently feel inadequate. Maybe we're not far wrong at that!" *(Green.)*

"It is one thing to talk on an intellectual level about this material, and another thing to actually live. I'm trying to really live in light of what I'm learning about personality development and it's not a simple matter." *(Grinnel.)*

"I could go on and on but these examples prove to illustrate what I get out of the chapter. Plant remains a constant amazement for me. His wisdom is overpowering. I say this because every line has meaning for me, helps me to see my position in society, my relationships with people, helps me to understand some of my problems. It's like our tutorial meetings. I just feel as if I grow every time I attend tutorial or read Plant.

"This is what I've wanted out of school — something that is living. This is growth food and I'm trying to stuff as much in me as I can. I want more and more because I understand so little." *(West.)*

"The last class discussion left me rather puzzled and uncertain as to the limits of the personality and as to where environment fits into the picture. Being unable to accept a new concept just because the professor or author says it's so, I have spent considerable time since the close of the last class period reflecting on the entirely new idea and discussing it with others, both classmates and outsiders, but must admit that it is still rather hazy and indefinite. I am a psychology major and have never thought of heredity and environment in this light. If Plant is sound I've certainly used a lot of words without much thought behind them. I don't like to think this, but I fear it may be so." *(O'Malley.)*

The material in this chapter shows differences in learning attitudes. The capacities and needs of every student vary. Hence, what the content of the course means to each student will be different. The use made of the subject-matter depends upon each student's need, capacity, and will-to-learn.

The instructor who is aware of such differences in learning attitudes on the part of the students will be on guard to observe those who tend merely to repeat the language. He will try to help them express in their own words what they have gained from the assigned material. He will also encourage them in self-expression during class discusion. (The previous chapter on The Activity of the Teacher can be re-read in light of this point of view.)

In the final analysis, all learning is a private, individual matter. In the following chapter, material will be presented showing the development of students' attitudes. The movement in learning comes from their own creative participation in their work.

Chapter 13

Development

Until the student himself has struggled with the problems presented in a course, he is not ready to comprehend the problems or to appreciate their resolution. By leaving them alone (with some guidance, however) to find their own way, at their own tempo, the instructor will help the students more quickly to come to grips with the material of the course. During this incubation period, the instructor observes the several students to see that they are meeting their responsibility in reading and reacting to assigned material, in handing in their weekly papers on time, and in contributing to class discussion. Those who fail to meet their responsibilities in these respects are interviewed with the view of helping them. During these interviews the student is not blamed, nor are the responsible students praised in class. Problems are presented. They will or will not engage the interest and effort of the class. That depends upon what the particular student wants to do about himself and the material.

Movement in Learning

The first illustration consists of an interview requested by Mr. Kerr. He spoke, briefly, only two or three times, throughout the entire semester. The interview was held three weeks before the close of the semester. Several weeks before the meeting, I had spoken to the class, as a whole, wondering whether each member was doing the kind of work which satisfied his or her sense of craftsmanship, whether each was making a contribution to the group. Mr. Kerr said:

Kerr: I wanted to know whether my work is satisfactory?

I: How do you feel about it?

Kerr: Well, I'm bothered about not talking in class. I talk in other classes, but this class isn't like any other class I've ever been in, and I've never had to write these kinds of papers. I'd like to know if my papers are what you want? Are they all right?

I: What kind of paper do you think would be all right?

Kerr: Don't most of the students write the same things?

I: Sometimes they do but, often, there are great differences.

Kerr: Can you tell me whether I'm getting the material?

I: What is your opinion?

Kerr: I think I am. I've learned some things.

I: Aren't you, then, the best judge of what the course means to you?

Kerr: I've had no courses in sociology. I guess I'm afraid to talk. I'm bothered about not talking and I feel inferior to the others.

I: Perhaps you'll feel better if you make your contribution to class discussion.

Kerr: But I might ask or say something silly.

I: This is your course, and anything you consider important *is* important so far as I'm concerned.

Kerr: But I might be bluffing.

I: Of course, but you are the best judge of that.

Kerr: That's right. I guess I wanted to be sure you thought well of me. I see now what's important is what I think of myself. Thanks a lot. Come to think of it, if I do bluff I just bluff myself. You really don't care and there's no point in kidding you. I'd be fooling myself. Gee, I get it. Whatever I do I've got to do myself. This is the nuts.

Mr. Kerr is not sure of himself. If he obtained my praise he'd be reassured. I refrained from reassuring him, giving him the chance to assert himself. His last remarks show improvement in that direction.

All of the following excerpts are taken from papers in the CS class.

They were written at the beginning of the second semester of the course.

(In the Appendix following the name of the writer is the number of the page where other contrasting comments of the writer appear. The reader, by comparing the comments with those presented here, will observe the movement in learning which has taken place.)

"More and more, I feel that I am looking at the criminal from an entirely different point of view since entering the class." *(Kuhn.)*

"I'm getting more out of the class discussion these days. I don't know whether it is a change in my own attitude toward the type of discussion, a realization of the importance of a clear understanding of basic essentials, or whether it results from a better organized and directed discussion. At any rate, from this past week's discussion I think that I have gained an appreciation of some of the difficulties involved in making the probation system work more in conformance with its theory than it does." *(Grinnel.)*

"The present chapter on treatment and correction is, to me, the most enlightening chapter which we have come across. At last, some of the major issues which we have been wrangling about are elucidated." *(Sims.)*

"This chapter meant a great deal to me in that it seemed to conclude and straighten up so many problems which were stated in previous problems. I now find I am able to integrate much of our class discussion and outside readings with the chapter, and actually understand what I am about. It's a great feeling.

"I honestly can say that this chapter has been a joy to read. I have not been so convinced about a chapter in a long time." *(Lawrence.)*

"This chapter is the one that I have been waiting for. For some time, I have tried to keep an objective viewpoint, but I have been conscious of some opinions which, although slowly crystalizing, I have tried to prevent from being tied up with too much feeling tone and thus, become belief. However, I now believe that I can objectively support my contentions, not just because of affective satisfaction to me, but also because of logical justification from the facts."

(Tylor.)

"This week's chapter in my opinion is one of the most important in the book. It was suggested in class by others that the chapter should have been at the beginning of the book. I think the suggestion is silly. If I would have read the chapter at the beginning of the term, I know the points in it would have been totally lost to me. With my limited background, I often find it difficult to gain the most out of the matter, but now, after the past few months, I see that I am becoming more capable." *(Leiser.)*

"Should this course be open for second semester registration? It appears to me, *now,* that the work of the first semester is essential for a clear and intelligent understanding of the second semester's work. This may seem, at first, a very selfish viewpoint. Repeatedly, on Wednesday, questions were asked by *those* students who were not fortunate enough to be with us (italics not in original) last term. Their questions were mostly, or should I say, in part, pertaining to last semester's work, and I believe that the time spent in answering them could have been made more profitable for a greater number of people." *(Morse.)*

Mr. Leiser and Mr. Morse were among those who, during the first semester, complained of the confusion resulting from class discussion. By the beginning of the second term, the point has been reached where they realize what had taken place in their thinking. Students Grinnel, Sims, Lawrence, and Tylor comment on how enlightened they now feel concerning their previous difficulties. There is now "a clear understanding of basic essentials" (Grinnel); "The present chapter on treatment and correction is to me the most enlightening chapter which we have come across" (Sims); "This chapter . . . seemed to conclude and straighten up so many problems" (Lawrence); "This chapter is the one I have been waiting for" (Tylor). Mr. Leiser, for one, understands what had taken place. "If I would have read the chapter at the beginning of the term, I know the points in it would have been totally lost to me."

The following series of comments is taken from early papers in the PC class.

"I wish I could feel more satisfied after reading these chapters. Instead of knowing more, I know less and less. This may be a good sign, but it is very unpleasant, especially as it is happening too much to be comfortable, especially at the family dinner table. But I wouldn't have it otherwise."
(Frank.)

"You wondered whether some students would remain in the course even if no credits of any kind were given. I know I'd be one of them. I feel that the course is doing something to me, and I have gathered the same impression from lengthy discussions with other students. It is very stimulating." *(Stern.)*

"I used to think that writing my reactions would be more or less simple. But the more I try to write, the more difficult it is. I get confused because there are so many ways of looking at the problems in the chapter. These problems were all simple before entering this course. In fact, there were no problems. Now I find problems and no answers." *(Green.)*

"Plant, at least for me, has taken away the feeling that life is easy to solve. I realize now that education of the mind is only education of the mind. I know now that I need experience both first and second-handed before being of any use whatsoever. This means a loss of the sense of being secure because of not knowing, but in return he gives us a deep problem to work out, and makes no secret of the perplexing dilemma that we face. I have reached a point where I am sure of my ignorance." (Roby.)

"How true it is that in our society we have so great an opportunity for acquaintanceship, and so small a one for intimacy. Of all my friends on campus, I don't believe I know one intimately. It's all very strange, when one stops to think about it. I can say truthfully that I never had before now. This course certainly does something to one!"

(Syne.)

"This course is like none other that I have ever had. It isn't just a classroom discussion. I feel free to voice my opinions at all times, and I also feel that I don't have to agree with anyone if I can present as strong an argument as he has.

"The minute our discussion period is over there are some of us who just don't forget about the course until the next hour. I, for one, have discussed with my parents, and friends in the Sociology Department, some of Plant's ideas and also some of the ideas set forth in our discussions. I can see some of the things that we have been discussing in my own family and among my associates. I have been growing more and more conscious of these things about me."

(Underwood.)

"It's very odd; something has happened to me in the last few weeks. I have carried some of the inspiration this course has given me over into some of my other courses, particularly my tutorial sessions. The course seems to have given me a little confidence in myself; I think it has already taught me to observe better and, in time, I think it may even help to resolve some of my personal problems although at first it complicated them. At the moment I am writing this I am supposed to be studying for a history exam. I shouldn't be doing anything else — yet here I am. I cannot study history when I have this course on my mind."

(*MacKenzie.*)

"I don't mean to seem smug, but I think I'm beginning to understand the relationships among my family members and the relationship between my family and me . . . Ever since I started this course, I have realized more and more how little I knew about these things and how little I understand what was going on. Too, many things I was aware of I could not give voice to, until such chapters as this came along. You can take this for what it is worth — I spend at least four hours reading these chapters each Sunday. I have to stop after every other sentence or so and struggle with the meaning. I can't let go." (*Caldwell.*)

"I sincerely feel that I have a comprehensive grasp of the subject matter of Plant's thesis. I don't know—yet. However, I have noticed that in my observations of life— that is, of human beings living—about me, there begins to pop in various ideas expressed by Plant, which become an aid towards my interpretation and understanding of the social milieu in which we live. And I think that, slowly, I am becoming aware of a new attitude on my part not only towards social construction, but further—towards social reconstruction. There isn't anything concrete about it all yet; there is simply a feeling of something within stirring, or shifting, a revised set of emphases on aspects of relationship between individuals and their society. I might almost say that it feels like an antiseptic, a cleansing agent which makes room for a new and—for want of a more fitting word —*better* viewpoint. Frankly, I appreciate the course for this enlightenment which is slowly making itself obvious."

(*Riddel.*)

The above remarks of the students reveal movement in some direction. The change, such as it is, comes from the student's own activity. It is difficult to understand what happens to any one individual, that is to say, how significant the movement in re-organization of the self is. I do not think it possible for the instructor to evaluate its significance. The least that can be said, however, is that the classroom situation and the relation between instructor and students is such that the individual feels freer to do something to and with what happens to him than is usually the case in the average classroom.

In the following section I believe the reader will agree there is some evidence in the remarks of the students that self-motivation does follow or accompanies the movement in learning described above.

Self-Motivation

Miss Robert appeared on time by appointment. She was flushed and tense as she seated herself.

I: I suppose, Miss Robert, you're a little scared at my calling you in?

Robert: I am frightened. I don't know what this is about.

I: I thought we might discuss your work in the course. Do you sincerely feel that you're doing the best kind of work you are capable of doing? Perhaps you are. I wanted to discuss that with you.

Robert: Yes and no.

I: Would you try to make that a bit more clear?

Robert: Well, I read the material carefully but I don't seem able to say much about it. I don't know enough, I guess, to see the problems.

I: And how about the class discussions?

Robert: I guess I'm in a rut. The questions I want to ask are so simple compared to those the other students raise that

I'm afraid to ask them. I'm that way in all my classes. What can I do about it?

I: I think you will have to settle that for yourself. You do agree, do you not, that you yourself are not quite satisfied with the kind of papers you hand in and with your lack of participation in class discussion?

Robert: Yes, but there are a few students in class who do a lot of speaking and who annoy me because they talk so much.

I: I suppose they have their problems, too. But that doesn't help you, does it?

Robert: No, I guess not. How can I help myself to get into the material more, to feel it more?

I: I'd like to, but I can't, help you with that. You'll have to decide that for yourself.

Robert: I think I know what you mean. I suppose you know that I haven't missed handing in a single paper on time. Do you remember, last fall, I wanted to give you Friday's paper on Monday morning and you wouldn't accept it?

I: Yes, indeed, I remember.

Robert: I thought, what's the difference if I hand in the paper due on Friday a day or two later. You said to me that if the paper was due on Friday it was due on Friday and not Monday. That was all you said. You didn't bawl me out. That made such an impression on me that I've made it a point to have all my work in on time. It's a matter of pride on my part, I suppose. But that's the way I feel. You didn't bawl me out and I felt I had to make good.

I: I think I understand that.

Robert: Well, I imagine that's the same thing with the chapters. It's up to me to decide what to do about them.

I: Yes, I think that's so.

Robert: Well, I guess that's all. Thank you very much.

"The trouble is with me—I don't seem to have any creative ability to grapple with these facts and apply them as they deserve to be applied. I'm not patient enough to study the facts carefully and thoroughly. I'm beginning to realize the necessity of this though." *(MacDowell.)*

"This I will say, that the present course has helped me measurably, and thru it, I have seen certain parts of me that I thought did not exist. My capabilities, I think, are many, and now I realize all I could have done. Suffice it to say that I have not done the best I am capable of doing— not even come close. Although I am disappointed in myself, I am thankful to have discovered certain things. Perhaps I can do something about it." *(Turner.)*

"Wednesday we discussed the point of how different ideas, acts, etc., aren't accepted because they are new and unheard of. I don't know if you realized it (you probably did though) but that was just one of Bentham's fallacies of authority that I had just been reading for Logic. These fallacies were just a lot of words to me until I heard you talk about that very thing. It gave me new ambition to go back to the library and finish reading these fallacies. I think I must have walked out of class beaming." *(Jaffre.)*

"Before making this report I wish to clear my conscience, of one thing. My readings on this book were not complete. Maybe I shouldn't be so bold and hand in such a report, but I feel that an incomplete report is better than no report at all. This is not to be taken as an excuse. I was simply lazy. I don't expect this to take place again."

(Morse.)

"I must ask myself whether I am doing the best work in this course that my capacity warrants. It is much more comfortable not to ask this question because the answer is so definitely no. I suppose the way to get rid of my discomfort is for me to do better work." *(Clark.)*

"For the first time in my life, I have come to the point where I can speak in a class with ease (of course there is room for more ease). I still am not perfectly relaxed but I feel that I am on the road to improvement. From both this class and tutorial, I can see a change in many of my actions and in many of my attitudes. I'm trying to realize that my capabilities are as they are and must not be hindered by the A students. I really wish that I knew what my capacities are and what I can do. I hope that the attitude I'm learning to develop, because of my acquaintance-ship with your courses, will carry over in other courses." *(Sievert.)*

"In previous class discussions, I never took part because I was afraid to talk. I was afraid of you, Professor Cantor, and of the other students. I never wanted to say anything in class because I thought I would probably say the wrong thing and the other students would laugh at me. When you first began to call on me, I didn't mind it so much, but when you called on me several days in succession I began to hate you more and more everytime. I felt you were heckling me, and it bothered me terribly. You see, this had never happened to me before and I felt so embarrassed that I almost dropped the course. I would have dropped the course if you hadn't said several times that anyone that wanted to could. I took this as a hint for me, so I stuck. I am very glad now that I didn't drop the course because you helped me to conquer my fear of talking in a classroom and I want to thank you very much.

"I was very much impressed, too, by the way that whatever I said was O.K. It removes the fear of talking."

(Moran.)

"Two things before I start. First, about the paper I wrote last week. Last Monday you talked with Mr. Gerber about his papers and said, to admit that you are shirking responsibilities is only a way of shirking them — unless you really do something about it. That really put me in my place, because then I realized that my whole paper wasn't a paper, but just an excuse to get out of work. Secondly, concerning your attitude in class last Friday when you suggested that those who wanted to drop could get partial credit, etc. Knowing that you are first and foremost a teacher, I believe that little act was a technique to get more interest in the class by artificially stimulating interest. If it wasn't an intentional stimulation, I suggest you use it some other time, because I saw how it made me and others just go home and tear into this next chapter with new zeal."

(Bird.)

"Prior to this, I had been prone to take a position on social views, more often than not, merely for the sake of the argument. Now, however, I find myself thinking about these problems at almost any time. What a change from the happy-go-lucky-carefree youth of but six months ago! I see but a sad picture of myself tearing my hair for the rest of my life and even winding up possibily a soap-box orator, unless I get the chance to do something about these problems. And that I must, for I feel these problems too keenly."

(Chaplin.)

"I'm always a little bit amused (although I don't know why I should be) about the child being bent to the needs of the parents. Dr. Plant brings it out very clearly in this chapter in that parents always want their children to live as they (the parents) had wanted to, and accomplish what they themselves had hoped to. This is what has happened in my family. My mother always bought my clothes, did everything for me, told me just what to do and what not to do. After I graduated from high school, they decided on where I should go to school and all to every detail. I wasn't even as much as asked about what I would *like* to do. My clothes were again bought for me, an adequate allowance was given me, and off I went to make the best of it. At the time, I didn't think anything about such procedures.

"Being only sixteen years old and a small-town girl I was quite immature. But in the last couple of years I have thought about it. Both this course and our tutorial session

of last year have opened my eyes.   I just came to the conclusion that I wasn't going to be pushed around by other
people and was going to do what I wanted to for a change.
Just about a week ago, I did do one thing in this way.   I
bought a new coat, just the kind I've wanted for three years
and could never have because my mother thought they
weren't proper, got dirty too quick, and I don't know what
all.   I've written and told her some of what it is like, but this
Wednesday when I go home I'll see her reaction.   I know
right now that she isn't going to approve, and will probably
make life miserable for me every time I wear it, but, at least,
I'll have the satisfaction of having what *I* have long wanted.
(The constant, hampering problem of, Who's going to win?
We'll see!)"   *(Syne.)*

"Last week's session, conducted in the absence of Professor Cantor, seemed to offer conclusive evidence that the
class as a whole has grown.   Had we been faced with a similar
situation last October, the class would have been dissolved,
and no meeting would have been held.   Later in the term,
one such session was held but the class split into groups and
discussion wasn't continuous.   Now, the class seems to have
developed a great deal more.   Not only did the entire group
participate in the discussion, but discussion continued for
the whole class period.   No one wanted to leave after the
period was over.   I counted only four who did not contribute
to the discussion.   To come thus far, I know, has been
achieved often through discomfiture and tension.   Probably, now, those feeling states can be viewed as growing
states.   Most of us were surprised at the end of the discussion
because of what happened.   We hadn't realized how interested we were until it was time to dismiss."   *(Fry.)*

It is almost impossible to predict to what use any particular student will put the material, and how it will affect
him.   The above excerpts illustrate several directions toward
the re-organization of the self.

I had quietly refused to accept the late paper of Miss Robert. I did not know until the above interview what this refusal had meant to her. Apparently, not having to struggle against me, since I did not "bawl her out," she disciplined herself. This helped her to realize that the problem of participation in the class discussion would also have to be settled by her.

Miss MacDowell, Mr. Turner, Mr. Morse, Mr. Bird, and Miss Clark admit quite frankly that they are not doing the best kind of work of which they are capable. Admitting this is, of course, not improving the quality of their work. The frank admission, however, may be the beginning of a more serious effort. Each one of the students will have to decide that for himself or herself.

Miss Sievert and Miss Moran have succeeded in partially overcoming their fear of self-expression. They find it easier to join in the class discussions. I did nothing other than encourage them. Miss Moran "almost dropped the course" but didn't because I suggested that "anyone that wanted to could." The opposition between student and instructor was avoided and instead the student was left free to decide what to do. Miss Moran states that she made the decision.

Mr. Chaplin finds his interest developing in the social scene. Miss Syne uses what she is learning, to help her in her family relations.

In whatever direction movement in learning takes the student, it follows from what the student does for and to himself. What the material will mean to the student cannot be predetermined by the instructor. The function of the instructor is to present the material of the course and accept (within limits) the class' reactions to it.

Criticism against the instructor is obviated since he avoids criticizing the students although he does make clear, in general terms, what one's responsibilities are. In this way standards are set up by which each student can measure his effort and development, if he wants to. Self-criticism is stimulated. Students become aware of their shortcomings, personal or social, and want to do something about them. Others become aware but have not reached the point where they will to change. The instructor can do nothing about this. He can only create an atmosphere which permits the student to express himself. He cannot will for the student.

Motivation is essentially a private matter reflecting the resolution of an inner struggle between the positive and negative will of an individual. The teacher who in one way or another *compels* students to learn certain things at a particular time and in a particular way, complicates an already confused situation, viz., the struggle of the student to find himself. He unwittingly projects his own will-struggle into the learning-teaching activity, not skillfully and professionally, but as one who, personally, has something at stake. This robs the student of the chance to discover himself. The struggle becomes one between the student and the instructor's demands, instead of an inner struggle on the part of the student to accept the responsibility of his "good" and "bad" sides.

The excerpts in the following section, taken from the PC course, are intended as a further illustration of what happens when students feel they are accepted, and feel relatively free to express their negative as well as positive selves.

"This chapter is also a very exciting, stimulating one. His discussion on the 'inviolability of the self' and the 'status-preserving mechanism,' made me tingle with a feeling of satisfaction and contentment. I am beginning to discover myself.

"I know now, in a flash of Van Gogh brilliance, what I was doing and what I was feeling during the few times I morbidly questioned myself. Just what is Gerber without that look of conceit which he wears? Fundamentally, what is he like when there are no people to impress, etc.? Why

does he act and think in the manner he does? Underneath
this entire social veil or cultural veneer, is he not just an
ordinary blundering, insecure, inadequate individual?"

(Gerber.)

"I don't like the way he talks about a wall—a status-
preserving mechanism. I see what he means, but I think it
would be clearer without talking about a wall. That it is
built by fear is interesting. It was interesting to note the
walls that were built up in class on Monday. When you
started trying to find out what was the matter with us, I
started building up a wall to protect myself right away. I
had several excuses to hide myself from the real reason —
that I was too lazy to think that morning, for some reason,
unknown to myself. It was a mild sort of fear. I was hiding
something from you, but mainly from myself." *(Frank.)*

"I have been considered, and have considered myself,
an introvert, but upon reflection, I find that the signs of
this introversion have been especially marked since our family
moved from the country to a suburban residential town.
We never seemed quite to fit into the new pattern, and although I was accepted into the most prominent crowd of my
age, I always felt those differences between their families and
mine, their clothes and mine, their manners and mine, etc.
Considering it all now in the light of Plant's discussion,
it seems clearer and less baffling. Also, it hurts less. The
more objective consideration seems to have given me a better
perspective, for which I am grateful." *(O'Malley.)*

"To thine own self be true and it must follow as the day
the night, Thou canst not then be false to any man" —

Shakespeare.

"I have always been the smiling-faced boy; smug, com-
placent and burdened with many pretensions. I have pulled
the wool over my own eyes and I *think* I have pulled the wool
over other peoples' eyes — but now's the time to let my hair
down — you see, for the past few months I have sat around

a table with other students and a *director* and through a
process that words are futile to describe, I have gotten the
courage to be true to myself and to any man. It's a funny
thing! I have read these Shakespearean words a hundred and
one times and never understood them. As I read the quota-
tion now, the words seem to vibrate and come to life.

"I don't think I'll ever forget the times, when you questioned certain individuals in the course — and as I watched
the struggles mirrored in their faces, how I feared that I
would be next on the list — I went through all the inner
agonies with each one of those students — and as each
emerged with a conflict resolved — so did I. It was like a
shower after a visit through a coal mine.

"And those terrific silences for minutes that seemed
like hours — oh, what a relief when some brave voice finally
broke through — and what a release of pent-up tension
was evident in the sighs that followed.

"It's pretty refreshing to feel that I am now the captain
of my soul—and it's no longer disturbing to accept myself
despite my weaknesses. At least I'll know it — there won't
be a cloud over my eyes. I think I can really start growing
now because at least I realize that the grass isn't greener
in someone else's pasture — that we are all only humans,
that the greatest part of our makeup is emotional and because
of this we suffer keenly at times — thus there *is* a brother-
hood of man — it is a wonderful feeling to realize this. If
everyone felt it as I know I do, I think this world would be
a better place to live in.

"Somehow I feel that the words I have written are inadequate; that they cannot possibly convey *all* that I feel—
but for me — well, it's the best I can do with words. This
has been a wonderful year for me." *(Rush.)*

"It is my private opinion that Plant's chapter on *The
Family* should be printed in pamphlet form and distributed
free to anyone interested, maybe even dropped on an un-

suspecting city from an aeroplane in the blue heavens. As I read it, however, I thought perhaps a bit petulantly, Why am *I* reading this so much? My mother is the one who should be reading this. So she did (the first page) and said perfunctorily that it was very nice. And now I know that people really do learn only what they want to learn!

"In connection with Professor Cantor, it suddenly occurred to me that you are the only person, without exception, whose approval I have never consciously tried to secure. You seem really to take people actually as they are, not as you wish them to be. If I could learn that lesson, my entire college education would become priceless." *(Doran.)*

"One day I watched a friend of mine who was busily engaged in embroidering a pillow-case in needle-point. As the process seemed to be a very interesting one, I resolved to purchase the necessary materials and to proceed to make a similar pillow-case. The work was very fascinating and I heartily enjoyed myself for the first three evenings. But then I grew bored at the steady task of thrusting the clumsy needle in and out of the heavy material. As a result the following evening found me at an altogether different occupation. But I resolved to finish the work I had so enthusiastically begun. Therefore, every once in a while I would distastefully take it out and labor over it.

"Until I read Plant's chapter entitled *Recreation* I had every intention of completing the work at some future time. But now, realizing that leisure time should be employed at doing something for the sake of doing and enjoying it and not for the sake of accomplishing something, I do not believe that I shall ever complete the task.

"Instead of boring myself with the pillow-case I intend to abandon all efforts in the direction of its completion." *(Leonard.)*

"This chapter inspired me. It presented a completely new outlook on *Recreation* as far as I am concerned. Upon breaking down and criticizing the "perfectionist philosophy" in regard to leisure time activity, Dr. Plant gave me renewed interest in activities which I have often wanted to engage in, but never did because I knew the results would not be satisfactory — (as compared with standards set by others). Such a task is drawing; I have frequently desired to sit down and draw but because I am not gifted in this field I considered it a waste of time. Now, I know differently and am acting differently." *(Suor.)*

"My whole being seems to rise up in defense when I read of the entire field of recreation being taken for such a ride as Dr. Plant has done in this chapter. His whole program is indeed commendable, if the circumstances existed at present as Dr. Plant says they do. But I believe that he has not presented a true picture of the field as it really exists for, if this were so, there would not be thousands of youngsters, young people, and adults crowding into social group work and recreational agencies as they are today." *(Waller.)*

(Miss Waller is in the physical education department of the school system.)

"If you will pardon the personal implications, I shall tell you how the chapter has affected me. I am unfortunate enough to have a hand which I cannot use. Because of this physical disability, I very often feel self-conscious and uncomfortable. Fortunately, so far in my life this defect has not caused me to interpret everything in life in terms of it. Perhaps this is so because my parents and friends have wisely refrained from making me feel that I was different from them. But occasionally, when an incident occurs which makes my disability apparent, I feel very sorry for myself.

"Plant's chapter has given me courage and insight. *It has made me realize that my hand is not me* and that I can live a full life despite it. These last few years have made me quite discouraged but Plant has given me much encouragement. My case is somewhat like that of the boy mentioned in the chapter, but I do not think that my crippled hand means to me what that boy's meant to him. The difference lies in the fact that the boy kept his hidden and I do not."

(Leonard.)

"Plant writes, 'One thinks of many cases of stammering as excellent pictures or symbols of some more general factor of maladjustment.'

"The above statement caught my interest more than others because it seems to apply to my life. Stammering or stuttering has played a large part in my life, as Dr. Plant says, it is a symbol of some general factor of maladjustment and has affected my mental life and social adjustment to some degree. I think it's the result of the strict discipline I got as a child. We had no social life in our home. Stuttering had always restrained me from reciting in class, and asking questions that bothered me. I have always been aloof and listened to discussions instead of participating in them, afraid to answer or talk through the telephone, and getting very excited when I do. In fact it wasn't until I entered your class that I gained enough confidence to talk in class, and I suppose you noticed how much I've improved. Now I talk with confidence in any class I go to. My stuttering has almost disappeared. What was it from which I obtained my confidence?" *(Darby.)*

Mr. Gerber, Miss Frank, Miss O'Malley, and Mr. Rush have reached a point in their development where they dare face their weaknesses. They have obtained, in their several ways, new insights into their behavior. The instructor, at no time, discussed their personal problems with them. Discussion was limited to the basic text and assigned readings. The by-product of the material came as a consequence of what each student did to the ideas. Miss Doran applies the chapter on *The Family* to her relations to her mother. Miss Leonard, Miss Suor, and Miss Waller use the chapter on *Recreation* to help them understand their problem of using their leisure time. Miss Leonard and Mr. Darby use the chapter on *Medicine* to help them face a poignant physical disability —and the use to which they put it seems to help them. (I noticed during the first meeting that Mr. Darby stuttered. I made it a point to seat myself next to him during many of the class meetings, and to encourage him whenever I sensed he felt like speaking.)

What ideas mean to students, only they can determine. The instructor can determine that ideas shall not remain useless tombstones to dead experience.

Self-Acceptance

It is extraordinarily difficult to assume full responsibility for one's decisions. It is easy to understand why this is so. Feeling and willing are ambivalent. Decisions are reached only after conflict. One part of the self struggles with another part. The side which controls must perforce deny and defeat the other side.

In back of the conflict or doubt lies some kind of fear and some degree of guilt. When we affirm our independence, we deny that the dependent self seeks social approval through conformance. Guilt at not conforming, and fear of being blamed, are present. When we conform, the part of the self which seeks self-expression is denied. Now guilt and fear are felt because one's independence has been denied.

To accept oneself, therefore, means to accept this inevitable conflict. It means one must learn to live *with* one's fears and guilts which accompany positive or negative willing. If the "bad" self is accepted with the "good" side, neither aspect of the personality has to be denied, and there is no need for justification or rationalization.

To accept oneself means to be responsible for one's decisions without feeling too much guilt. This can be accomplished only through being given the chance to work out one's conflicts without praise and blame of others. The person who is afraid of what others might do, say, or feel about his actions cannot make his own decisions. He excuses his compromises on the ground that he is considering others. Self-criticism, however, is often a form of avoiding responsibility. To blame oneself, or "to think of others" and not mean it, is easier than changing oneself. When self-criticism is genuine, it is painful. When specious, it is merely a way of protecting oneself from facing oneself and being found out by others. Saying, but not meaning, "I guess I'm no good," is a way of having others reassure you that you are good or convincing yourself there is no use in being better so you will not have to make the effort. Doing something about conflict is much more difficult than thinking about how to escape doing something about it.

Praise and blame, reward and punishment, which play such a tremendous role in our language, ethical practice, and child training, should be considerably reduced as the motivating factors in conduct. The individual must learn to motivate himself. There is little danger of individuals becoming anarchic.

Family life, the neighbors, and the police can always be depended upon to provide a medium of reward and punishment as ultimate motives for behavior.

The teacher is in a favorable position to assist the student in disciplining himself. There is a controlled situation in which the responsibilities of instructor and students are clear. Furthermore, in functioning professionally, the instructor can, much more easily than the parents, remain emotionally undisturbed by the decisions of the students. He need not use them for his own needs. In brief, he does not have to blame or praise them. He accepts them as they are, qualified by their understanding that certain consequences follow certain decisions. The students, aware of their responsibility, may do what they wish. The decisions are entirely their own.

Will students utilize this kind of opportunity? Do they accept their responsibility? In a word, do students recognize their attitudes, and to what extent? The following chapter seeks to answer these questions.

Chapter 14

Evaluation

Standards

This study has been concerned with describing the dynamics of the learning-teaching process. *What* changes occur in learning are independent of the question *how* one learns. The belief is implicit, however, that the kind of learning and teaching described in this volume is an improvement over the traditional type of academic instruction. The assumption is made that, if teachers better understand what takes place in their relationship to students, instruction will become more skillful and learning more vital.

The problem of evaluating the process described here should, therefore, be met. There are two aspects to the problem of evaluation. First, what standards are to be used to meet the practical administrative problems of grading students?

The first question is, strictly speaking, not inherently related to the soundness of the learning-teaching analysis which has been made. The first problem is really one of evaluating the student's work rather than the methods by which he is taught and by which he learns. In other words, the standards used in the traditional type of instruction are used to evaluate the kind of development which follows from a different kind of instruction. Until the college of arts and sciences are aroused to the realization that there *is* a teaching problem, the traditional standards will remain in force even in the relatively few classrooms where something different and, perhaps, better, is tried. Hence, the question of grading under the new approach should be discussed.

Schools generally certify a student's successful completion of his work by standards which are uniform for all courses. Numerical ratings, A, B, C, D, or comparable quantitative devices, signify the standing of the student. The passing grade is a "C" or a "D" or an average mark of 65 or 75. The passing grade represents a statistical average. It is determined rather mechanically, being based upon such factors as class attendance and oral or written responses to questions of fact. The true-false, multiple-choice, or matching type of question, or similar developments in examination technique test the student's ability to "reason" or measure the amount of information acquired.

A few progressive colleges recognizing individual differences in students have developed honors work, the tutorial system, credit for individual projects, and student selection of some course. The differences in students which have been recognized, however, relate to intellectual ability or interest and not to the differences in learning.

The point of view developed in this study emphasizes the quality and level of learning as against merely acquiring factual knowledge. The information of the course, the factual data, is not disregarded but the important objective is to help the student use data in developing liberal attitudes. How is one to determine whether this has been accomplished?

By this time the reader will appreciate that by "liberal attitude" I do not mean the kind of student attitudes which are subject to statistical investigation (such as those made by Farnsworth, Thurston and Chave, and others). Such studies tell us what the students' *replies* are to *questions*. There is a world of difference, however, between meaning what one says, and saying what one means. The *genuine* test for "an attitude," as I use the term, is found in important, vital behavior, not in language. Perhaps one of the reasons we talk and write so much these days is that, often, we really do not believe what we are talking or writing about.

The individual student with given capacities and interests learns what he wants to learn — and by learning we mean organic learning. The capacity and ability of any student is what it uniquely is. Is the test, then, to be whether the individual makes the best or good or poor use of his talent? Should a student with less than "average" ability who does the best he can rank "higher" than one who is very capable and hardly exerts himself?

The instructor must be responsible to the administrative policies of his college and, at the same time, loyal to his conception of learning. When the standards of performance required by the college conflict with the standards of development set up by the instructor, the problem of meeting both is not easy to solve. The college, properly, certifies that a student has satisfied its requirements. The responsible instructor must accept these standards.

The professional teacher recognizes that learning is not merely intellectual but organic. He understands that the genuine test of development is found in what a student does with his capacities in re-organizing himself in light of the particular course; how he meets the responsibilities of the course; the contribution he makes to it; how the course has altered his attitudes; what use *he* makes of the knowledge acquired. He judges this in several ways, by noting progress in the development of the particular student through what he says and does and writes from the beginning to the conclusion of the course, by his judgment of the range of ability and achievement of all the particular members of the class which helps the instructor gauge what might be expected from the several members.

There are dangers in such standards, that of subjective bias being the most obvious. Experience in teaching over a number of years helps in refining one's judgment as to what should be expected. It may be argued that the teacher's judgment, nevertheless, remains impressionistic. This is only partly true. His impressions are corrected by the student's class behavior and written work.

The degree of responsibility the student assumes for his work can be objectively evaluated by his regularity and promptness in attendance, by the doing of his assignments, handing them in on time, and contributing to discussion. Progress in his development can be evaluated by comparing his weekly written assignments with each other and observing his performance in class.

I have tried a device for several years and found it very helpful in evaluating a student's growth. When the students assemble for the first time in the criminology course I ask them to answer several questions such as, "What is a crime?" "Who is a criminal?" "How would you treat a prisoner?" The answers to these questions involve the basic factual data of the course. Each student is assigned a number which I record next to his name in my classbook. The papers, identified only by number, are handed in. At the last meeting of the course, I ask the students to answer the same questions, sometimes differently framed. Each is assigned the number given the first day. I then compare both papers, bearing the same number, to judge what difference being in this course for a year has made in the expressed attitudes brought to class at the beginning. I give only two grades, an "F" (fail) or a "P" (pass).

The reader may persist that such evaluation remains too subjective. Grant (which I do not) that this is so. I am of the opinion that subjective judgment of this kind, with the attendant probability of error, when made by a skillful teacher, represents a sounder evaluation of the quality of performance of students and of what they are getting out of a course than the mechanical rating scales of examinations which primarily test "memory." Evaluation is so much more complex than measurement. Certainly no standardized measure exists for learning as it has been described in this study. One must evaluate, and the written and spoken word have to be used. This is the test of what one says about one's attitudes.

Some elementary and secondary schools of education, and many progressive schools, are, in effect, moving in this direction. Instead of retaining or using the grade system they issue progress reports noting that the student's work is "acceptable," "satisfactory," "improving," and the like.

The university graduate schools, as a rule, consider the work of a candidate for a higher degree either acceptable or not acceptable. Does not this final decision rest upon the judgment of the instructors who worked with the candidate, supervised his work, and finally, gave their *opinio*n as to its value?

The reader who maintains such an evaluation is subjective, is free to make his own interpretation about what the courses have meant to the several students if he does not want to accept what the students themselves say and the judgment of the instructor as to what the papers indicate. If so, however, the reader will now be asserting what he formally denied, viz., that *his* subjective judgment is valid, as against the judgment of the instructor and the statements of the students. The logic of the one position, with regard to evaluating the students' comments, is not any better or any worse than the logic of the other. So much with regard to the practical problem of grading students.

The more important question regarding this study is, what proof have we that the kind of teaching and learning described here is an improvement over the traditional academic instruction? I do not know what kind of "proof" to offer other than this entire volume.

The reader, who is acquainted with the work of students and instructors, is asked to compare what is described in this study with his general knowledge of what occurs in the average classroom. The average instructor lectures, assigns material, conducts recitation periods, has some discussion, gives periodic examinations, corrects the papers, and reports the grades of the students. The average student attends class, takes notes, reads assignments, and prepares for the examinations. He does more or less what the instructor asks him to do. By and large, the work of both teacher and student is rather cut and dried. As one student expressed it, "A fellow student in one of my classes said that he never did the assignments in that particular course because the professor did not inspire him to do the work. Indeed, the lectures were dry and uninteresting — our prime incentive to study for the course was to get an A. And, to be sure, those who memorized their notes verbatim with no thought toward retention or full comprehension of the subject matter did get an A.

"It is bad, I know, to attempt to commend something by degrading its opposite. Nevertheless, I am sure that it would appear altogether too insincere were I to express outright my opinions upon the course in criminology. However, I realize that more profound and complex incentives to study exist. Whether it is the personality of the teacher, so enrapt in the subject that this vital interest is extended to the student and inspires him, or whether it is the method of presentation of the material or both, I do not know. Nevertheless, I do know that the interest and the delight in studying criminology is equaled in few other courses.

"If the above expression seems incoherent and meaningless, it is only because of the difficulty of translating my feelings upon the entire subject into words." *(Koenig.)*

On the other hand, the instructor who understands the *profession of teaching,* and the student who is led to recognize his own part in learning, have to put into this instructor-student relationship a great deal more of themselves.

The professional teacher recognizes his responsibility for the quality of his teaching. He is aware of his function. He knows that teaching is a ceaseless struggle. He must examine and re-examine what he is about, during and after class. No two classes are alike. Each hour brings different problems. The instructor must sense whether he should take over or permit the students to carry on. He must judge whether students are too confused or too willing to agree, whether their interest is genuine or superficial. Each student must be helped and, yet, not at the expense of other members of the class. The contribution of each student must be viewed in light of its meaning to the student, his fellow-students, and the subject-matter. In addition, the instructor must be on guard to recognize, to admit, and to do something about his own mistakes. He, too, must learn from the students in order to develop new skills and to make better use of his old ones. In brief, the instructor must attend to the subject-matter, his relations to the students, and the relation of the students to each other.

The student must educate himself. He is in class to make use of the instructor, not to be used by him. The student must discover what he wants from the course and how he proposes to get it. He is not permitted to lean on authority to escape his responsibilities. Interpretations of the material must be shared. The instructor leads but students do not necessarily follow. Together, they explore by-paths discovered by all. The student is given freedom to express his opinion and is expected to be responsible for it. Material is assigned, not to be merely read, but to be understood. The student is responsible for that understanding in light of his development. Matters of interest or points not understood are properly discussed by him in class.

College students do not relish being spoon-fed. If they are *sincerely* respected, with all their individual differences, they will become self-respecting. If each one is made to feel that he or she counts, an effort to justify such confidence will be made. The positive constructive self of the student, often deeply hidden behind timidity, inadequacy, or aggressiveness should have the chance to show itself.

I believe this demonstrates the value of this teaching-learning approach. The basis for a fair evaluation is not found in questioning the reliability of isolated statements or in judging them to be insincere student expressions. I do not doubt that some of the comments are to be taken with a liberal supply of salt. The entire volume should be surveyed to observe the movement on the part of the students in reorganizing the self. The sincerity of the papers is to be judged by the form of expression as well as the context.

Unfortunately the reader has not had personal contact with the students nor with their written work throughout the entire course. This helps one in judging the sincerity or speciousness of the reactions.

The "Data"

What happens to students who are exposed to the teaching-learning technique described in this study? Do they really change in outlook, understanding, and maturity? How extensive is the change? The following papers help to provide the answer. *They represent living data showing something of the change which occurred in students who had participated in only one or two courses conducted in the manner described.* Considering the kinds of "relationships" students carry on outside of the college, the different type of instructors in other classes, and the attitudes brought to these courses at the very outset, it is extraordinary that any kind of fundamental re-organization occurs at all. *The kind of change*

*and growth which takes place is sufficiently clear, I think,
to indicate what could take place if teaching and learning
were carried on in this manner on all levels of education.*

The CS papers are presented together, followed by the
PC series. I offer no further comment on the papers which
follow. The reader is free to make his own interpretations.

"It is difficult for me to take this course in criminology
out of all the material I studied this semester and comment
on it alone. You see, for the first time in my college career,
I found that everything I studied was integrated, that a distinct relationship existed among all my courses. I suppose
that every student experiences this burst of insight when
he begins tutorial work. This past semester, my introduction to you and to criminology, and to tutorial work filled
me so full of new ideas, new viewpoints, new relationships
that I sometimes felt I might burst before I had begun to
digest them all.

"I was saddened after almost every class, because I felt
that there was such a tremendous amount of work to be
done, and I could do so little right now. Perhaps I was saddened because my security, my peace of mind about so many
phases of life, had been jolted. This is hardly one of the
courses that sets the college graduate off with confidence
in his boots. I feel less confident in the world and in others,
but I do feel a little more confident in myself — confident
that I shall be more skeptical and more befuddled as I look
a little deeper into crime and society, which I definitely intend doing.

"P. S. One day when you failed to come to class without previously notifying anyone — it was the day after visiting the County Jail — the class carried on a very interesting
discussion, almost everyone present participated freely. I
was very proud of us, for I am quite certain that any of my
other classes would have walked out after the ten-minute
period. I don't know whether credit should go to you or to

us, but that doesn't matter, I guess. Let's say we both achieved something." (*Thorn.*)

"When I think of some of my ideas and convictions when I entered this class and then realized that I might have been chosen to represent the typical layman, I find it hard to believe that I and others could be so narrow, so short-sighted and so utterly ignorant of the essential conflicts existing in ourselves and in society. When I look at the picture now, I can almost literally see the dynamic process of individuals interacting upon each other and society which in its very complexity creates such a grand mess of mixed motives and self interests, that it creates chaotic behavior in some which we call criminal. I can now see how ridiculous it is to try to separate, out of dynamic living, one field and try to stay within its limits to solve the problems existing there.

"In order to derive meaning from the how or the why of human action, it is necessary to seek clues from the total living scene. This terrific complexity which I am aware of now has made it impossible for me to become dogmatic in my relations with others." (*Lawrence.*)

"If memory serves me, I believe that in one of the weekly reports I said something about our not learning much criminology in the course. This statement I wish to retract. I know a great deal more about crime, criminals, and criminal justice than I did nine months ago. I can say this with all due humility, because most of my newly acquired knowledge arises from the realization of my ignorance. Many things which I once unquestioningly accepted no longer impress me as being beyond doubt. My simple faith in some of the eternal verities has been sadly shaken.

"There has, of course, been a positive side to this learning process. I shared the common ignorance in regard to the legal and penal institutions of the various units of government. As part of the course, we were shown what was, what is, and to some extent, what should be in our treatment of crime and criminals. On the destructive side, some of our rather naive beliefs about the cause of crime and treatment of prisoners were debunked. We discussed efficient and sufficient factors and arrived at conclusions quite different from those we brought into the course. We viewed realistically the limitations of necessity imposed upon the field of criminology. We defined the area within which we could successfully hope to operate, and within that field we studied major patterns and practices, rather than attempting to acquire information of the type supplied by any *World Almanac*. So, again, I must offer my apologies for asserting that this was not a course in criminology." *(Selig.)*

"I have always gotten something out of writing a paper for this course in Criminology for I learned very early in class that my opinions, my ideas, unless false, are accepted for what they are worth. The unique method of teaching accepts freedom of expression, a freedom which is so unusual, that it is at first difficult to accept. I suppose it's been different because we had to examine just where we ourselves stood on these questions." *(Sims.)*

"What did I get out of this course in Criminology?

"I feel that I got more out of this course than anything else in school thus far.

"As far as criminology goes, I feel that I am now aware of the problems in the field and can discuss the subject more intelligently with others. I have found, though, that the only people I can discuss the subject with and discuss the ideas I have gotten this year, are with students in the class now or kids that have taken the course in prior years.

"Two clear illustrations prove how much I have gotten out of the course. They are, first, my re-reading the papers I wrote on the three opening chapters of the book, and secondly, my trip to Industry. (A New York State Training School for Boys.) I asked some stupid questions on these first papers, that is, they seem stupid now. One was: What causes crime? When are we going to get on to the subject? Now after a year's experience behind me, I think they were really stupid.

"I think that the method of conducting the class is far better than the ordinary way and I mean this. I can not imagine another class that I have had since I have been in the University that would continue with the instructor's absence and go just as if he were there. I know for a fact that in any class I have had, we have waited the ten minutes allowed for instructor's lateness and then left. I think the reason we don't do it with Crim, is that in the class, the class does the work, (most of the time) and for that reason, we can carry on a class without your presence. (*Edwards.*)

"To be sure, I've garnered some actual material on criminology. I don't think that was so important. I have assimilated more real stuff than in all my other courses put together. I doubt very much if I will ever go into the field of criminology or even social work, for that matter, but I am going to be very busy being a woman and a human being for the rest of my life — and this is a very good preparatory course for that." (*May.*)

"Throughout the year, I have wondered why definite answers were seldom given when questions were asked. Now at the conclusion of the course, I can understand what a complex and complicated world this is. The multitude of unanswered questions and problems in criminology alone, gives one an idea of the greater problems which await solving in the world about us. Each one of us, I have learned, must individually, try to find answers to the many complex problems which life presents." (*Finegan.*)

"Before I took Crim. I thought I could see the problem, whatever it might have been, if I could see one side or possibly both sides of it. Now I think that I cannot understand a problem without seeing between both sides. The course has helped me in matters not pertaining to the field of criminology. Believe it or not, I did not realize that I did not know how to read a book until I started to write my reaction to the chapters. I have tried to carry over that idea to my other readings. No doubt when you read my reactions or reviews you will question whether I have gained anything. Now that I am writing this, it seems strange that so many people read materials and can give it back almost verbatim without really understanding the meanings." *(Goddard.)*

"In writing this last paper for Criminology it occurred to me that in this last year more than any other year, I acquired more information in the Crim. Course than from any other course I had on the campus where we *had* to do the work whether we liked it or not." *(Koenig.)*

"Another very important part of this Course is that it is taught in such a manner that I feel I can apply it in my everyday life. By this, I do not only mean those instances in which I would have some connection with the field of criminology, but the principles are made known to me in such a way as to be applicable to things I do every day. I can honestly say that this is the only course I have taken in my university career that is so living for me. There is no doubt in my mind that the reason for this is that it is not taught to the students, rather, they do the teaching themselves. The facts are gathered by an actual struggle with them and not by a question-and-answer method. This makes evident the fact that a student can get as much or as little out of the course as he puts into it. This seems to me a very intelligent way to present material, for when, if not now, are we ever going to learn. The Criminology Class is merely a cross-section of life's experience." *(Cole.)*

"What did I get out of Crim. this year . . . *It only switched my whole life around from disinterested acceptance of my ends to a motivated acute interest in social work* with a definite leaning toward the field of criminology. The class was marvelous because what we learned can be applied to all fields of human action. What you investigated was the meaning behind the symbols of criminal action; you delved into non-rational action; you made a universalistic course out of a particular body of data. . . and to me it became one of the most fascinating courses I ever took. Of course I bogged down in a few places, yet I still stuck to the previous statement. If I don't get another chance, thanks for setting the conditions of some swell courses. I've never been so emotionally disturbed in my life — and I love it."

(Bird.)

"Yesterday I finished my course in Chemistry, and when I say finished, I mean completed. But in Criminology I have nothing of this feeling of completion. I am still forced to think about its problems because they have been made part of me. I mean, the way in which we tried to answer the problems in criminology seems to be the way we have to try answering the problems we meet in our everyday living." *(Leiser.)*

"Last September, I thought the subject matter of the course was being made unnecessarily hard, that a simple thing was being twisted and turned to make it appear more difficult when essentially it was easy. Now I can see how all that was necessary in order to make us see how very much was involved behind the words that seemed so clear in the text. This struck me particularly and was very hard for me to become accustomed to because I have been so used to taking things at their face value. I really thought in September that it was making a mountain out of a molehill.

"I have become aware that each one should have a feeling of social responsibility. It is very difficult to throw off the shackles of an attitude so different from this. Since this was first brought out in class, I have thought about it many times because it is such a new idea. It never occured to me that I should do something for society because I feel a responsibility and not for what I receive from society."

(*Robert.*)

"In the first place, I don't think it was necessary to get us so very confused right at the beginning of the course, though, come to think of it, I guess I enjoyed it a little bit. In reading my first papers, I find that I sound like little miss-know-it-all. This can be accounted for by my previous training in which everything I learned was set into formulas, and explicit statements. It must have stuck out like a sore thumb in my papers that I faked a lot and really didn't know what I was talking about." (*Gilbert.*)

"I have been going to college for almost four years and every year I have had a considerable amount of Social Science courses — especially in Sociology and Psychology. In each course I have had men of different personalities and varying points of view. Most of the subject matter in these courses is of necessity abstract, and many of the courses are in complete disagreement with each other, in fact, I believe that there is as much disagreement as agreement in the various courses. My head has been crammed with this knowledge which I had to know fairly well and agree with to a certain extent, in order to pass exams. It seems that the more courses I took, the more confusion reigned, and I needed one course to act as a sort of compass, to steer me in one direction so that I might at last choose a course and keep what I needed to follow this course, and place away the rest to be used if needed. I am not saying that this course in Personality and Culture, and, of course, Plant, is a panacea for all my ills, but I believe it offers the first crude compass for my understanding of the past four years in college." (*Fields.*)

"As soon as I heard what was required from me for a final term paper, I rubbed my hands together with anticipation on the simplicity of my task. Now, after three solid days of having tried to write this paper, I wish I could have taken a tough three-hour exam and have done with it.

"What did I get out of this course?   After much sincere thought, I can frankly say, I don't know — that is my answer. The more I think about this question, the more I feel like a person who is trying to describe a color to another who has been blind since birth — a startling, awesome, beautiful sunset — the intricate color patterns on the leaves of trees in fall — the dazzling whiteness of fresh snow in sunlight — all these things I can visualize and I can feel, yet if I could only describe them in their true qualities, I would be among the world's best authors.

"I have said before and I say again with utmost honesty —this semester's work in Personality and Culture Patterns has been a highlight in my education.   There is no question in my mind but that it has been interesting from its first class until the last.   This type of work was a novelty to me. I had never had anything like it in all the time I had gone to school.   Now I wonder if my interest in it was due to the fact that it was a novelty in my education.   I say, I wonder, yet I get the feeling that, although it was a novelty, the things I have read or discussed will stick to me.   Whenever any-one asks me which studies I am taking, I never fail to mention it and invariably the questioner is stuck with several minutes of your writer's opinions on personality, environment, the church and its effect on the individual, the school and its systems, both right and wrong, and so forth.   This was not possible before.   Of course, I have at one time or another, been involved in arguments on the topics mentioned above. But that was merely to hear myself talk and give the general impression of my mastery over certain witticisms and a few words.

"Now, I find myself discussing these points and respect-ing others' opinions, whether I agree or not is another ques-tion.   The main issue now is, once I argued about personality for the sake of argument.   Then I took this course and found myself involved in a discussion about the same subject.   I felt a slight resentment when my beliefs were in antagonism with the general trend of opinion found in the class. Gradually as the weeks slipped by, my resentment progressively lessened. I had begun to realize that this feeling was without basis because I began to listen and concentrate on other's opinions, where before I may have scoffed. I realized that my beliefs were respected as such . . . That actually no one was trying to undermine them. It was immaterial whether they correlated with the author of the text, they were not valued as much as Dr. Plant's, naturally, but nevertheless they represented an individual's opinions. It is not only in personality where I may have been at odds but in other points of discussion. And wherever my differences may have laid, they were respected.

"If you had asked me to write a paper such as this two or three months ago, I'm sure I would have submitted a thesis several pages long. Now, I have been thinking about those things which several months ago would have made an ass out of me if I undertook to write such a paper and the more I think, the more hesitant I become in trying to express my true feelings — I've got to be sure now and I'm not. Yet, the course must have left something or this mental disturbance would not be occurring and recurring — what is it —maybe I'll find out later — it might be years, but this I do know — there is *something* there! I certainly have come a long way in my understanding of what makes us tick. I finally realize how silly it is to ask for simple definitions of the complex relations of individuals." *(Turner.)*

"Being a person who has lived an extremely sheltered life with everything handed to me on a platter, this course at least has been a new experience for me. Every other course has meant, take notes for an hour, learn them, and hope to remember them until after the final. So, it has been a relief to get away from that old routine and to do something new and different. But this course has been difficult, too, in a way. I'm afraid of the new. I've been taught to be afraid of it. I'm timid, and when I talk with so many people around to look at me and hear me, I blush, which makes me self-conscious and end up rather frustrated. If other classes, both in high school and here, had been similar to this one I'd been conditioned to it, but none of them have been. We were to accept the teacher's opinion and our opinion should be the same as his, so that left no room for questioning. I'd never had the opportunity before and now that I got it, a few months ago, I found it very hard to take. I simply didn't know how, even though I did try to some extent.

"I won't say that I've gotten stacks and stacks of knowledge out of this course and that it's changed my whole outlook on life for that's not true and I believe that the truth is wanted here. After all, one semester of about fourteen weeks is a pretty short time to undo and change what has taken twenty years to build up. That is why I wish I had started sooner. I can, however, sincerely say that what I have gotten from the semester's work has greatly impressed me and changed me. So many little things, which may be small but, to me, they are awfully important and vital to everyday life.

"There's the incident about my buying the coat (incidently, I did not take it back) something I wouldn't have dared to do a year ago. But, I'd dare to do it again. My mother has had her say in the last two decades, I'm going to have mine in the next two.

"So you see, it has been little things like that which I've gotten from the course. So many little things which have touched my own life, opened up my eyes and cleared up things for me. Some of these points have made me a bit frustrated. On the one hand, I had seen what I should do to make life better; on the other hand, there was what I had always done. It's darn hard to make a change like that. It can't be done just all of a sudden. Then, after it's done, I still worry about whether I did the right thing. I've always been terribly chicken-hearted anyway, and hate to hurt other people. I suppose my mother was hurt when I disobeyed her and bought the coat. But one can't please all the people all of the time. Of course, all of this changing has to be taken with a grain of salt and done bit by bit so as not to make an anomical mess out of the given person and his associates. It seems to be human nature to stick to the old no matter what their effect. But I do think that the little I've changed has been for the better in myself and will lead to more changes in the future. I do hope so.

"Other than this, I've also gotten to the point of reading material much more carefully. In other courses, I've read the assignments through rather rapidly and got the general idea of them which was enough to get a pretty good mark in the quiz. After all, the whole set-up is based on marks. But, this can't be done with Plant. I would spend more time on one chapter in Plant than I would on all of Durkheim, for every sentence, even every word, of the former had to be hung onto or the whole thing would be lost. Then, if I didn't understand it quite enough, I would re-read it. Something I've NEVER done before." (Syne.)

"First of all I would like to say a few things about the discussions themselves. For the first few weeks, I didn't know what was happening. The discussion was above me. I was completely lost. A lot of the talk went over my head. So I came to class and quietly shivered thru the discussion in a remote corner. Then one day you asked me what I thought about something or other. I think it was about people trying to show their individuality, how each person is different as a result of his previous experience. Boy, I guess I did all my stammering and shivering for the rest of the term in that short interval in which I was trying to say something. Well, from then on I didn't do any more shivering but I didn't talk much either. The only time I felt awkward was during a lull in the discussion and you looked around at everybody who stuck their heads into the book trying to find something to say. Several times I did have something to say but just couldn't bring myself to say it. I know that outside of the classroom I could talk about such things with a small group of the students, and it didn't matter who they were either. But in the classroom I felt that I could learn more just listening to the discussion and also to you. I also realize that that's a poor excuse for not talking in class. To justify myself, I'm going to take your Criminology Course in my senior year and see what happens. I've learned from this course that if I'm ever going to do anything I must do it for myself.

"In closing, I would just like to say that I wasn't trying to write a paper. What I said I really and truly meant. I feel for my own personal justification, that I should do something about myself. I really don't know what is the matter with me (if there is something.) I feel there is, for I see if not all of me, at least part of me. I'm just beginning to know myself." (Richmond.)

"And so the paper and class are brought to a close. Finis? No just a start. I have suddenly realized that since I no longer feel the need to talk so much in or out of class, I find that when I do talk I talk clearer. I also have improved the quality of my reading and thinking in that I don't read or talk merely to criticize!!!" (Rush.)

"For three years I hated college. I came because my parents insisted upon it. This course has redeemed those three years and made me determined to return for my senior year, finish school, and enter the School of Social Work."
(Sievert.)

"I do not believe that I would have written the above at the beginning of the semester. I probably would have given you what I thought you would like, and I do not think that I would have been as honest, even with myself. It is true, at least, that I have never before attempted as definitely to analyze my feelings about a course.

"Again, in general, I feel that the biggest thing that this course did was stir me up. It has made me think. I feel that I have a long way to go yet, but I am sure that I have at least been started. My only regret is that I did not start earlier. I should like your permission to repeat the course." *(Grove.)*

"I got my first glimpse through this course of what is meant by liberal education.

"By last summer, I was definitely dissatisfied with school yet could not really discover the cause for my discontent. I was persuaded to return to the University for at least one more year, since I held a two-year scholarship. I am a three-year student and so had to decide upon my major by the beginning of this school year. Although I had no real desire to teach, I had for some time had a vague notion of majoring in math with the intent to teach. The one subject which had really caught my interest in my first year here was psychology so I decided upon a double major in math. and psych. and embarked upon a prospective two years of nothing but math. and psych. courses — *one semester was enough to convince me that if this was a college education I wanted none of it.* I decided to quit school if I could get a job. In my discouragement, I hit upon the idea of making use of the last semester of my scholarship and then having the whole summer in which to get a job. Since I planned no further education, there was no need to continue the courses prescribed for my joint major so I proceded to make a number of changes in my program. Among the new and varied courses taken was Soc. 456. This, together with the very individualized work done in psych-tutorial, has given me an entirely new slant on education and I am determined to return next year, even if I am forced to borrow the money to finish. Thanks to Soc. 456." *(O'Malley.)*

"I feel that you, as a professor, have contributed more
to me than any other teacher with whom I have ever come
in contact. The reason for this feeling is that we are ourselves in this class. We are living. We are not spending an
hour of having someone else live for us. We are not stuffed
with concepts and ideologies which take on no meaning to
us. The material, which could easily be lectured to us in
very abstract terms, is discussed by all of us in a very human,
natural way. *I have learned not to be afraid to listen to
those who disagree and not to be afraid to express myself.*"
                                                    (Kryle.)
"This has been my first experience with the institutional
approach to and its inter-relationship with the personality. I
thought my course in Psychology taught me a little about
people, but this course has opened up a new world to me.
I am sincere when I say that I feel that I understand, a bit
more, my family relationships, my school-friend relationships, and the need for tolerance in one's dealings with other
people and their ideas. This course has helped me to understand the world a bit more than I did, and perhaps it won't
be as difficult finding a place in it as I once thought. Maybe this is why I find myself so personally involved in the
course! From as *many* different backgrounds as the students
manifested, there was as much in evidence of a crippling of
our minds by the family, the church, the school, and the
home. We all had a tremendous amount in common to unlearn. I have never experienced this feeling in a classroom
before.
"Someone asked after class, 'Now what can *we* do about
an individual-centered culture?' I have heard others ask,
'What are we going to do about all this material that we have
learned in class?' I have been asking myself what I could
do about all this, and what was Plant really trying to get
across to his reader. This is the conclusion I have come to.
I—all of us—as teachers, lawyers, doctors, social workers,

or what not, have the answer. If, when your life touches another life, you can bring to that life understanding, tolerance, and kindness, then there is peace, happiness, and beauty. Then there is an individual-centered culture; then there is harmony and people doing yeoman's work in a world in which events and institutions are seen in the light of what they mean to the lives of people." *(Caldwell.)*

Chapter 15

The Dynamics of Learning

Toward the close of Chapter I (p. 12) I wrote, "the problem of getting an author's insight across to the reader is always present—especially in a work of this kind which deals with *processes* of growth." This entire volume stands as a simultaneous description and illustration of the process. No description and no illustration, however, is identical with a living process. Insight includes much more than verbal description or even intellectual awareness. The reader must bring himself to the material; do something to what he reads, and permit what he reads to do something to him.

It has been my experience and that of other teachers[1] who have used this volume that readers often have the *feeling* that the learning process described has been demonstrated. Yet when asked to translate their insights into a more exact *statement* of the dynamics of learning they find it difficult. The usual reply is, "You've got to experience the class meetings and discussions to realize what this is about." The obvious reply to this is, "Well, you've had the experience and so have I . Tell me, what are the dynamics of learning?"

I am quite certain that many readers derive *some* insight into the process of learning without being able to communi-

F. N.[1] Milton C. Albrecht, friend and colleague at the University of Buffalo, has repeatedly challenged me in numerous discussions to clarify the basic concepts of this study. I am very grateful to him for the trouble he has caused me. He has been exceedingly helpful.

cate how they have gotten such insight. I am equally certain that the measure of insight is proportional to the ability to articulate clearly and consistently the basic dynamisms involved. The profounder the insight the more discriminating will the intellectual awareness become.

I assume that the reader has read through, or better perhaps, struggled through the material. In light of this assumption it may be helpful to bring together in one place a description of the more important dynamisms of learning.

1. The Dual Nature of the Self

The human organism seeks adjustment, finds balance, and is again exposed to a different situation for which a new adjustment must be made. There is always an organic potentiality or readiness to respond in a given direction under given conditions. What principle integrates activity and directs change toward a given end? *The fundamental construct selected in this study is the human will.* Whenever an individual is faced with the need for change, for a better balance between his present organization and what troubles him, he will face the challenge or seek to avoid it. Fundamentally the organism resists change. Once we have achieved a certain organization there is a tendency not to alter it. The organism strives to remain in equilibrium. We tend to assimilate new experience in accordance with our former habits and experience. We fight against disturbing our present wholeness. The reason for this will be considered in the discussion of resistance.

Change, however, is inevitable. Adjustments of many kinds, inner and outer, must be made if the individual is to survive. We must reorganize our ways of responding. We must yield, at times, to the demands of persons, places, or objects.

The human will, the integrating factor in selfhood, in other words, is dual. On the one hand, the self resists changes, it fights *against* anything which threatens the present organization of self. On the other hand, the self must be modified in normal association with others and in adjusting to a changing environment. Individuals want to be independent but they also have to or want to be dependent. This leads to fundamental and inevitable conflict in ourselves and in relation to others.

2. *Conflict*

A simple way to appreciate the inevitability of intrapersonal and inter-personal conflict is to reflect on the tremendous role which fear, guilt, hostility, and anxiety play in our lives. What and whom do we fear? What makes us feel hostile, guilty or anxious?

We often fear expressing our independence. We dare not will as we think or feel because we fear condemnation, punishment, parental or social disapproval. We are unwilling to accept the risks and consequences of independent self-expression. The "pleasure principle," doing just as we please, we learn very early, must be qualified by the "reality principle." The wishes and ways of others upon whom we depend must be taken into account; the world of objects and events limit us in self-expression.

In the earliest years, as the sense of independent selfhood develops, the youngster tries his powers and seeks control. He soon learns that his own independent willing gets him into trouble. Authority blocks him in many directions, authority of parents, places, playmates, and objects. The price of acceptance by others is submission to them. We gradually discover (mostly, without being conscious of the process) that the very exercise of one's independence is accompanied by a gamut of disturbing emotions. "If you do as you please you'll get into trouble. Don't will as you feel but behave as you're expected to or else . . . " Hostility develops because we feel blocked. Guilt arises because we feel hostile toward those whom we love or because we do or want to do that which is forbidden or frowned upon. Anxiety and fear are present because we don't understand and cannot easily assimilate the mixed up feelings.

As childhood passes into adolescence we learn somehow and some way to cope with the inner conflicts. We submit and conform to the demands and expectations of others. The religious beliefs of the culture, its literature and morals, label certain conduct "good" and contrary conduct "bad." Parents, teachers, and friends support these traditions. The "bad" side of us (our independent willing) is condemned as evil, wicked, sinful. Hence we are led to feel wicked, bad, sinful, and guilty. We develop feelings of inferiority in relation to what others (who feel inferior) think of us and say to us. In merciful self-protection we are led to deny that we are "bad" or wilful (full of our own independence). This need to appear socially acceptable and one of the group is the source of lying, rationalizing, projecting, and the long list of defensive mechanisms which characterize "respectability" and standing in the "community."

The maintenance of pretense becomes a life-long tortuous task. To pretend to be upright, consistent, noble, loving, kind, (that is, "good") and, at the same time, to pretend that one is not unkind, inconsistent, ignoble, hateful and unkind, (that is, "bad") doesn't heal conflict. It exaggerates our splits and calls for further defenses of the pretension. Conflict isn't resolved. It is concealed, but remains disguised. We thus fail to realize just what troubles us.

A psychologically more healthful approach is openly to recognize the dual aspect of self; the need, at times, to be independent and the need, at other times, to be dependent. *The way to deal with our conflicting self is to recognize its* likely to cause too much psychological disturbance. The *existence.* Conflict is part of living. Conflict, in itself, isn't disturbance arises chiefly because we seek, futilely, to deny conflict, and then seek ways of justifying the denial.

If we were aware of the fundamental needs to be independent from others as well as dependent upon them, and of the resulting ambivalences, we would recognize, for the first time, the real source of disturbance and be in a better position to struggle for more comfortable balance. We would accept conflict and not resist changing.

3. Resistance

Psychological growth involves change. Psychological change involves disturbance. The greater the change the greater the disturbance. When a person has reached a point of satisfactory adjustment in relation to another person or situation he feels comfortable. There is a balance. One is in equilibrium.

Why, then, change? The answer is simple. Situations change and re-adjustments to them are necessary. Directed change requires effort. Change requires admission that answers which we thought sound and satisfactory are no longer valid. Change requires self-criticism; we are not all that we thought we were. The idealized image of ourselves or others which we have built up are discovered to be false or distorted. Sometimes we are shocked to discover that the ideas and ideals we incorporated in our lives are not absolute.

Why not, then, change? We have been taught (emotionally) to believe, and we feel that yielding our authority, prestige, or power, or admitting our limitations, inadequacies or inconsistencies, is debasing. We pretend to be mature adults. We spend much effort, time, and money trying to convince others and ourselves of this pretension. Our many defenses are fairly well established. We resist change to avoid the pain of self-disapproval and social condemnation. Is it any wonder that we wish to avoid the pain of self-discovery and the fear of social disapproval?

4. Identification

If the polar needs of dependence and independence, and the resulting ambivalences of individuals were recognized *and accepted* the fear of change and disapproval would be lessened. What is needed is a recognition and acceptance of the fundamental psychological nature of the human being. From a psychological point of view he is not "good" (what society demands) or "bad" (what society condemns). He is independent and dependent. Learning to balance these polar needs for self-expression and group approval will, even under the most favorable conditions, be accompanied by disturbed feelings. To realize this is to help the individual in the struggle and not to add to his load by condemning him for being "bad" or wilful. A better ethical balance will be achieved by the individual if the psychological description of his behavior is not confused with a moral evaluation of it.

Relatively few adults, including teachers, genuinely accept the dual and ambivalent process inherent in the development of personality. All certified psychiatrists, however far apart in theoretical orientation or clinical practice, are in accord with this view although they may differ in their formulations of it.

They also generally agree that *the keystone of helping the individual to develop is communicating to him an understanding of how he feels without moral condemnation or praise.* Very few individuals have ever experienced the therapeutic release of heart and mind which accompanies the utterly spontaneous and unscreened expression of genuine feeling. Interpersonal relations involve vested interests. How different dare one be? What is at stake? What risks are involved? How dependent must one appear? What rewards are forthcoming? Individuals become actors playing many roles, and, hence, fail to discover their own.

How can the individual be helped to discover his "real" needs and to make use of the proferred help? If, in relation to the helper, the person feels accepted no matter what he utters, and understood whatever his attitude, he becomes free squarely to face his ambivalence. His fears and anxieties are gradually reduced. He needn't remain or become defensive. No one is attacking, blaming, or condemning him. He doesn't feel threatened or coerced. No one insists on making him other than he wishes to be or to become. His integrity is respected. He is left free to decide what, if anything, he wants to do about the help he seeks.

In a word, he feels at one with the helper. He is identified with the other. He can afford to express his feelings and explore his problems with the understanding support of one whom he trusts. Not having to fight against the imposition of a foreign will he is left free to struggle or not to struggle with his own.

5. The Teacher

Anyone dedicated to the wondrous adventure of professional education becomes increasingly humble in carrying on this exhausting task. Problems unfold as insight increases. Professional educators with insight into modern clinical psychology, cultural anthropology, and sociology are learning how very little is understood about the teacher, the student, and what goes on between them. Nevertheless, a few significant generalizations seem warranted in light of present knowledge.

(1) The teacher should be aware of his professional role. *In any educational setting the teacher is the helper, not the master.* He is not in the classroom to "control" or to "discipline" the students. He is there to be used by the students within the limits defined by his superiors, and in accordance with the purposes of the institution.

Both teacher and students assume responsibilities. The teacher is responsible for knowing the material to be learned and the student is responsible for learning the material to be known. The teacher is responsible for directing the movement of learning since, ideally, he is the one who understands the learning process. The student is responsible for fulfilling the official requirements of the course. Responsibility for the course cannot be forced upon or demanded from the student without perverting his growth. Genuine learning is always, in the final analysis, self-motivated.

The teacher who respects the dignity and difference of each student will not only win the latter's respect but will also help the student develop his own.

(2) The teacher, who is clear about his professional role, will keep at the center of the teaching process the importance of the student's problems and feelings, not his own. *The subject matter of the course is the student, not the knowledge.* The knowledge of the teacher is the tool, not the product. The teacher should not be in the classroom to ask the students questions about what he, the teacher, already knows. He is there to use his knowledge in answering the questions the students put to him or to help them to raise the significant questions and to discover the important problems.

A teacher with professional skill learns to keep his personal feelings in the teaching situation under control. He refrains from becoming emotionally entangled with his students, using them as a target for his dissatisfactions or irritations. This is *the* educational sin. The need to be right, to have one's way, to play God, is unfortunately so much a part of most adults and teachers that it becomes the outstanding obstacle in acquiring professional teaching skill. Students are a convenient and tempting target for the relief of the teacher's needs and tensions, especially in an undemocratic school structure. At least in the classroom, if nowhere else, the teacher can hold court and win a crown! Teachers, too, must learn that the Kingdom of God lies within themselves and not in a classroom. The crown is one of thorns. The teacher who learns to control himself will discover less need to "control" students.

(3) The teacher who realizes that constructive effort must come from the creative forces within the individual student recognizes the importance of the student's needs. *He will accept the differences of the students.*

The teacher who understands the dynamics of learning in its individual and social aspects also realizes that common goals must be acquired, that a common body of data must be translated. The school and classroom require formal structure and organization. Rules and requirements are necessary to define functions and limits and to prevent chaos in education. This is proper and sound. It becomes improper and unsound when rules and requirements and organization become the goals of educational practice. The machinery is made for the protection of the student. The student is not in school to be fed into a well-oiled machine.

The fact remains, however, that the student has been lost in the maze of machinery of the large overcrowded schools, staffed by underpaid and little-respected teachers. Mass education is a contradiction in terms. Ten to fifteen in a classroom is optional, thirty should be the maximum. With such limited numbers it is possible for the teacher to observe more carefully the individual members of the group, their different needs and abilities. Less time will be given to paper work and more energy devoted to helping the student.

This study has not been concerned with the structure and organization of the schools and colleges. The problems are briefly mentioned to indicate my awareness that more meaningful learning on the part of students and more skilled teaching on the part of teachers require extended modifications in the formal organization of the physical plant and the professional preparation of teachers. The need for many more better prepared teachers and larger expenditures of money is, I believe, indisputable.

Given a more favorable classroom arrangement the teacher will become more free to attend to the principal task of helping the individual student to release *his* creativity in becoming a responsible and dignified human being.

6. *The Dynamics of Learning*

In conclusion I should like to present an overall picture of "the process of learning" hoping that the reader will see how the above concepts are used in the classroom.

The physical setting for a discussion group will in itself produce some ambivalence in students accustomed to the traditional rows of seats and the teacher's desk. The new seating arrangement around tables with the instructor casually taking his place in the group is something strange and makes the students slightly uncomfortable. It's different and the students do not know what to make of it. They're not certain of what to expect.

The instructor opens the discussion by a friendly greeting, "good afternoon," and then, "Would you like to tell me what you expect from this course?" The usual response to this question will be silence, which grows heavier if the instructor also remains silent. The attitude of the instructor is of key importance.

Tension mounts. There may be discomfort, anxiety, or annoyance. The previous habits of the students have not prepared them for this setting and procedure. They are disturbed. This is precisely what the instructor aims at. He is gingerly disturbing their traditional orientation of passively sitting and listening, ready to take notes. It is as if he said, "Your accustomed way of being 'educated' by placing the burden upon the instructor to do the work, to do the explaining and the question asking, is not the way of this group. The responsibility of this course rests largely where it belongs, with you. It is your course and unless you actively participate and indicate what you want out of it nothing much will happen." In brief, the instructor has started to help the group by skillfully opposing and challenging their prior habits of skilled inattention.

The silence generates a defensive attitude. Negative willing is aroused. The students resist. "What's going on? What's this all about? The guy must be a 'screwball.' Doesn't he know his stuff? What's he expect us to do?" The students simply do not know how to meet the strange setting. The safe thing is to run away by remaining silent, to protect oneself by criticising the instructor.

It is necessary that the students be helped to overcome their defensiveness if learning is to occur. In a sense, their learning has already started in that their accustomed negative classroom habits have been cautiously challenged. The instructor, therefore, has to judge the moment to break the silence. Too much silence can lead to too much confusion and to a battle of his will against theirs. This of course, is to be avoided. The instructor breaks the silence by asking, "I'm sure there are many different reasons why you are here and that what you want from the course will differ. Some of you may want credit hours or a few points. That is certainly a legitimate reason. Some others may find this a convenient hour for their schedule and that is certainly understandable. I wonder if we can help each other to explore what one might obtain from this course?"

This will, almost always, bring several responses. The ice has been broken. The instructor creates a permissive friendly attitude. He accepts all comments without praise or blame. He treats each remark or question as important and gives equal consideration to any statement made by any student. By showing his understanding of what the students say the tensions are released. Students gain confidence that they may speak freely. The risks of exposure are less than they anticipated. Not all students gain equal confidence in a given time. Some feel somewhat more comfortable during or at the close of the first meeting. Others may require two months of meetings before they feel free to participate. A skilled instructor understands this and permits the individual student to develop at his own tempo. He rarely, if ever, drags or coerces a student into the discussion by calling on him. All that can happen if he does is that the student finds himself on a spot, feels embarrassed, if not hostile, and answers the questions with the least risk to himself.

Contrast the above with the traditional procedure. The teacher lectures, gives "answers" to questions not raised by the students. The instructor is supporting the student habit of passive acceptance of the authority of teacher or text. Outward conformance to imposed requirements is the best than can be hoped for. This leads to trained incompetence, not to self-discipline and enlightened understanding.

The tradtional teaching process becomes a contest of wills. The teacher will have his way. "Remember, now, there'll be exams and grades coming along. I'm warning you. You've got to get this stuff—or else." And the students, "What does *he* want us to know? What *must* we know or do to get by?"

How often teachers remark, "The students aren't interested. They don't know how to study. They don't want to work. They're lazy." Such comments reveal more about the teacher than the students. This has not been my experience. I found the majority of students excitedly interested and eager to study *once they feel that the course is theirs,* that what they have to say and do is important, and that *the instructor can learn from them* as well as help them to learn.

As the weeks pass the students' confusion is reduced. The instructor, in time, can communicate his genuine regard and respect for student difference. Sensing his attitude the students do not fight against him when, at appropriate times, he challenges their points of view or presents other sides of a question, or calls attention to contradictions in student contributions. There is no trace of blame or condemnation, no ridicule or badgering or humiliation. It all takes place in a warm friendly atmosphere of inquiry and exploration engaged in by all.

New ambivalences are aroused, new disturbances set up. The students, however, are emotionally free to consider whether they agree or disagree. They challenge the instructor, to. They point out his contradictions. Often the instructor agrees that he can't answer, he doesn't know or he simply states he is wrong.

Identification with the instructor, the materials, and with other students occurs. The students no longer fight *against* the instructor or the data. Negative projection or resistance gives way to positive willing. They struggle *with* themselves to reorganize their ideas, attitudes, and feelings. They gain self-respect, self-confidence, and a willingness to be responsible for their opinions. New integrations of data and self are achieved. Learning is taking place.

Not all students devolp alike. Some may persist in writing formal, stultified papers to please the instructor. A few sit silently withdrawn during the class discussions. Through comments on the papers or through personal interviews with the instructor such students may be helped to discover how they can improve their performance.

Learning probably takes place in small increments which accumulate into insights. The final product may become evident only after a period of weeks or months or even years. Whatever genuine learning does occur is the product of the positive and creative effort of the learner. He must pass through the stage of being disturbed in his given organization, and then helped to resolve his ambivalence by struggling *with* himself not against the teacher. Through the latter's acceptance and understanding of the struggle the student is supported and encouraged to continue. Ambivalence and tension are resolved. A new organization occurs.

The cycle repeats itself many times throughout the course, indeed, throughout one's life. If something didn't stand in man's way what would he do with himself?

Part III

Chapter 16

Education, for What?

Democracy as a way of life had been threatened in many parts of the world. The challenge to democracy as a form of government has been successfully met.

The preservation of political democracy, however, makes possible but does not guarantee a living democracy. There are defects in American society, the diseases of concentrated power, poverty, and wealth which threaten the health of its members. The removal of this inner infection requires the vigilant and creative efforts of leaders in every area of community life.

Leaders in industry, business, and government are attacking the illnesses in different ways. This is as should be in a democracy where conflict of opinion is the life-blood of progress. *The conflict,* however, *must be open in order for the balancing of interests to be fair.* The existence of formal democratic political rights does not in itself guarantee their proper exercise. Opinion must be enlightened and interest recognized before legislation can operate equitably for all.

Freedom of speech is hollow if one can but join the chorus of propaganda. Freedom of the press is a trap if newspapers fail to present, fairly, minority points of view. The right of suffrage is an illusion if the citizen has neither the capacity to understand, nor the knowledge of policy, nor the choice of candidate. Civil liberties are specious if those in power protect only their interpretation of the Bill of Rights.

The exercise of freedom will be effective if one has something to say and feels free to speak, if one is capable of distinguishing between propaganda and fact, and is motivated and permitted to act. Herein lies the essence of a living democracy. To respect and to express one's difference and allow others to express their differences is the very lifeblood of a democratic society. The Federal and State Constitutions in guaranteeing political, civil, and religious liberties are, in fact, protecting a way of living together in difference.

How is one to acquire a living faith in the democratic way of life? The answer is simple. One becomes democratic by living democratically. The attitudes of adults are, in large part, developed through their early experiences, especially those of family life and schools. This study has been concerned primarily with the role of the liberal arts college in educating young men and women towards a way of living with others. If they are not given the opportunity to live democratically in the classroom, i.e., to express themselves and to respect differences of expression why should they be expected as adults to believe in and make sacrifices for a democratic way of life?

I should like to list some of the dangers for democracy that inhere in our present school system and to indicate the qualities which should be developed for the making of genuine democrats.

Education by Authority

The American school system is one of the most regimented social structures in American life. The school program is laid down by adult boards who administer the school system. Relatively little choice is allowed students in the selection of subject-matter or activities. The way to learn, when to learn, what to learn, how much to learn, and how to test that learning, are generally standardized. The relation of teacher to superior and of pupil to teacher is that of subordinate to authority, not one of co-workers. The fear of authority implanted in the home is aggravated by the fear of the teachers in, and the standards of, the classroom.

American schools generally support the *status-quo*. The traditional ways of managing the ills of the country in the past are supposed to be good enough to meet present crises. New ideas, new objectives, new methods and a questioning of the old, are dangerous for children. Change is feared, and innovation is resented. A willingness to experiment when challenged by the unexpected is not fostered. For solutions, one turns to accustomed arrangements and traditional techniques. To teach about the past, in order to illuminate the problems of the present, is foreign to the spirit of the American school. The classroom teacher who presents a realistic picture of American life jeopardizes his reputation and his position. It is not to be wondered that the average American citizen fears any extensive transformation of basic institutions. There has been little in his school experience to prepare him for accepting the inevitability of change. He remains unreceptive to, and suspicious of, ideas which depart from what he has been adjusted to.

The school rewards individual, not cooperative effort. Grades and reports are given to the individual student for the acquisition of intellectual and verbal skills. The classroom, generally, consists of a group of children each of whom is in an insulated individual relationship with the teacher. The "I" growth, not the "we" development, is emphasized.

Fear of authority, fear of change, and emphasis upon individual "learning" are only a few of the dangers to subsequent intelligent citizenship inherent in our school system.

I recognize that the picture of the schools presented here is somewhat out of focus. Throughout the country, on all levels of education, many courageous efforts are being made to remedy the defects pointed out. Such experiments are relatively few when viewed against the background of the educational institutions as a whole. The schools can provide millions of children with the opportunity of making (within limits) their own decisions and of questioning authority.

Students can be encouraged to express their own opinions. They can be helped to appreciate the value of the past while at the same time recognizing the need for change. They should be encouraged in co-operative effort even while expressing differences of opinion.

To experience this sort of freedom in association with others is to act democratically. It becomes superogatory to verbalize about the value of democracy. The students, the future citizens of a democracy, will believe in it because they have lived it.

The American schools can create this democratic spirit provided two important steps are taken. First, the information about man and his world must be realistically presented. If there is genuine value in the democratic way of life it can acknowledge its weaknesses. One need not fear a diagnosis revealing disease if the body is fundamentally vigorous and sound. Millions of school children leave the secondary schools without much understanding of the society in which they live. We need material which will vigorously and honestly present the workings of our institutional life and their effects upon the lives of the people.

Secondly, we must find and educate enough teachers who, by living classroom example, will transmit their faith in democracy, as a way of living, with others.

The first step has been taken. Professor Harold Rugg of Teachers College, Columbia University, conceived of a brilliant idea many years ago (1928). (Professor Rugg's work is selected as an outstanding example of the preparation of realistic materials for use in the schools. While he deserves credit, he by no means stood alone. Many other individuals and local, state, and national educational associations have been interested in working for a more vital curriculum in the schools and colleges of the country). He carried out this idea and published to date a fourteen-volume series on *Man and His Changing Society* used by millions of American children in the schools of the United States.

The fact that Professor Rugg's volumes, and the writings of other progressive-minded authors, have been "best sellers" for many years is some evidence of an awakening on the part of school administrators and teachers that traditional curricula can be improved upon. Progress, so far as text material is involved, has certainly been made. It is the spirit and underlying purposes of instruction upon which we are commenting.

During the past several years, Professor Rugg has been personally abused, his books have been thrown out in some instances, and publicly burned in others. The Rugg controversy made the headlines of the daily press. School boards of education throughout the country were compelled by pressure to call special meetings to discuss "the Rugg books."

Professor Rugg was finally prevailed upon to answer his attackers and in 1941 he published a volume, *That Men May Understand*, in which he describes his faith in America and how he tried to crystallize his beliefs for millions of American school children. For many years, Professor Rugg has, through his books, tried to help young people understand the kind of society in which they were living. He sought to examine American civilization, pointing out its virtues and its faults. He wanted the future generation of adults to have an appreciation of the tremendous changes brought about by our industrial society and to realize their significance. If they could be helped to understand, men could control the machine rather than helplessly witness the machine enslave men.

Professor Rugg raises the critical question, "Can our people solve the American problem?" In his own words,

"I restate the problem:

"To bring forth on this continent that civilization of economic abundance, democratic behavior and integrity of expression which is now potentially available . . . To operate a technically efficient and sustained-yield economy and at the same time preserve the democratic principle of sovereign individual personalities . . .

"We stand indeed at the crossroads to a new epoch; in various directions lie diverse pathways to tomorrow. Some lead to social chaos, and the possible destruction of interdependent ways of living. One leads, however, to the era of the Great Society. There is no way to short-circuit the buildings of the new epoch. There is only the way of education, and its great purpose is THAT MEN MAY UNDERSTAND." (pp. 349-350).

Men must understand what they are about. That is Professor Rugg's theme reiterated throughout his writings. Professor Rugg does not indicate (and that was not his undertaking) how the significance of American civilization can be translated into the lives of 25,000,000 school children.

Where are we to obtain the teachers who will take this material and help to make it a part of the living reality of students? This is the primary interest of the Commission on Teacher Education of the American Council on Education which in 1938 started a five-year program of research, demonstration, and evaluation.

This leads us to the second problem: How to prepare teachers to understand what they are about. This country faces the gravest crisis in its history. No one can foretell what the future holds for the democratic peoples of the world. The immediate problem is the preservation of democratic institutions. But the more important problem is: What kind of world shall we build to give men and women, old and young, a chance to realize themselves? In the words of John Dewey, "The serious threat to our democracy is not the existence of foreign totalitarian states. It is the existence within our own personal attiudes and within our own institutions of conditions which have been given a victory to external authority, discipline, uniformity, and dependence upon the leader in foreign countries. The battlefield is also accordingly here with ourselves and our institutions." *(Freedom and Culture*, 1939).

We must have planning while at the same time we provide for active, positive participation by individuals. We must have centralized economic control while at the same time permitting individual initiative to operate. The dignity of man and not merely the quest for profits must become the chief goal of the post-war, world-wide reconstruction.

How shall we go about creating a faith in the mass of citizens that the task of building a new world is theirs; that the power of dictators, political or economic, over the lives of people can be transformed into the free and willing, not blind and hopeless, delegation of authority by those governed?

Organizations are the creations of men and women; they do not run by magic. The kind of world we want can be shaped by the desires, beliefs, and will of every one of us. We can, if we will, subordinate the machine to man. We will, however, only if we are imbued with the faith that the democratic way of living is the only principle which can guarantee "sovereign individual personalities."

Toward this end, teachers, more than any other professional group, can contribute. But they must understand what they are about. This study is a contribution toward such understanding. The teaching-learning process described here is based upon the belief that the individual has the right to differ from and to criticize others. In this way, there develops a genuine respect for one's own personality and, hence, a regard for the difference and dignity of others.

Such self-discipline will lead one to act positively and creatively. The individual will feel free (within limits over which he has no control) to do with himself what *he* wants to do and not what he is supposed to do. He will become responsible for his decisions and for the acceptance of the consequences.

The student must learn for himself how to get along with other students, with the instructor, and with the ever-changing problems which confront him. He is given the chance to become an integrated, cooperative, and creative individual, *unafraid to express what he stands for and confident enough in his own integrity to respect both the strength and weakness in others.* This is *being* democratic. This is what education is for, the making of Man.

Appendix

The reader who wishes to trace the development of the several students will find the page number, on which comments or excerpts appear, next to the name of the student.

Index

A

Adequacy,
    sense of; 59
Alexander, 34
Allen, 86
Allport, 51
Ambivalence, 117-119, 127
American College,
    goal of; 13-16
American Council on Education, 13
Arnold, 32
Attitudes,
    formation of; 6, 16-19
    fundamental changes in; 2, 22
    racial; 2-5
Angyal, 53
Authority,
    attitude toward; 90-91
    exercise of; 87
Aydelotte, 13

B

Basch, 78
Bates, 133
Beccaria, 208
Benedict, 147
Benjamin, 25
Bertolanffy, von, 53
Browder, 65

C

Cantor, 53, 78
Chave, 246

Classroom,
    physical setting of; 95
Clinical Method, 54
Coghill, 53
Cohen, 46
Coignard, 61
Cole, 23
College,
    curriculum of; 14, 21, 81-83
    freshmen; 16-26
    problem of; 45
Community,
    values of; 29
Crisis,
    in modern society; 35-49
Culture,
    character of; 42-44

D

Data,
    limitation of; 98
    non-verbal; 98
Definition,
    education by; 152-153
Democracy,
    as a living faith; 270
Dewey, 275
Dies, 65
Differences in Learning, 185-219
Dollard, 147
Dynamics of Learning, 55-76